OVER THE WIRE

OVER THE WIRE

A Canadian Pilot's Memoir of War
and Survival as a POW

ANDREW CARSWELL

Library and Archives Canada Cataloguing in Publication Data

Carswell, Andrew, 1923-
        Over the wire : a Canadian pilot's memoir of war and survival in a POW camp / Andrew Carswell.

ISBN 978-1-118-10968-7 (bound).–ISBN 978-1-118-10969-4 (pbk.)

        1. Carswell, Andrew, 1923-. 2. Air pilots, Military–Canada–Biography.
3. Canada. Royal Canadian Air Force–Biography. 4. World War, 1939-
1945–Personal narratives, Canadian. 5. World War, 1939-1945–Prisoners
and prisons, German. 6. Prisoners of war–Canada–Biography. 7. Prisoners
of war–Germany–Biography. 8. Stalag VIII B Lamsdorf. 9. Prisoner-of-war
escapes–Germany–History–20th century. I. Title.

D805.5.S723C36 2011   940.54'7243092   C2011-902167-6

PRODUCTION CREDITS
Copy editor / proofreader: Judy Phillips
German translation: Elizabeth M Schwaiger
Book design, production: Counterpunch Inc. / Peter Ross
Photo research: Peter Ross, Owen Cooke, Annabel Ossel, Anna Wickiewicz
Front cover illustration: Geoff Bennett, 1988
Printer: Friesens Printing Ltd.

John Wiley & Sons Canada, Ltd.
6045 Freemont Blvd.
Mississauga, Ontario
L5R 4J3

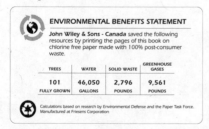

ENVIRONMENTAL BENEFITS STATEMENT

John Wiley & Sons - Canada saved the following resources by printing the pages of this book on chlorine free paper made with 100% post-consumer waste.

TREES	WATER	SOLID WASTE	GREENHOUSE GASES
101	46,050	2,796	9,561
FULLY GROWN	GALLONS	POUNDS	POUNDS

Calculations based on research by Environmental Defense and the Paper Task Force. Manufactured at Friesens Corporation

Printed in Canada
1 2 3 4 5 (FP) 15 14 13 12 11

Previous text spread: Three Avro Lancasters from No. 44 Squadron, RAF, based at Waddington, Lincolnshire, flying above the clouds. September 29, 1942.

To my wife of sixty-three years, Dorothy, without whose strong encourage-
ment and support this book could not have been written, and to my son,
John, without whose support it may not have ever seen the light of day.

And to the German farmer's wife near Zerbst, who took me,
a half-frozen young man, into her home on a bitterly cold night.

Recruit Andrew Carswell photographed at the manning depot,
Toronto. July 1941.

CONTENTS

Avro Lancaster B Mark I about to cross
the western perimeter of RAF Waddington,
Lincolnshire. April 14, 1942.

FOREWORD

In just the last six months of 1940, RAF Bomber Command lost 330 aircraft. Fourteen hundred aircrew were listed as killed, missing, or captured. As losses mounted, the demand for aircrew soared, and the British Commonwealth Air Training Plan answered the call. Young men from all over Canada and the Commonwealth enlisted to serve in the exciting realm of air combat.

Andy Carswell enlisted in June 1941, just after his eighteenth birthday, and found himself as an operational bomber pilot in England by the fall of 1942. The pace of training was so frantic that from the time he began training until he was deployed to Europe the next year he was given no leave. Then, on only his fourth mission, in January 1943, he was shot down on his way to Berlin.

His story exemplifies the courage and integrity of the generation that sacrificed so much for the cause of freedom. The aircrew of his generation risked death daily, against almost impossible odds, because it was their duty. The average crew lasted only several missions before succumbing to night fighters and anti-aircraft fire. But the survivors persevered.

Throughout this story, Carswell never puts himself forward as a hero. Instead, he credits the men around him as he recounts their stories too. He provides an even-handed assessment of the Germans he meets, both civilian and military. Without glossing over the evil at the heart of Nazi Germany, he still acknowledges the basic human decency he found in many of the German civilians as well as the common soldier.

The greatest single attribute these men who enlisted possessed was the virtue of high moral character and a willingness to do their duty. These were not empty phrases to Andy's generation. They were real values that men lived by and fought to maintain. Even after being shot down over Germany and parachuting out of a burning Lancaster bomber into enemy territory, Andy escaped from the POW camp twice because it was his duty to escape. In the end, as he is marched across the country, he observes the agony of Germany in total defeat and the horror of war for the civilian as well as the soldier.

After the war, he returned to school and to work without asking for thanks or help. He marries, raises a fine family, and continues to live a life of courage and integrity. Andy's wartime experiences resonated with many, including his son, who also joined the air force in his teens.

Canadians need to remember the sacrifices made, just a generation ago, by men and women who put their country and their duty before comfort, safety, or gain. The world has changed dramatically since the day in 1941 when the teenage boy signed on to do a man's job. But, if the need for sacrifice returns, I believe Canada will again produce a generation of men and women who will meet the challenges, and persevere to protect the freedoms and values that Andy's generation bequeathed to us.

It is my pleasure to recommend this book wholeheartedly. Read it, it will make you proud to be a Canadian.

T.J. Lawson
Lieutenant-General, Canadian Forces
Deputy Commander NORAD
Colorado Springs, Colorado

OPERATIONS RECORD BOOK

APPENDIX................   R.A.F.
FORM

DETAIL OF WORK CARRIED OUT

By .... No. 9 Squadron

SECRET

PAGE No. 6

FOR THE MONTH OF January 19 43.

DATE	AIRCRAFT TYPE & NUMBER	CREW	DUTY	TIME Up	TIME Down	DETAILS OF SORTIE OR FLIGHT	REF
17/1/43 (Contd)	LANCASTER R. 5894.	SGT. I.M. MARSHALL. SGT. S. NANCEKIVELL. P/O. W. SWINBURNE. SGT. J.J. MIESEN. P/O. R.A. NEWTON, D.F.M. SGT. J.L. ELLIOTT. SGT. O.G. ERASMUS.		1703.	2355.	Task abandoned owing to engine trouble. Bombs jettisoned 54.32N. 11.28 E. containers also jettisoned to maintain height. 1955 hours.	
	LANCASTER W. 4379,	SGT. A.G. CARSWELL. SGT. J.W. MARTIN. SGT. GALBRAITH. SGT. H.C. HIPSON. SGT. E.J. PHILLIPS. SGT. J.W. DE SILVA. SGT. C.E. CLEMENS.		1654		Aircraft missing - no signals received.	
	LANCASTER W. 4820.	S/L. G.S. FRY. SGT. S. BOCZAR. SGT. A. RITCHIE. SGT. J. LEES. SGT. A.R.H. THOMPSON. P/O. C.D. PERKINS. SGT. A.E. PELLY. SGT. J. PULLMAN.		1657.	0036.	Primary attacked 2049 hrs. 18,000 ft. Moonlight. Vis. fair. Target identified by large built-up area on ETA from BARSSER POINT. Target in sights but own bombs not definitely seen. Four or five small scattered fires seen but nothing of note. Aircraft slightly damaged by flak.	
	LANCASTER ED. 436.	SGT. CHILVERS. SGT. L. WHITESIDE. SGT. B. NAYLOR. SGT. A. McCANN. P/O. C.B. HASLAM. SGT. T.W. JONES. SGT. M. LACASSE.		1656		Aircraft missing - no signals received.	

Squadron 9 Operations Record Book, page 67, listing four of the bomber crews participating in the January 17, 1943, mission. Sgt. Andrew Carswell was pilot and captain of aircraft W. 4379.

X

Preface

This is a true story about RAF Bomber Command and a nineteen-year-old Lancaster bomber captain shot down on a raid to Berlin on January 17, 1943. It was written many years ago, while the names and events were still fresh in my mind. Five of the seven crew members on that mission, including me, survived. And became prisoners of war in Hitler's Reich until we were liberated by the British Army in April 1945.

I joined the Royal Canadian Air Force upon turning eighteen in 1941 and proceeded through the usual "training mill" in Canada and the United Kingdom without any leave. This reflected the severe casualty rate of Bomber Command in 1942 and the steady demand for replacement crews. I arrived in England in April 1942 and after considerably more training on larger and more complex aircraft, culminating in the Lancaster bomber, a four-engine, sixty-thousand-pound aircraft with a crew of seven, and two second-in-command operations over Germany with more experienced captains, I flew my third and fourth mission as captain, and was shot down on my fourth trip, on the way to Berlin. I was nineteen.

My friend, Harry Levy, another POW and sole survivor of a Wellington bomber shot down in 1942, sent me a book called *RAF Bomber Command Losses of the Second World War* by W.R. Chorley that provides a picture of those terrible days. During the five and a half years of war from 1939 to 1945, Bomber Command flew over 300,000 sorties. Over 125,000 aircrew served in the various units and, of those, over 55,000 were killed and 18,000 were either wounded or taken prisoner. In addition to the enormous human cost, over 9,000 aircraft were lost. A simple calculation shows that over 40 percent of all Bomber Command aircrew who flew on operations were killed.

The Red Cross organization will always have my undying gratitude for the work it did for all prisoners of war. It not only was responsible for supplementing our diet of bread, potatoes, and turnip soup with good food from Canada and Britain but also acted as a neutral go-between in supplying us with mail from home, including individual parcels containing clothing, art equipment, chocolate, cigarettes, and the like, as well as overseeing shipment of uniforms and overcoats from our governments. When I first arrived at the POW camp, the issue of Red Cross parcels was one-half parcel per week per prisoner.

Unfortunately, the Germans did not treat all of their prisoners equally, particularly when it came to the Russians, the Poles, and the Jews, whom they treated brutally and even sadistically. But the Geneva Convention was respected, for the most part, as it applied to Allied prisoners of war, and the International Red Cross was allowed access to our camps. Having seen the emaciated state of Russian prisoners from a nearby camp, I can only conclude that it was the Red Cross intervention that meant the difference to us between starvation and survival.

Sitting here in my comfortable study some fifty years later, watching the Severn River flow by my back garden, I find myself questioning if all this really did happen to me. Could people really have been that cruel and evil? But whenever I have doubts that these things really happened so long ago, I remember the feeling of fear and hopelessness that came over me when I thought that I was about to be despatched in some Gestapo basement, and that fear is very real, even now.

But we shouldn't feel too smug, even today. Under the right circumstances when "the best lack all conviction, while the worst are full of passionate intensity," any country can succumb to the blandishments of power-hungry leaders who feed on people's fears and humiliations.

Because of what I've been through, I promised myself that I would always be sympathetic toward any poor soul unfortunate enough to be incarcerated in any kind of prison or jail. Whenever I hear someone say that so and so only got five, or ten, years, I think, "What does he know!" Five months, or even five weeks, in some prisons is a lifetime.

It still amazes me that most of us in the POW camp at Lamsdorf were barely twenty years old. I was lucky. Unlike many who died in Bomber Command operations, which saw one of the highest casualty rates of any service during the war, I made it through healthy and reasonably happy and lived to tell this story.

Andrew Carswell

Seven Thousand Feet and Falling

There was no sensation of falling. I seemed to be floating motionless in space as I heard the high-pitched scream of Rolls-Royce Merlin engines rapidly fading away into the cold blackness of the night.

Suddenly a slight popping noise interrupted my dreamlike state, there was a rustle like a flag in the wind, and I was jerked straight toward the stars at 120 miles an hour as the parachute harness cut painfully into my crotch. The faint scream of engines in the distance stopped. There was a muffled explosion. Then, except for the sound of my parachute, a deathly silence.

In contrast to the blackness of the sky, the stars were so bright I felt as if I could touch them with my fingertips. It was deadly cold – twenty or thirty below zero Fahrenheit. Here I was, a nineteen-year-old boy, not long out of high school, thousands of feet up in the air, swinging from a parachute not far from Berlin, floating down into the middle of enemy territory.

A mile or so below me were dark woods, moonlit fields, and a silvery river. The swinging had stopped and everything was motionless, silent. I felt very alone. A few seconds ago there had been nothing but noise: the roar of four 1250-horsepower Rolls-Royce Merlin engines trying to tear themselves apart at more than three thousand revolutions per minute. The thump of exploding

Aerial view over the Schoeneweide district of Berlin near the Landwehr Canal; the white patches are from heavy anti-aircraft guns. January 16–17, 1943.

anti-aircraft shells all around us. The scream of air rushing by when Paddy Hipson, our bombardier, pulled the emergency releases on the escape hatch, exploding it out into the roaring darkness. The flames from number three engine eating into the leading edge of the wing, flickering brightly, inches away from the main fuel tanks, with their thousands of gallons of high-octane gasoline.

I had just dived through the forward escape hatch of a burning Lancaster bomber, hurtling toward the ground at more than three hundred miles an hour, with my parachute chest pack hooked onto my harness by two flimsy-looking hooks, and my right hand firmly clutching the D ring. Being left-handed, I had listened to many a story about lefties who had panicked in just such situations and had hit the ground still clawing with their left hands at a nonexistent D ring. I had also heard stories of those who had panicked and pulled the D ring too soon, filling the cabin with parachute silk, and not getting out at all. This was my fourth operational trip over enemy territory, with only a few hundred hours of flying experience, captain of a four-engine bomber with a crew of seven, and I was the only one on board who knew how to fly the plane.

A little more than a year previously, I had graduated from high school, having just passed my eighteenth birthday. It was the summer of 1941. Being of legal age to enlist, although too young to legally drink beer, full of patriotism thanks to the propaganda of the day, like most young fellows I enlisted in the RCAF – the Royal Canadian Air Force.

I had recently seen James Cagney in *Captains of the Clouds*, a Hollywood movie about a hotshot Yankee bush pilot who joins the RCAF as a pilot and proceeds to win the war almost single-handedly, so I decided that I would be a pilot.

By pure luck I was chosen as a pilot trainee, not having obtained sufficient marks in mathematics to qualify as a navigator. Being very healthy and also very fast – I'd been trained in running by the school bully – I easily passed the physical tests.

"G" Flight, No. 2 Squadron, No. 5 Initial Training School, Belleville, Ontario. Andrew Carswell is in the third to last row, second from right. October 1941.

Andrew Carswell in front of a Fleet Finch training aircraft, number 12 Elementary Flying Training School, Goderich, Ontario.

In those days, in the normal scheme of things, you joined the air force as an aircrew candidate, then waited your turn for selection and training. It took months, and sometimes years. You were given a blue RCAF uniform with a little white flash in the wedge cap, to signify that you were an aircrew trainee, filled full of vaccines and serums, and immediately marched around in the hot sun in a heavy wool uniform until you almost passed out. You were taught how to march and how to curse and swear and tell dirty jokes by disgusting little men called "discip." corporals, who seemed to be just slightly under God in the powers assigned to them by the government.

The trusting souls would then be given a rifle and assigned security guard duties at some obscure aerodrome in Saskatchewan until a course came up at the ITS (initial training school), where he would be tested, trained, and selected for one of the three aircrew categories.

In 1941, new schools were opening regularly, and while our group was at the manning depot in Toronto, anxiously awaiting a

Fleet Finch aircraft in formation.

posting to security guard duty, a new ITS had opened in Belleville,
Ontario. Magically, our group was sent there instead of some more
deserving group that had done its stint of security guard duties and
that would logically have been next in line for the course.

Naturally, we didn't complain. We considered ourselves to be
the lucky ones, short-circuiting the normal procedures. None of us
realized that a fast track through the training system for many of
us was just a quicker ticket to oblivion.

After a couple of months in ground training and selection at
the ITS, some of us were selected as pilots, some as navigators, and
the rest as air gunners. Most of my classmates were killed, one way
or another, before the war ended, and I would have been too, I suppose, except for my "bad luck" on January 17, 1943.

My "luck" persisted, and I was selected as a pilot trainee. More
"good luck." No leave, no waiting; a new course for pilots was
opening up at number 12 EFTS (elementary flying training school)
at Goderich, Ontario, and there I was posted. Sixty or so flying

Left: Andrew Carswell flying an Avro Anson at three thousand feet on his second cross-country training flight. Canada, 1942. Right: Avro Anson in flight.

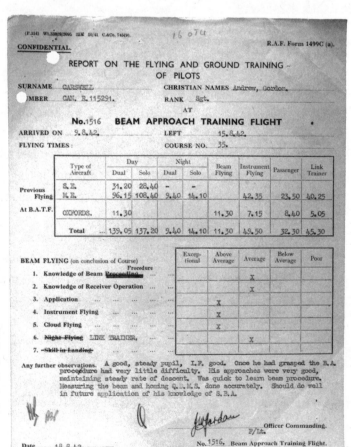

Blind Flying Training (BAT) course report for beam approach flight training, Leconfield, Yorkshire. August 1942.

(P.354) W1.53829/2095 55M 10/41 C.&Co. 745(9).   R.A.F. Form 1499C (a).

REPORT ON THE FLYING AND GROUND TRAINING OF PILOTS

SURNAME CARSWELL   CHRISTIAN NAMES Andrew, Gordon.

NUMBER CAN. R.115291.   RANK Sgt.

AT

No. 1516 **BEAM APPROACH TRAINING FLIGHT**

ARRIVED ON 9.8.42.   LEFT 15.8.42.

FLYING TIMES :   COURSE NO. 35.

	Type of Aircraft	Day		Night		Beam Flying	Instrument Flying	Passenger	Link Trainer
		Dual	Solo	Dual	Solo				
Previous Flying	S.E.	31.20	28.40	-	-				
	M.E.	96.15	108.40	9.40	14.10		42.35	23.50	40.25
At B.A.T.F.	OXFORDS.	11.30				11.30	7.15	8.40	5.05
	Total ...	139.05	137.20	9.40	14.10	11.30	49.50	32.30	45.30

BEAM FLYING (on conclusion of Course)

	Exceptional	Above Average	Average	Below Average	Poor
1. Knowledge of Beam ~~Procedure~~ Procedure			X		
2. Knowledge of Receiver Operation			X		
3. Application		X			
4. Instrument Flying		X			
5. Cloud Flying		X			
6. ~~Night Flying~~ LINK TRAINER.			X		
7. ~~Skill in Landing~~					

Any further observations. A good, steady pupil, I.F. good. Once he had grasped the B.A. procedure had very little difficulty. His approaches were very good, maintaining steady rate of descent. Was quick to learn beam procedure. Measuring the beam and homing Q.D.M.S. done accurately. Should do well in future application of his knowledge of S.B.A.

F/Lt.   Officer Commanding.

Date 18.8.42.   No. 1516. Beam Approach Training Flight.

6

hours later on a biplane called the Fleet Finch, I graduated from elementary flying training and was reassigned to number 5 SFTS (service flying training school) in Brantford, Ontario, to learn how to fly twin-engine planes on the good old reliable Avro Anson. So I was to be a bomber pilot!

We envied those who had gone on to service flying on single-engine Harvard trainers, for they were destined to be fighter pilots – a glamorous job that everybody in the air force wanted. Despite this, I felt lucky. Others who had enlisted with me were still waiting for their initial training, or had "washed out," and here was I, well on my way to getting my wings.

I was still a fairly innocent young man when I got my wings in the summer of 1942 – a not uncommon condition in those days. My idea of a wild night on the town was to invite a girl to the corner drugstore or to the White Spot hamburger joint for a milkshake or a Coke, which would set me back about fifteen cents. The Beach district in Toronto where I grew up was like a small town in those days, and still is to some extent. Most of us there went to the same high school and bummed around on the beach in the summer. There was a boardwalk along the lake, exactly a mile long, from Beech Avenue to Woodbine Avenue. Most of us could jog down to Woodbine and back without even breathing hard. The couples smooching on the benches in the park facing the boardwalk paid us no heed, nor we them.

Now I was more than a mile above the brightly lit countryside, and just floating. I could tell by the speed at which I was drifting across the ground that a strong wind was blowing from the northwest. We had passed through the top of a weather front, with clouds, turbulence, and icing, and had entered the clear, cold, and moonlit night sky of northern Germany. The temperature was about forty below zero Fahrenheit at twenty-five thousand feet and the cockpit windows had been so badly frosted on the inside that, when the searchlights hit, all we could see was the inside of the aircraft, and our own white, frostbitten faces. The aircraft heaters were ineffective at that altitude, and even the sheepskin jackets, pants, and flying boots, called Irving suits, couldn't erase the chill from our bones – or was it fear? There was a lot of that also.

I had been anxious at the ops briefing when I saw that our target was Berlin again, for the second night in a row. Same route, same altitudes, same turning points, exactly the same in every respect as the night before. The rationale was that the Germans wouldn't believe that the RAF – the UK's Royal Air Force – would be stupid enough to use the same route two nights in a row.

After the briefing, my crew and I had filed into the mess hall for our traditional bacon and eggs, a big treat in wartime Britain, where the average civilian might see an egg once or twice a month. One of the experienced captains at the next table was expounding to his crew on what a great opportunity this was going to be. He was a flight lieutenant with twelve operational trips to his credit, the crew one of the most experienced on a squadron that had been decimated so many times recently that twelve was a pretty respectable number. Nobody had completed a tour of operations (thirty trips) for quite some time and was not likely to for some time to come, unless we could find a way to keep the Germans from shooting down our squadron members in such numbers.

The more inexperienced the crews, the more unconcerned they tried to act. The bravado and the wisecracks only covered up the creeping realization that there was a good chance all of us were going to die. No one on the squadron had finished a tour of ops for a long time, the most experienced captain having survived only twelve operational trips.

But I couldn't believe it would happen to me. In the books and movies, and the war stories, the "good guys" always survived. So we all believed, or tried to believe, that we would be the ones who survived, and that the "other guys" would be the unlucky ones.

January 1943 had been a bad time for Bomber Command.

Whenever the enemy brought out some new weapon or improvement in its air defence, we would lose some more bombers.
When the RAF countered with an advanced technique like "G,"
a radio navigation device that allowed our forces to navigate in
bad weather and bomb through clouds, we would lose fewer aircraft. Then the enemy would counter with another new device, like
radar-directed searchlights, and more of our crews would be lost. It
was like a game of chess, played by generals and air marshals, and
politicians. We were the expendable pawns.

January 17, 1943, was one of those nights when the Germans
seemed to have all the cards, including the weather, and they
were waiting for us all along the route. Our route was from a
point on the east coast of England, straight across the North Sea
to Denmark, with its heavy German flak batteries, and out across
the Baltic Sea, to a point more or less due north of Berlin. There
we were to turn south and fly directly over Berlin, where the
Pathfinder force was to have laid down all sorts of marker flares,
and drop six or seven thousand pounds of high explosives and
incendiary bombs on a given marker.

History would later show that most of these bombs never hit a
specific target, but when you drop tens of thousands of pounds of
high explosives over the middle of a large city, there is bound to be
very heavy damage, particularly to the civilian population.

I had heard tales of British aircrew who, when rounded up by
the irate German citizenry after a particularly heavy air raid, were
strung up on the spot. I heard similar stories about hapless German
crews, arriving by parachute in East London after a particularly
bloody raid, done in by the local populace. These stories may have
been apocryphal, but I suspect there was more truth than fiction in
some of them, considering the circumstances.

So here I was, in a plane diving almost straight down, near
a town called Magdeburg, not far from Berlin, with a fire in the
starboard inner engine that was burning into the wing. I hauled

back on the almost useless control column with all my strength, trimmed back the elevator trim as far as it would go, and tried to appear calmer than I actually was.

"Jock" Martin, my Scottish flight engineer, was acting pretty cool too, methodically picking up the parachute chest packs from the rack on the starboard side, reading the names in the flickering orange light of the fire, and handing them out to the navigator, bombardier, radio operator – and me. Considering the careless way some of us treated our chutes in the crew room, I think he wanted to make sure he got his own.

I had managed to get the crippled and burning aircraft into a more moderate dive and gave the order to "bail out," in what I hoped was a fairly professional tone. The fire in the starboard inner engine had refused to go out, despite the engine fire extinguisher, and was rapidly eating its way toward the main fuel tanks still containing hundreds or more gallons of high-octane aviation gasoline. In seconds the fuel tanks could explode!

Paddy Hipson, our Irish bombardier, pulled the release pin on the forward escape hatch, and the pad on which he had been lying minutes before, as well as the hatch, was ripped downward into the roaring darkness. The front cockpit of the Lancaster was now full of engine noise from the three remaining Rolls-Royce Merlin 1250-horsepower engines screaming above the roar of the wind, with papers, maps, and debris being sucked into the dark void. Paddy hesitated, then stepped into the black hole, and disappeared.

Jock Martin carefully folded up his jump seat on my immediate right, opening up the way to the nose compartment, and proceeded forward. Without a pause he dived head first through the opening, clutching his chest pack with both hands. Our English radio operator and air gunner, Eddie Phillips, followed him out smartly without even a nod in my direction. I was glad to see them going out so fast, as the aircraft seemed about to explode, with bright

Left: A flight engineer on board an Avro Lancaster B Mark I checks the readings on the aircraft's control panel. February 1943. Right: Interior view of the cockpit of an Avro Manchester Mark I from an RAF squadron at Waddington, Lincolnshire. September 1941.

orange flames steadily eating into the wing, only inches away from the fuel tanks.

A strained voice over the intercom from the mid-upper gun turret – Joe de Silva, an Englishman, older than the rest of us, married with kids – "I'm stuck! I can't get out!"

Then Claude Clemens' voice, our Canadian rear gunner: "Hang on, Joe! I'll go and yank him out!" A long pause, then Clem's voice again: "He's okay now, Skipper – he's out of the kite now, and I'm right behind him." Then silence on the intercom.

We were below ten thousand feet now, and the altimeter needle was spinning down at an alarming rate. The cockpit was full of noise and wind. I was straining with all my strength to hold back the control column. The airspeed indicator was past the red line, and the noise from the open hatch was deafening. The four throttle levers were back to idle, but the props were still winding up. There were only two of us left, John Galbraith, our Canadian navigator, and me.

John's intercom was unplugged, the cord dangling from his leather flying helmet. I grabbed his shoulder, pulled him to me, and screamed in his ear, "Get out, you dumb bastard!"

He looked at me with a strange expression on his face and shouted back over the noise, "We can get her back home!"

I grabbed the dangling wire on his helmet, pulled his head over to mine, and shouted into his ear, "Look at that fire, you fucking idiot! We're going to blow up any second and you're standing there arguing! Get the hell out! The controls are shot and I can't hold it any longer! If you don't get out, I'm going anyway!"

"Turn onto a heading of two seven zero, due west," he yelled in my ear, "and we'll get out of here."

"Don't be an asshole!" I yelled. "We're heading straight for the ground!" We were now at about seven thousand feet.

He stood there, his parachute chest pack already hooked on, and looked at me with a strangely wild stare that I had never seen before. My parachute pack was still on my lap where Jock had dropped it. I let go of the control column, picked up the parachute pack, and clicked it in place on my chest harness.

"Out of the way, then!" I yelled and pushed by him. I grabbed his collar and pulled his face close to mine. "You'd better follow me now – you've got about ten seconds!"

He stared at me with wild eyes. Then I dived through the open hatch into the roaring black hole, clutching my parachute pack to my chest.

In all of the heroic aviation stories that I had ever read, the captain was always the last man to leave the ship, even if he was only a sergeant pilot. And I was the second last man to leave my ship! I didn't have time to argue with John. I knew that in seconds we were going to blow up in the air, or crash into the ground. I hoped that he would come to his senses if I clinched the argument by diving out ahead of him. I had another strong motivation: I didn't want to die!

James Cagney or other movie heroes of the day probably would have knocked John out with a clean punch to the jaw and carried him out of the burning aircraft. I wasn't built in such a heroic mould.

We found out later that he wasn't in the plane when it hit the ground and exploded. And I figured that I'd seen the last of my Rolex Oyster wristwatch that John was wearing that night. My father had given it to me for my eighteenth birthday. It had been inscribed with my name and service number, and date of my first solo flight. I had lent it to John that night. So many crews had been lost on the squadron in the past few months that the supply section had run out of standard-issue navigation watches. John, needing a good watch to navigate with, had borrowed mine. He still had it on when he went out the hatch – *if* he went out the hatch.

I'd never made a parachute jump before. In those days, para-troopers spent months training for their jumps, seldom jumped at night, and never jumped when the wind was strong. This, my first, last, and only jump, was at night, with a bitterly cold surface wind at about forty miles an hour from the west, and twenty-below-zero-Fahrenheit temperatures. When the plane was at twenty thousand feet, the wind had been close to a hundred miles an hour. No wonder we were well off course, and over Magdeburg instead of Berlin.

By now, in the bright light of the moon, I could make out the fields, woods, some little villages, and a river. As far as I could esti-mate, I would probably pass over the woods and land some dis-tance past the river. I was hoping that I wouldn't land in the river when, with a crash, I tumbled through the treetops almost in the centre of the forest. It happened so fast that I had no time to pre-pare for it. One moment I was drifting rapidly over the woods, seemingly thousands of feet in the air, and the next moment I was dangling high above the ground with my parachute hooked in the top branches of a large pine tree.

After the noise of crashing and branches breaking, there was a sudden and eerie silence. I found myself swinging gently and helplessly a few inches from the trunk of a tree, twenty feet above the ground. The wind had been knocked out of me.

I hung there thinking that half of Germany must have heard the racket and would be coming after me. Minutes passed, and the silence was deafening. I could hear the blood thudding in my eardrums. I couldn't be dead because I was starting to feel the cold. And my crotch hurt!

When I was a small boy in the Beach district in Toronto, I spent a lot of time climbing trees. I'd scaled a few sixty-foot elms and chestnut trees in my neighbourhood. That skill now paid off. I swung myself over to the trunk of the tree, climbed up a foot or two to loosen the tension of my parachute shroud lines, and punched the quick-release button over my belly.

My harness swung clear, and I slid carefully to the ground, leaving my parachute and harness dangling from the top of the trees. I sat down on a large root at the base of the pine tree, lit a cigarette, and tried to take stock of my situation.

I seemed to be deep within a pine forest. The trees were tall and fairly close together, with patches of moonlight in the clearings lighting up the deep snow, which reflected into the woods around me, casting everything in a ghostly light. A full moon shone down and the stars seemed brighter than usual. There was no wind inside the forest, although I could see the tree tops above me swaying. It was deathly quiet, and extremely cold.

I began to wish that I had worn my full Irving suit. Although I was wearing the sheepskin jacket and boots, I hadn't bothered with the heavy sheepskin pants because they restricted the movement of my legs and feet and affected the quality of my rudder control, especially when landing. I had been rather vain about my ability to "grease in" the sixty-five-thousand-pound "kite" without bouncing it on the runway. Now, doing a smooth three-point landing didn't seem very important.

I had ripped off my leather helmet, earphones, and oxygen mask just before diving through the forward escape hatch, so my head was bare. I was glad that I hadn't been able to get a haircut for the past three weeks, for my thick brown hair was now keeping my head reasonably warm. I pushed the fur collar of my bomber jacket higher around my head and warmed my ears with my hands. My thin, RAF-issue leather gloves had a silk or nylon lining, great for flicking cockpit switches and pushing throttles, but not exactly designed for winter cross-country hiking.

I examined my escape kit, a standard issue to all aircrew: some chocolate bars and pills, a very large jackknife, bottle and can opener, compass, hacksaw blade, hard candy, emergency rations, a large silk map of Europe, and some French and Dutch money. I removed my right flying boot and one of my two pairs of wool socks, then carefully folded the silk map and placed it so it would be between the two layers of socks. The combination hacksaw blade/compass I put between the two socks on my left foot. (The two-inch hacksaw blade was magnetized; to use it as a compass you were supposed to hang it by a thread from a hole in the middle of the blade. The sharp end would point north.) There was a "wakey-wakey" pill to keep one alert, supposedly to be used in an emergency. This seemed to be an emergency. I wasn't particularly sleepy – but I took the pill anyway.

I finished off the chocolate bar, distributed the rest of the escape kit in various pockets of my uniform, and walked into the middle of a clearing. Most of the northern constellation, including the Big Dipper and the North Star, was exactly where it was supposed to be. I was probably not the only person looking at the North Star that night, but I was pretty sure that few others could have felt as alone and insecure as I did.

I could hear very faintly in the distance the sound of an air raid siren sounding the All Clear. The reality of the situation was beginning to sink in. This was no Hollywood movie scene, where the hero miraculously stumbles onto an Me 109 Aerodrome, fools all the Nazis with his flawless German and perfect disguise, jumps into a waiting Messerschmitt – which just happens to have its engines running and enough gas to get it to England – and flies back into the waiting arms of his girlfriend, after shooting down a couple of enemy squadrons on the way.

This was for real! A boy pilot with a few hundred hours' flying time, no knowledge of the German language, a very elementary knowledge of European geography, and no particular talents except the ability to run, climb, swim, camp, paddle a canoe, and fly a four-engine bomber, stuck in the middle of Germany!

"If that's north, then this must be southwest," I thought, lining myself up in the proper direction, and starting out in a generally southwesterly direction. I knew that Holland was in that direction, about four hundred miles away, and I couldn't think of anything better to do other than to sit where I was, and it was much too cold for that. Walk I must, or I would freeze to death.

The large sheepskin collar of my jacket, when turned up, almost covered my ears, and I thanked the designers for having such foresight. With my hands stuffed into the jacket's side pockets, I trudged through the deep snow in the silent forest, trying to maintain my direction.

The brilliant moonlight fell in pools in the small clearings, the reflected light making every tree and bush stand out eerily. The only sound was the crunch of my boots in the crisp, new snow.

I came across a road, crossed it at right angles, and re-entered the forest. I ploughed through many deserted fields and quite a few frozen creeks. Trying to jump a small creek, my foot went through the ice, up to my knee. I could feel the cold water seeping in. I pulled my boot off, shook out some water, and stuffed it back on. My hands were numbed by this small operation, and the toes of my wet foot were losing their feeling.

Keeping moving seemed to be the only way to keep warm, so I trudged on. My watch said that it was two o'clock in the morning. It didn't seem possible that I had been walking for more than four hours. I wasn't sleepy or tired – probably the result of the pill in the escape kit that I had taken. God only knows what powerful drug it contained – and I had never taken anything stronger than Aspirin.

The rest of the night was an icy horror, staggering and shuffling through the empty woods and fields. There were no Free French, Dutch, or Norwegian Resistance workers to smuggle me out of the country.

The truth was that I was an unimportant, expendable sergeant pilot who happened to be lost more or less in the centre of Germany, with no idea of how I was going to get out, not to mention that I had just recently attempted to drop several thousand pounds of high explosives on its capital city, a fact that might annoy some of the more excitable citizens.

These thoughts were going through my mind as I dragged myself across ditches, over fences, and through fields and woods, falling regularly and brushing off the snow mechanically. The sky was growing light to the east behind me when I fell for the last time in a field just short of what appeared to be a fairly well-travelled road.

I got up, looked at my ice-encrusted legs and half-frozen feet, pushed my numb hands back into my jacket pockets, and headed for the road. A basic survival logic took over.

I could hide in the woods, and the Germans would never find me. Not till spring, anyway. And then all they would likely find would be a half-rotten corpse, nibbled at by wild animals. Or I could walk down the road, and maybe someone would capture me and lock me up in a nice warm jail! The sun was starting to come up. I had been walking for seven or eight hours and it was now about five or six o'clock in the morning. I'd eaten all my chocolate, candy, pills, and everything else edible in the escape kit.

My mind made up, I walked boldly down the deserted country road, fully expecting at any moment to hear the sound of a military vehicle bearing down on me. Nothing. I might as well have been walking on the moon. In the distance, about a quarter of a mile down the road, I could see that there was an intersection of two roads. The road to the left appeared to lead to a small village.

When I arrived at the crossroad, I stopped, looking toward the village. A few hundred yards down the road, on the right-hand side, was a small-frame, two-storey house, with a short driveway on the far side and some sort of outbuilding behind. A dog barked in the distance. There was no other sign of life. I walked toward the house.

Even now, sixty years older and a lot smarter, I still can't think of any alternative to what I did except freezing to death in the woods. Still, I felt guilty about simply surrendering to the first German I came across, particularly after the scene with John Galbraith. I had thought about it all night as I stumbled along through the snow, and hoped and prayed that he had made it out of the escape hatch – he would have had plenty of time. The aircraft had been in a shallow dive and had not exploded until it crashed, quite a while after my parachute had opened.

2

"Engländer"

It was a very ordinary-looking house, with two windows on the upper storey in front, and one window on the main floor on the right. The front door was on the left, solid wood. There was a small cement porch with three steps, and a very fancy wrought-iron railing led up to it. The house was dark and silent as I walked up to the front door and knocked.

There was no sound. A dog barked somewhere down the road. I knocked again, louder this time. There was a flurry of movement somewhere upstairs. A window opened, and a woman's voice called out something unintelligible. I stepped back so that I could see the window. There was a face, indistinct in the darkness. More strange words that I couldn't understand.

"Let me in!" I said. "I'm very cold, and I need some shelter." I couldn't think of anything else to say.

"Engländer!" she screamed in a voice that surely could be heard for miles, and the window slammed shut. There was an even deeper silence. After a few moments, I could hear a muffled conversation in urgent tones, a shuffling as people moved about, and doors opening and closing somewhere in the house. I strained my ears, and thought I could hear the stairs creaking inside. Then silence again.

I was completely exhausted. I didn't care much what happened anymore. I sat on the top step, my elbows on my knees and my chin in my hands. Suddenly I heard the creak of a door at the back of the house as it was carefully opened and closed. I stood up. I could hear stealthy footsteps coming down the side driveway. I was too tired to be frightened.

The stealthy crunching in the gravel drive came closer. A little old man, clutching a rifle almost as tall as himself, leaped into view, pointing the gun at my chest, his finger twitching spasmodically on the trigger, and yelled at me in German.

Even though I had never had a gun pointed at me in anger, I had certainly seen enough movies to know what to do. I put my hands up and said, "Don't shoot!"

We stood in that position for what seemed like hours – probably two or three seconds. My hands were freezing under my skimpy gloves, and I was so tired that I couldn't hold them up any longer. So I put them back in my pockets, shrugging my shoulders in what I hoped was an unthreatening manner.

The old man, obviously not accustomed to threatening people with a gun, looked a little sheepish and lowered his weapon. He came a little closer and peered at my uniform. Speaking rapidly in German, he pointed to the sky, pantomimed an aeroplane, then pointed at me. I nodded, pantomiming a parachute coming down, and pointing at myself. Then an awkward silence as he seemed to ponder his next move. I was beginning to shiver in the intense cold when the door behind me opened, and a motherly-looking woman of about fifty came out. She took one look at me, looked at the old man, and lapsed into a stream of German. Although I had no idea what her words meant, by her gestures and tone I was sure that she had said something like, "What are you doing, you stupid old man? Can't you see that this poor boy is freezing to death. Bring him in the house this minute!"

Whatever she said, I was grateful, for the old man immediately motioned for me to go inside. The woman took my arm and led me over to a sofa in a small but comfortable parlour. I sat down grate-fully and immediately lost consciousness.

I awoke gradually but was wide awake before I opened my eyes. I could hear a babble of voices. I was lying on the sofa with a cushion under my head. Through half-opened lids I could see that the small room was packed with people, all talking, and all star-ing at me. I was the guest of honour, the corpse at my own wake. Someone noticed that my eyes were open and said something in a loud voice. The room became deathly quiet. I sat up on the sofa and looked at my captors.

There were about twenty people in the small room. Young, old, middle-aged. They were all gazing at me with some apprehension, as if they expected me to leap up and bite someone.

When I attempted to stand up, they all reared back nervously. My legs were still stiff from the previous night's hike, so I sat down again. A boy of ten or eleven peered curiously at the "Canada" flashes on the shoulders of my RAF uniform.

"Kanada!" he announced.

A noisy discussion ensued among the group. Several others came over and examined my shoulder patches. Someone asked me a question in which the one word I could understand was "Kanada."

"Yeah," I answered, "I'm from Canada." The response was sur-prising. It seemed that someone thought I could understand German because I answered with "ja." Later I discovered that a lot of German phrases sound similar in English. "Meine mutter," "Mein vater," "Mein bruder," for "my mother," "my father," "my brother," and so on. Everyone then started firing questions at me, which, of course, I couldn't understand. I just shrugged, not know-ing what they were talking about.

Suddenly the room became quiet. Something was happening outside. A black, expensive-looking automobile had pulled up in front of the house. I stood for a better look. Two uniformed men strode purposely up the front walk and into the parlour. Their uni-forms were dark, police or SS, I imagined. How was I to know?

They looked at me with some curiosity. I was clearly unarmed and harmless. The larger of the two motioned for me to put my hands above my head, which I did while the other frisked me, rather perfunctorily, I thought.

Satisfied that I was not carrying any weapon, the policemen allowed me to put my hands down. After some discussion they indicated that I was to put on my flying jacket. Escorted to the waiting automobile, I was seated in the centre of the backseat between the two men. One of them unholstered his pistol and in very plain sign language indicated that he would shoot me in the head if I should attempt to run away.

The driver did a U-turn in front of the house and drove back down the road. Soon we joined a more well-travelled road and entered the outskirts of a large town. One of my captors stated tersely, "Zerbst." I remembered that we had been in the general area of the city of Magdeburg when we were shot down. I had never heard of this particular town.

We stopped in a square, outside a large building, which I learned later was the Zerbst town hall. It was a stone building of three or four storeys, with a central tower and clock. An impres-sive entrance in the archway at the top of several steps led from the square. I was hurried up the main steps, through the main hall, up more stairs, and along another hallway to an empty room with a door on one side, a window on the other, a bench along one wall, and a chair near the door.

The men pushed me into the room and closed the door. I sat down on the bench. Shortly after, a young man in civilian clothes appeared. On his right arm was a yellow armband with some sort of insignia and he held a rifle in his hand. He sat down on the chair next to the door, smiled in a friendly way, and went through the same pantomime as had my initial captors, indicating

Low-level view of the centre of Magdeburg, Germany, from over the River Elbe; the buildings near the wharves suffered severe bomb damage. June 7, 1945.

graphically that if I attempted to escape I would be shot. I smiled back weakly, hoping to convince him that escaping at this moment was the last thing on my mind.

An hour or two went by.

My new captor leaned his rifle against the wall, stood up, and disappeared through the door. I looked at it stupidly. This was the stuff of Hollywood movies! Any half-assed hero would have leaped up, grabbed the rifle, and shot everyone in sight. Interrupting my fantasy, my youthful guard returned with a half-opened brown paper package in one hand and half a sandwich in the other. His mouth was already full as he plunked himself down beside his rifle and continued eating.

By now I was more than slightly hungry myself, having had nothing substantial to eat since my bacon-and-eggs dinner at the aircrew mess the previous night. As if he had read my thoughts, he broke his sandwich in two and offered me half. I accepted gratefully. The greasy sausage and black bread tasted very good, and I realized that I was very hungry. When I indicated that I would like a drink, he escorted me to a drinking fountain in the hallway, and when the inevitable call of nature came, he escorted me to the toilets, standing guard outside the stall.

By now it was early afternoon. We were both becoming bored. Suddenly there were voices outside the door. A good-looking man in a blue Luftwaffe uniform strode through the door. He dismissed the guard, closing the door behind him. I stood up as he approached me. He held out his hand.

"I am Oberleutnant Karl Schmidt," he told me in heavily accented English, briskly shaking my hand. "And what is your name?"

"I'm Sergeant Andrew G. Carswell," I replied. "Service number R115291," remembering all of the briefings I had listened to where it had been emphasized that name, rank, and service number were the only information that one was allowed to give if taken prisoner.

More than one lecturer on the subject had stressed that the German interrogators would be skilled interviewers, with degrees from British or American universities, and that any attempt to give them misinformation, or to outsmart them, would simply lead to more problems. The point had been relentlessly pounded in on more than one occasion: "Do not give the enemy *any* information other than name, rank, and number!"

Oberleutnant Schmidt was friendly and jovial. "I am a pilot in the German Air Force," he announced. "You are a pilot too, ja?" he added, looking at the RCAF pilot wings on my tunic.

I nodded, then remembered my lectures. "I'm sorry," I said, "but I am not allowed to tell you anything but my name, rank, and number. My name is Carswell, my rank is sergeant, and my service number is R, 115 –"

"That's enough!" he interrupted, raising his voice a little. "I know that you are a pilot from the insignia on your chest, and your Lancaster bomber is just now a pile of burnt wreckage in a field outside this town. Why would you not want to tell us things that we already know?"

"Why indeed?" I thought. "Why shouldn't I agree with the simple facts that they already know?" But I recalled the voice of my lecturer saying, "If you let yourself get sucked into any kind of conversation at all with your captors, you will soon find yourself tricked into giving out information, or perhaps merely confirming information that they are not quite sure of. So say nothing, even if it seems stupid to do so."

"I don't know," I said, trying to play dumb again. "All I know is that I am only allowed to give you my name, rank, and number. My name is –"

"We know what your name is!" he roared, "But why can't you and I just have a friendly conversation? You are a pilot, I am a pilot, we could be friends, ja? Your Lancaster bomber is a very good plane, ja? It is better than the B17, ja?"

"I'm not allowed to talk about such things," I replied. "My orders are to give only my name, rank, and –"

"I know," he interrupted, "'and number!'" He stood up, turned his back on me, and stamped out of the room.

My young civilian jailor returned, leaned his rifle against the wall, shrugged his shoulders, and sat down. A few minutes later I heard tramping outside the door, and two more blue Luftwaffe uniforms marched in. This time it was two younger men, both officers, who introduced themselves in broken English as Messerschmitt pilots. One offered me a cigarette, which I accepted gratefully. The other lit it for me. My young guard was dismissed again.

Soon they were telling me about their Me 109 and how much they liked flying it. Then they asked me about my aircraft.

"You were flying the Lancaster bomber, ja? Is it not your best bomber, ja?" one said.

I could see that they were not trained interrogators. Their English was poor and difficult to understand. I was not sure that they could understand me very well. But they were quite nice chaps. In different circumstances, I think that I would have enjoyed sitting down with them over a beer or two and discussing the relative merits of various aeroplanes … but I was beginning to learn the game.

"You are soldiers," I said, "and I am a soldier. I must obey orders. My orders are not to give any information except my name, rank, and number. My name is –"

"Ja, ja," said one of them. "We understand! We also must obey orders. We must now go." And after shaking hands with me, they departed. My young jailor returned once again.

Hours went by, how many I don't know, but I guessed it was still afternoon because of the light coming through the small window. My guard was dozing off, and I was half-asleep on the bench on the opposite side of the room. His rifle was leaning against the wall beside him.

Then there was a commotion in the hall outside, and the sound of marching feet. A voice called, "Halt!" or something very similar, and the marching feet crashed to a halt. A uniformed German marched into the room, pointed to me, and said, "Kommen Sie mit mir!" indicating with his arm that I should follow him. I walked out into the hallway, where a squad of soldiers was standing at ease, each soldier holding a bayoneted rifle.

The leader pointed to me, then down the hallway, and motioned to me in unmistakable sign language to get moving. I moved.

I increased my pace a little to avoid being run over by this fierce-looking squad of armed Germans when suddenly I realized that I was alone. They had turned left, into the main hall where the staircase was, and I was marching alone down another hallway, like a character in a Keystone Kops comedy.

I stopped, wondering what had happened. A lot of shouting ensued and about half of the squad came charging around the corner with their rifles at the ready, convinced, I suppose, that their prisoner was trying to escape. I turned around, held my hands up, and tried to shrug my shoulders to indicate that I had made a mistake. Shrugging your shoulders with your hands above your head is quite difficult, I found, and looks rather like an erotic movement in a strip show, which was the last thing I had in mind. I tried to look as harmless and stupid as possible, which was not hard, as I really felt pretty stupid for making such a dangerous error.

We continued to march after this comic incident, this time down the correct corridor, with part of the escort party ahead of me and the other half behind. As we marched down the stairs and toward the main entrance of the town hall, I could see through the open main doors that the square was packed with people. As we drew nearer I saw a convoy of four military vehicles drawn up on the opposite side of the square.

Two lines of armed soldiers formed a path through this crowd, across the square, to the line of trucks. I had seen newsreel pictures of captured Nazis, most of them arrogant and sneering. I decided that this was not the picture I wanted to present to these spectators, for fear of catching a rock in the head or a rifle butt in the small of my back. On the other hand, I didn't want to appear nervous or frightened, although I felt both. I decided that perhaps no expression at all would serve the purpose by not antagonizing my captors, yet salvaging some of my pride from the shame of being shot down and captured before my flying career had really begun.

Some of the crowd were distinctly hostile, particularly the younger men and older boys. The young women and children merely looked curious, having never seen a real, live *Luftgangster* before. "Luftgangster" was a word coined by Goebbels, Hitler's propaganda minister, to refer to the American and British bomber crews.

The older people seemed a little sad, and perhaps somewhat fatalistic. They had been through all this about twenty-five years previously, I guessed, and may have been wondering if it was all going to end the same way.

I was marched across the square, past the curious, the hostile, and the sad, and halted behind a covered truck. I climbed into the back of the truck and found myself face to face with four members of my crew!

Jock Martin, our Scottish flight engineer, was there, large as life, and "Clem" Clemens, our Canadian rear gunner. On the other bench was Eddie Phillips, our English radio operator and air gunner, and Paddy Hipson, our Irish bombardier from Belfast. Missing were Joe de Silva, our English mid-upper gunner, the one who had trouble getting out of his turret, and John Galbraith, our Canadian navigator. We all started talking at once – until a guard stuck his head in, along with his rifle, and forcefully indicated that we were not to talk among ourselves.

Despite this warning, we whispered back and forth. Two had heard from the captors that Joe's parachute had failed to open and that he, in their words, "had been scraped up" from a field. Nothing had been heard of Galbraith. Apparently no bodies had been found in or near the wreckage. We wondered if somehow he had managed to evade capture, and decided for the moment to let Paddy Hipson pretend to be the navigator, since they both wore observer wings, and besides, bomb aimers were not exactly popular in the Third Reich in those days. We also agreed to give nothing but our names, ranks, and numbers to any interrogators, to avoid having to talk about who was in what crew position. Two armed soldiers climbed in the truck with us and sat at the rear of each bench, nearest the exit, effectively stopping any further talk.

Twenty minutes later, the convoy entered a large German air base and stopped at the guardhouse, unloading the five of us. We were then marched through the main offices and down a corridor to a cell block, which appeared to be similar in design to those of RAF stations in England. They assigned us two to a cell, Jock and me in one, Clem and Paddy in the other, and locked us in. The cells were sparse but clean, each containing two bunks, a bucket, and a couple of stools. Eddie Phillips, who was limping badly from a strained or broken ankle, was taken to the Luftwaffe hospital for treatment.

During the next few days in the Luftwaffe guardhouse, we were well treated and reasonably well fed. A series of well-meaning but incompetent interrogators visited us, attempting various ruses to get us to talk about our aircraft and the RAF in general. Our decision to take the "I am a soldier, you are a soldier" routine to its utmost and give nothing but our names, ranks, and numbers worked very well, and probably gained us some respect from the Luftwaffe, who no doubt were trained to respond in exactly the same way.

After three or four days we were told that the next morning we would be moved to an interrogation camp at Frankfurt-on-the-Maine. This seemed like good news, as Frankfurt was near both the French and the Swiss borders, and by now I was already thinking of escape, partly in atonement for giving myself up so easily, and partly because I had heard some escape lectures and had read a few fictional stories involving escaping. I didn't know at that time that there was a vast difference between fictional escapes and real life.

But even at age nineteen I knew enough to realize that although the heroes of literature and film usually shot their way out of confinement, leaving a trail of bodies along the way, my best chance of escaping was in slipping out, without leaving any trail at all.

In my youth I had spent a lot of time hiking, camping, and canoe-tripping in Ontario's lake and bush country. I had hitch-hiked, hopped freight trains, was a strong swimmer and runner, and had plenty of experience during my childhood of climbing fences, trees, and even cliffs, so I felt that if I could only get into open country, in warm weather, I might have a chance.

The next morning, a young Luftwaffe officer accompanied by two armed guards informed us that he would be escorting us to the "Interrogation Camp" at Frankfurt. The word "interrogation" had an ominous ring to it. The young officer, who spoke passable English, assured us that we would be well treated and that the camp was strictly for the purpose of screening and classifying Allied air force prisoners of war before assigning them to permanent prisoner-of-war camps. This sounded reasonable and made us feel a little better.

The two guards were stolid conscripts who regarded us with considerable curiosity, much as they might have inspected some new breed of pig freshly arrived on the farm. We were told by the officer that they had been given orders to shoot us if we attempted to escape. Although one of them looked as if he was having a little trouble staying awake, the other looked at us with some relish, as if he were hoping that we would give him an excuse to use his gun. "Nothing personal," his manner seemed to imply, as though he were the type who would enjoy killing anything, and in particular an air force prisoner of war attempting to escape. I mentally resolved not to give him that opportunity!

We were loaded into the back of a truck similar to the one that had transported us from the Zerbst town hall, two on each side, with two guards at the back, blocking any chance of jumping out of the truck. The officer rode in front with the driver. After a short drive, the truck stopped, and we were ordered out. We were at a railroad station. Our appearance on the platform caused a bit of a stir. A small crowd formed around us, our blue uniforms identifying us as *Luftgangsters*. Perhaps they had read about a recent bombing in their local paper.

A middle-aged woman in the crowd started screaming at us. Although none of us understood German, it was clear that she wasn't saying anything complimentary. It looked as if she was going to hit Jock with her cane (he was the largest target), when our officer shouted something at the woman. Whatever he said it was effective, and she faded back into the crowd. The rest of the mob drew back a little, intimidated by our Luftwaffe protector.

A train pulled into the station and stopped. Our escort walked along the platform, selected a compartment, opened the door, and motioned the four of us inside.

The trip was uneventful, except for the stops during the next several hours, when civilians would try to get into our compartment and would be repulsed by our guards. We were supplied with drinking water at one of the stops, and given some sausage and black bread by our host, who by now was becoming almost affable.

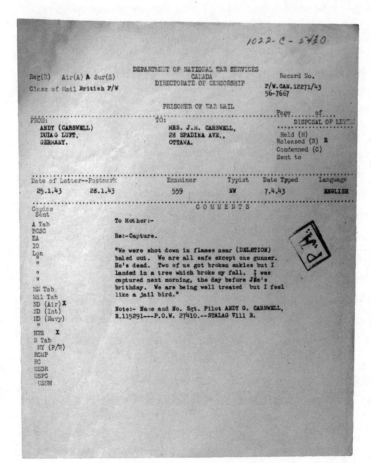

"To Mother: RE: Capture." Dispatch from Department of National War Services Canada. January 25, 1943.

3

INTERROGATION

It was late afternoon when our train rolled into Frankfurt am Main (Frankfurt-on-the-Maine). I could see the name printed clearly on the side of the station building. I could also see that German trains operated much like British trains in that passengers bought their tickets at the start of a trip, and handed them in at the destination station. There were few, if any, ticket checks on the train. I made a mental note.

The train stopped, the guards opened the doors, and we were ordered out onto the platform. Our escort motioned us toward an army truck parked by the curb. Twenty minutes later, after a bumpy ride through the back streets of Frankfurt, the truck came to a jarring stop, and again we were ordered out.

This time we were in front of a large stone building, two armed soldiers guarding the main door. It looked like a jail. It *was* a jail. Through the door, along a short hallway, and into a twelve-foot-square room we went.

Our friendly Luftwaffe officer poked his head in the door and said goodbye. He shook hands and told us that we were now in the hands of the Wehrmacht – Germany's army – and that they would look after us from then on. The tone in which he said "army" indicated that he, like all good air force people, looked on the army as being an organization several levels below the air force. He told us

Aerial reconnaissance photograph taken over Frankfurt am Main, Germany, three days after the heavy attack by RAF Bomber Command aircraft on the night of October 4, 1943.

to stay where we were until we were called and again graphically pointed out the hazards of trying to escape by pantomiming shooting us in the head. We got the picture.

Although the hallway outside seemed full of soldiers and guards, no one seemed to be paying any attention to us. I got up and looked out the one heavily barred window. There was a thirty-foot drop to a courtyard below, which was surrounded by a high wall.

A large, burly soldier appeared in the doorway and pointed at Paddy Hipson.

"Kommen Sie mit mir!" he said, crooking his finger at Paddy, and Paddy disappeared down the hall with him. A short time later, we looked up just as Paddy Hipson was marched by, no longer in his RAF uniform but in an ill-fitting grey Polish army uniform.

We looked at each other. Clearly, if they were taking our uniforms, we were going to be searched. Our Escape and Evasion lectures had mentioned the efficiency of the German searches. I reached into my flying boot and pulled out my RAF-issue folding knife. What to do with this monster? My eye fell on the stove, and in one motion I got up, stepped over to the stove, and placed the knife underneath, behind one of the legs. It looked as if no one had cleaned here for months, and I was hoping that the practice would continue. My other two surviving pieces of contraband, my silk map of Europe and my hacksaw blade/compass, were still between the two layers of my wool socks. It was too late to do anything about them now.

I was still wearing my flying jacket and black leather flying boots, which had drawn covetous glances from various Luftwaffe officers and German guards. The rest of my crew was similarly attired. After seeing Paddy in a Polish uniform, looking more or less like an itinerant street cleaner, I began to think that perhaps they were going to strip us of all our clothing and leave us for the duration of the war in some ill-fitting, cast-off uniforms from another war.

Ten minutes went by. The burly guard appeared again. This time he motioned to Jock. They disappeared down the hallway. Then it was my turn.

We stopped by an office, separated from the hallway by a counter atop a half-door. My escort exchanged some documents with a soldier on the other side of the counter, signed a couple of documents, then took me to a small room farther down the hallway.

The room was about ten feet square, with whitewashed walls, a bench in the centre, and benches along either side. Another soldier came into the room with shapeless grey clothing in his arms. He indicated that I should strip.

As I took off each article of clothing, one of the soldiers went through the pockets and lining carefully. I knew that some uniforms were being produced with built-in compasses in some of the buttons, maps in the lining, edible buttons, and the like, and all kinds of sophisticated escapeware, but I was sure my uniform contained none of those things. My Uncle Edward, a veteran of four years in the trenches in World War I, had given me a solid gold Queen Victoria sovereign as a lucky keepsake, and I had sewn it under the centrepiece of my gold-embroidered RCAF pilot wings, the very wings that were sewn on the battledress jacket the guard was now examining very closely. He hadn't discovered it yet. Would I ever see my uniform again?

My boots came off and were very closely inspected, as well as admired, by the two guards. Goodbye boots! Then my shirt was turned inside out and discarded on a bench. My pants were next, the pockets cleaned out, and the legs turned inside out. I was left standing with nothing on but my underwear shorts and socks. I could feel the hacksaw blade in my left sock, between the two layers of wool. Although I couldn't feel the silk map, I began to be painfully aware of its existence. The guards indicated that I should drop my underwear, which I did reluctantly, never having exposed myself in this fashion to anyone, let alone a couple of ugly strangers.

I soon realized that the inspection of my underwear was just as distasteful to them as to me. My underwear was somewhat grimy after being in the cockpit of a burning Lancaster, traversing twenty miles or so of freezing German forests, riding in German lorries, and sleeping in German jails, not to mention our most recent, day-long train trip. In retrospect, I can see that no self-respecting soldier of any nationality would likely enjoy poking through the dirty underwear and socks of a foreign prisoner of war.

After a short, distasteful glance, they pointed to my grey wool socks. I pulled them off together, one foot at a time, turning them inside out in the process, and held them out to one of my captors. He drew back in obvious distaste and indicated that I should put them back on. My feet were not only dirty but the stench was quite overpowering. A pair of wooden clogs was pushed toward me. Clearly, I had seen the last of my beautiful flying boots!

My captors hadn't noticed my double socks. I had a little trouble putting the left sock back on; the hacksaw blade/compass was now sideways between the two layers. While the two Germans were discussing the quality of my boots and flying jacket, I quickly straightened the hacksaw blade and slipped my foot into the wooden clog. A shapeless grey jacket and pants were handed to me, which I put on. A short length of string served as a belt. Finally, I was marched down the corridor by one of the guards, while the other guard disappeared with an armful of clothing, once the uniform of an RCAF sergeant pilot.

We went past another guard, around a corner, past more guards, and eventually we stopped in front of a steel door; it was unlocked, and I was pushed in. There was a loud *clang* as it shut behind me, and I could hear a bar dropping in place.

I was in a bare cell, about six feet wide by eight feet long, with a bunk, a small table, a stool, a slop bucket, and nothing else. There was a small barred window level with the top of my head. I pulled myself up to the window by grasping two of the vertical bars. Looking out between the bars I could see that six feet away was another concrete wall. I could see nothing else. I dropped down and sat on the bunk. It contained a straw-filled mattress, covered with potato sacking and a threadbare grey blanket.

I sat on the bunk and stared at the wall. So this was what it was like to be a prisoner of war! Soon I became bored with sitting and began to pace up and down the narrow cell. Then I sat down and again stared at the wall opposite me. I wondered how long it would be before the war was over. I wondered about my chances of ever escaping. This particular place seemed to be just about escape-proof! Not that I was planning on escaping at this particular time. I had already experienced the perils of trying to live outdoors in the winter. I resolved to try to escape when spring came. I felt sure that

I could live off the country once the weather was warm. While I was thinking these things, I became aware that my cell had become very hot.

I peeled off my jacket. It became hotter. I took off my shirt, then my pants. I sat there in my underwear, sweating. It became even hotter. I went to the door and banged on it. I shouted, "Hey, guard!" a few times.

After a while, an eye appeared at the peephole in the door and the guard asked, "Was ist los?" (What's going on?)

"It's too hot!" I yelled, vigorously pantomiming my predicament.

"Ja, ja," the eye said, and disappeared. I heard the squeaking of valves. The radiator in the cell became cooler. My cell began to feel cold. I put my clothing back on. Soon I had my blanket draped around my shoulders. Finally I went to the door and banged on it again. The peephole slid open and the eye appeared.

"Too cold!" I pantomimed. "Brrrrr!" I tried to indicate how cold I was. "Turn up the heat!" I pleaded.

"Ja, ja," said the eye, and disappeared. More clanking of valves. I could hear the heat coming back into the radiator. It started to get warmer. Soon it was too hot again, and I was stripping off my clothes. I banged on the door some more.

This went on all night. I was either suffocating with the heat or freezing with the cold. I never did figure out whether it was a deliberate tactic to weaken us so that we would talk more, or just stupidity in matters concerning plumbing. In any case, I got no sleep that night.

Although there was a bucket in my cell, I banged on the door when nature called and was escorted to the toilet. This gave me a chance to look at the geography of the place and try to get a general picture of my surroundings.

This was a prison, no doubt about it, and I was in a cell, in solitary confinement! This came as a bit of a shock, as I had always thought prisoners of war were kept in camps, in the company of their peers. On the way to the toilet, a primitive place down the hallway, I noticed that there were dozens of cells like mine, with a small peephole in each door, equipped with a cover that could be swung to one side for observation of the prisoner inside.

There was no way of seeing out. When the cover was moved to one side, all that could be seen from the inside was the eye of whoever was watching. I had a strong temptation, which I resisted for obvious reasons, to poke my finger into the eye that occasionally appeared in my peephole, but just thinking about it gave me a certain satisfaction.

The first day of solitary confinement went very slowly. I neither heard nor saw anything or anyone else. I had no idea of who, or if anyone, was behind those other doors. Sometime during the day I was given some thin turnip soup and black bread in a tin dish. It wasn't very appealing, but I was hungry and I ate it.

I stared at the wall. I noticed that someone had scratched a number of marks in some kind of sequence. Of course! I realized that six vertical lines in a row with a diagonal line through them must represent a week. And there were dozens of weeks, in neat columns! Is this where they were going to keep me for the balance of the war? From the way it had looked when I had last heard any news, it could go on for years.

I paced the floor. I measured the width and breadth of my cell with my wooden clogs. I practised chinning on the vertical bars of my cell window. Even without bars, it would have been too small to climb through.

On the third day, a bundle was thrown into my cell. It was my uniform. Although it was very wrinkled, I was happy to put it on again; it gave me a sense of identity, which I had lost in the tattered grey Polish uniform. The pockets had all been turned inside out, and some of the seams had been ripped open. The pilot wings had been partly removed, and the gold sovereign was gone. My

blue RAF shirt and my white turtleneck had been returned. No flying boots, no sheepskin jacket. (I learned later that these items
went directly to the Luftwaffe, who were very short of such "luxury" items of clothing.)

Even with my wooden shoes, which gave a rather bizarre effect
to my outfit, I felt like a human being again. Shortly after my uniform was returned, I was visited by a very friendly German officer.
He was tall, suave, good looking, and spoke perfect English with
an Oxford accent, although in those days the only Oxford accent
that I had ever heard was in a movie called *A Yank in the RAF*, star-
ring Tyrone Power.

He walked into my cell, closed the door behind him, and stood
facing me. "Good morning!" he said, a big, friendly smile on his
face. "Are you feeling better after your harrowing experience?"

I stood up and shook his extended hand. "Yes sir," I mumbled,
suspicious of this sudden friendliness. He was obviously an officer,
and as an NCO (non-commissioned officer) I had learned to treat all
officers with a certain amount of respect, if not suspicion.

"Sit down please, Sergeant Carswell," he said, sitting down on
the stool. I took the only other seat, the bunk, and sat down facing
him. He obviously knew my name, which was no surprise, as it was
pretty much the only information I had given any German so far.
As well, it was stencilled on my parachute pack, which must have
been found by now, given the clear tracks I had left in the snow,
and it was also stencilled on various parts of my uniform.

"You are a Canadian," he said, more as a statement of fact
than a question. I nodded. It was pretty obvious, with "Canada"
flashes on both of my shoulders, and RCAF pilot wings on my chest.
"Where do you live in Canada?" he asked in a conversational tone.
"Vancouver? Toronto? Montreal?" then reeled off the names of several other Canadian towns and cities.

I couldn't think of any reason why I shouldn't give out my
home address – it surely had no military significance, but our

CAN/R115291/P4/CAS

AIR MINISTRY
(Casualty Branch)
73-77 Oxford St. London W.1

2nd February, 1943.

Dear Mr. Carswell:

It is with deep regret that I must confirm the information which you have already received from Air Force Headquarters, Ottawa, which stated that your son Sergeant Andrew Gordon Carswell, was reported missing as the result of air operations on the night of 17/18th January, 1943.

Your son was Captain of a Lancaster Aircraft which took off on the above mentioned date for the purpose of carrying out a bombing raid on Berlin. No information has since been received concerning either the aircraft or any member of the crew, however, enquiries are continuing through the International Red Cross Committee and all other available sources and should any news be received it will be at once forwarded to you.

Please accept my deepest sympathy with you in your great anxiety.

Sincerely,

(Milton A. Foss) Flight Lieutenant,
R.C.A.F. Casualties Officer,
for Air Officer Commanding-in-Chief,
R.C.A.F. Overseas.

Mr. J.M. Carswell,
28 Spadina Avenue,
Ottawa,
C A N A D A

Letter from RCAF casualties officer informing Morrison Carswell that his son, Sergeant Andrew Gordon Carswell, is reported missing. February 2, 1943.

briefings had stressed the importance of giving absolutely no extra information of any sort. Even the most innocent piece of information, they had told us, when put together with a lot of other "harmless" information, could be used to convince a prisoner that the captors already knew everything about him – his squadron, organization, background, and training – and so render the discussion of day-to-day events, insignificant as they might seem, quite valuable to enemy intelligence. Tiny details of training procedures, travel arrangements, even the amounts and places of leave, all had their place in filling in the big picture for German intelligence.

I must have spent some moments with these thoughts when his voice recaptured my attention. "Well," he said, "what is your home address? I have spent some time in Canada myself. It is a beautiful country."

"I'm sorry, sir, my orders are to give only my name, rank, and service number. I'm not allowed to talk about anything else."

"That's ridiculous!" he said sharply. "What possible difference could it make to anybody if you told us your home address?"

"I don't know," I replied. "All I know is that I am under orders to give out no information other than my name, rank, and number." ("Orders," I thought to myself. "Any good German should understand that kind of logic!")

"Don't you care whether your family or loved ones are informed that you are safe? You must be a heartless brute!"

"I'm sorry, sir, but I'm not allowed to talk about anything with you except my name, rank, and –"

He got up abruptly and strode to the door. "If you do not cooperate with us, you will be here for the rest of the war!" He rapped on the door with his swagger stick, and departed without a backward glance.

The prospect of spending years in the tiny cell had sobered me. The few days that I had spent there already seemed like years. Being a nature lover and an outdoor enthusiast, as well as having little patience, I found the thought of pacing up and down in a barred cell for years unappealing. One of the reasons that I had joined the air force, I think, was a bit of natural claustrophobia. Trenches, underground tunnels, submarines, and the like were terrifying to me.

The next day, the same German officer visited me again. He was surprisingly friendly considering our last encounter and asked me if I would like some shaving equipment and a book to read. I thanked him and said that I would appreciate both having a shave and something to read.

Shortly after his departure, a razor, some soap, a bowl of water, a small towel, and even a small mirror appeared. An hour later, I was clean-shaven, and looked and felt civilized again. It was the first time that I had seen myself in a mirror since leaving England, and I was surprised at how normal I looked, considering the circumstances. I certainly did not feel normal!

I picked up the book that had been left by the guard. It was *A Tale of Two Cities* by Charles Dickens. I had read a lot of Dickens, but not this particular book. The story was engrossing, and I could hardly put it down. The part about the old man in the Bastille, who had been a prisoner for twenty-two years, got to me. I began to wonder what I would be like after spending twenty-two years in this cell! Looking back in later years I often wondered whether my friendly German interrogator hadn't deliberately picked the book for me.

The next day, he visited me again, accompanied by another officer. The usual questions, and the usual answers. He attempted to draw me into a discussion on the relative merits of British and American bombers. He asked innocent questions about my education, parents, home life, school, etc., and I retreated into my standard defence. I began to realize the wisdom behind the instructions that I had been given in those long-ago briefings.

These were two very intelligent men, these German officers; obviously university graduates, they probably spoke several languages and were trained to extract accurate information from the most innocent of remarks. And I, a recent high school graduate, with average intelligence and no great debating skills, was no match for these two. In a battle of wits I would surely come out last.

But my perfect line of defence could not be refuted by "Der Führer" himself. Duty! Soldiers (and airmen) must do their duty! And obey orders! This dogma had been pounded into every German boy from the age of five on. And even these intelligent German interrogation officers, with all of their education and language skills, could not disagree with such basic logic promoted by Adolf Hitler himself.

The two officers did not stay long. On his way out, the senior officer informed me that the next day I was to be visited by a member of the Red Cross, who was empowered under the Geneva Convention to visit prisoners of war to make sure that they were being treated in accordance with the convention.

We had been told in our escape and evasion lectures that in the interrogation phase we would probably be visited by a phony Red Cross man. They were right.

The next afternoon, after a day of pacing up and down in my cell, I was feeling more than usually depressed when the cell door was unlocked and in marched the "Red Cross" officer. He was a short, fat man, wearing a brown uniform with a military-type peaked hat, emblazoned with a large red cross on the front. There were several red crosses in various places on his tunic, and he had a white armband on his right arm, on which was sewn another red cross.

"Goot mornink," he said in heavily fractured English. "For you der war iss over, ja? Ve are glad to see zat you are not voondet or anysink like zat! I am from der Red Cross in Cheneffa, undt ve are here to make sure you get treated goot like der Cheneffa Convention says, ja?"

I shook hands with him and agreed that I knew of the Geneva Convention.

"Goot!" he said. "Your mutter and vater vill vant to know as soon as possible zat you are hokay. I have here mit me der form zat der Red Cross must haff filled out so zat zey can make sure zat all uff your luffed ones know zat you are hokay."

He handed me a form that consisted of two legal-sized sheets. I glanced over it. The first three questions were name, rank, and service number. Then came my home address. Then, "Type of Aircraft Flown," "Point of Departure," "Name of Squadron," "Range of Aircraft," "Bomb Load," etc.

I sat down at the little table. He handed me a pencil. I wrote down my name, then my rank, then my number. Then I stood up and handed the form to him.

"Vas iss das!" he said. "You haven't filled out der form!"

"I'm not allowed to give you any more information."

"Iff you don't fill out dese forms, ve vill – I mean, zey vill keep you here forever!" he bellowed. "You must fill dem out! Don't you care iff your mutter and vater know zat you are safe?"

"No," I said, suddenly tired.

"You are a heartless brute!" he yelled, using the same terminology that the intelligence officer had used. More than a coincidence, I thought.

He became almost apoplectic, screamed and yelled at me, called me names, threatened me with permanent incarceration, and stormed out, highly frustrated, and clearly very annoyed. He took his printed form with him, and it was the last I ever saw of it, or of him.

I was visited again the next day by my two interrogation officers. "I understand that you did not cooperate with the Red Cross representative yesterday. He was quite annoyed with you!"

"He's no Red Cross officer!" I blurted out. "He's a phony!" I had no sooner said it than I wished that I could have bitten off my tongue. I had broken the cardinal interrogation rule. Not only had I allowed myself to be drawn into an argument with an interrogator much smarter than myself, I had given away a valuable piece of information – that I knew about the fake Red Cross representative.

They looked at each other. "How do you know that?" the older officer asked, looking intently at me. I couldn't admit that it was because I had been briefed by British authorities – that was valuable military information.

"He doesn't look like a Red Cross man," I said. "He looks like a German and he talks with a German accent!"

"A lot of Swiss speak German," my interrogator told me gently, as if correcting a child.

"Oh," I lied ingenuously, "I thought they all spoke Swiss!"

They looked at each other with great amusement. What an amusing story to tell at the officers' mess. This stupid Canadian boy thinks that the Swiss actually speak "Swiss."

I breathed a mental sigh of relief. I seemed to be off the hook! I had almost divulged an important piece of information – that the Allies knew a great deal more about German interrogation procedures than the Germans realized.

The two then left, after suggesting to me again that if I didn't talk to them, I would likely be staying in my cell for the duration of the war.

The next day I had another visit from my chief interrogator. "Sergeant Galbraith," he said. "What position was he in your bomber crew?"

"Who?" I asked innocently. The crew and I had agreed previously when we were still together that we wouldn't mention John, if possible, to give him a better chance of getting away. If, indeed, he had been able to escape.

"Don't pretend that you don't know him!" he said. "We know all about him! We know that he was the navigator on your Lancaster bomber. We know his name, and we know his regimental number."

They must have found his parachute pack, I thought, and his harness. His name, rank, and number would be printed on the cover of the parachute pack, which would be still attached to the harness. The whole lot could have been stuck in a tree, like mine, or in a field, like some of the others'.

"Okay," I said, feeling that denying I knew him might somehow jeopardize his safety. "Where is he, then?"

"We don't know. We're still looking for him. But we'll find him. Tell me, what does he look like?"

My confidence returned. "You know that I'm not allowed to give you any information other than my name, rank, and –"

He laughed, the first time I had seen him laugh. I was actually beginning to like him a little. "I hope that our pilots, when they are captured, give as little information as you!" he said.

As the guard opened the door, he stepped out, then turned around. "You will be transferred to the reception camp tomorrow." He extended his hand. "Goodbye," he said, "and good luck!"

4

NEXT STOP LAMSDORF

The next day, my cell door swung open and the guard motioned for me to step out into the passageway. I was marched down the passageway past the toilets, turned right down another passageway, and halted outside a doorway. I was told to go into the room and sit down.

It was the same room where we had waited on our first day there. The same pot-bellied stove in the middle, covered with dirt and dust. Jock was there, and Clem. I guessed that we were waiting for Paddy. The guard had disappeared.

I walked over to the stove, reached under, and retrieved my giant jackknife, putting it in my pocket. The guard appeared with Paddy Hipson, deposited him in the room, and disappeared.

We exchanged small talk. All of us, it seemed, had similar experiences. We had all been relieved of our expensive flying jackets and boots so that the Luftwaffe pilots could be warmer. Even in 1943, while Germany still had a good chance of winning the war, a lot of consumer goods were already in very short supply.

Another guard appeared at the door and motioned for the four of us to accompany him. Down the hallway, past more armed guards, a stop to exchange and sign papers, out the door, and across the street, and into the ubiquitous German Army truck, with which we had grown so familiar.

A short trip through the city and we were unloaded in front of the entrance to a large camp, complete with barbed wire, guard towers, searchlights, and all of the accoutrements of a regular POW camp. Inside we could see hundreds of men in blue RAF uniforms, interspersed with the tan US Army Air Corps uniforms, wandering about in pairs or in groups, in seemingly haphazard fashion. Some near the main gate looked out at our little group with interest, perhaps hoping to recognize a friend or acquaintance.

Dulag Luft was the main collecting point for Allied air force POWs. After the usual paperwork at the guardhouse, we were taken in tow by a very efficient British RAF corporal. He welcomed us to Dulag Luft and explained that it was a collection camp for British and American aircrew POWs. He himself had been captured about the time of Dunkirk and apparently spoke German fluently. The whole camp was run by the British, he explained, and the British commander was an RAF wing commander.

We were taken to an office in one of the barracks to meet this man. He was a typical British officer, affable, polite, and very interested in the recent events that had led to our being shot down.

"You don't have to worry about talking here," he said. "There are no Germans around, and no hidden microphones." He was very friendly, and arranged for our temporary accommodation in one of the barrack blocks, plus an issue of British Army boots, Air Force greatcoats, and kit bags, all of which had been obtained through the Red Cross to replace our confiscated flying jackets and boots.

Rumour had it that another group was going to a camp in the east in a few days. Who was going, or where the camp was, nobody seemed to know. Some said that it was in Germany, and some said Poland. The permanent British staff didn't seem to know much either, or perhaps they were not allowed to tell us.

Two days later, a list of names was read out, which included my crew, and we were told to assemble the following morning with all of our personal gear for a train trip to our final destination. The name of that final destination was not given. As it later became clear, the officers were to go to one camp, and the NCOs, like me, were to go to another.

The camp at which I and my crew ended up, about fifty miles from Sagan, in occupied Poland, was a camp for enlisted men, the great "unwashed," and that included non-commissioned officers like me. It was to be the scene of what I like to call "The Not-So-Great-Escapes," for what the officers at Sagan accomplished and wrote about with such skill, daring, and imagination, the other ranks in camps such as mine made up for in sheer numbers, and with such pig-headedness that escaping was considered to be a major sporting event, jovially referred to as the Annual Spring Handicap.

After being counted, checked, and identified, we were told by the British officer in charge that we were being sent to a large prisoner-of-war camp near Lamsdorf, in Ober (Upper) Silesia.

We were again loaded onto trucks, larger ones this time, and taken to the railroad station. Here we were marched along a platform to the side of a waiting train.

These trains were different from the ones in which we had travelled from Magdeburg – passenger coaches that were quite old and originally French. On the side of each coach was printed "40 HOMMES OU 8 CHEVAL" (forty men or eight horses). The seats, removable to accommodate the eight horses, were simple, old, and uncomfortable.

I found a seat approximately in the centre of the coach, which was quickly filled. More prisoners were being marched down the platform to other coaches. They all appeared to be RAF or other British air forces. I saw no Americans in this batch. Perhaps they were going to a different camp.

The passenger coach, such that it was, appeared to be full. All of the occupants were clearly air force, and there were no officers in our car, only sergeants, flight sergeants, and warrant officers. I learned later, that because of the Germans' great respect for rank, officer POWs generally travelled first class, or at least in standard compartments. The "40 hommes ou 8 cheval" railroad cars had been resurrected from World War I stock as troop transports.

From the conversation around me, I assumed that most of the prisoners in my coach had been shot down over Germany in the past few weeks. I hadn't yet met any survivors of the raid that we'd been on, but just about every other German city of any size was represented, particularly those in the Ruhr valley, Essen, Cologne, and Duisburg.

About a quarter of our coach, occupied by about a half dozen guards, was partitioned off into a separate section. A large pile of Red Cross parcels were stacked in this compartment. This was to be our food for the trip. There were two more armed guards at the rear door.

Suddenly the babble stopped and there was a very loud silence. In the doorway in front of us stood an *Unteroffizier* (corporal) of the Wehrmacht, who was holding up his hand to gain our attention. "Quiet, youse guys!" he yelled in an unmistakable Bronx accent. "Youse guys better lissen to me, and youse better lissen good!"

He was small, dark, and had a weasel-like face with small shifty eyes and a built-in snarl. His uniform was immaculate, and on his belt was a large leather holster containing a Luger pistol. We were rapidly learning the German rank insignia, and this guy was only a corporal – but he had the airs of a general.

"Pay attention, youse bastards," he shouted in a gravelly voice, drawing out his Luger and cradling it in his folded arms. "Any of youse guys trying to fuck off from dis train is gonna get shot and shot good!" He raised his pistol and pointed it at us. "Dese guards are all packin' loaded guns and will shoot any guy dat even looks like he's tinkin' about escapin'! And if dey miss, I'll shoot da sonofabitch myself. So don't even tink about it!" Some of us had discussed the possibility of jumping off the train and making our way to the Swiss border, which was apparently quite close to Frankfurt-on-the-Maine.

Our *Unteroffizier* then went on to inform us in his own picturesque way that we would be on the train for the next few days, and that we would be given some food from time to time from the Red Cross stores that had been supplied from our previous camp. He also pointed out that the toilets, crude hole-in-the-floor affairs that dumped the stuff raw right onto the tracks, were another place where one might get shot, for trying to climb out the window. Having noted the window in question, I didn't think that anyone larger than a seven-year-old boy would have much chance of squeezing through.

The train slowly pulled out of the station and gathered speed. For the next few hours the trip was uneventful. There was drinking water, and the guards issued us some biscuits and jam. It seemed quite adequate, and I wasn't particularly hungry. The prospect of going to a prisoner-of-war camp six hundred miles deeper into Europe from our present position hadn't done much for my appetite.

Some of us had spoken to the German *Unteroffizier*, who by now had acquired the nickname "Yankee Joe," and discovered that he had spent ten years or more in New York City but had moved back to Germany in 1937 because he had been impressed with Hitler's "New Order." In New York he had driven taxis, worked in restaurants and factories. Now he was a corporal in the army of the Third Reich, and a "somebody." He was determined to make us aware of his importance.

One of the Canadians had returned from the front of the coach, where he had probably gone to see if there was any more food, and had just come back to his seat when he said in a loud voice, "Do you know what those bastards are doing up there? They're eating our Red Cross food! What a bunch of pricks! What a bunch of bastards! Why don't they eat their own lousy food?"

There was a loud yell. Out of the guards' compartment stormed Yankee Joe. "Who called me a bastard? Who called me a prick!" he yelled, stomping down the centre aisle, glaring at each prisoner in turn. By now he had pulled out his Luger and his bayonet and was waving them around, one in each hand. I stared straight ahead, as did the others (including the man who had made the statement in the first place – his face a little paler).

"Was it you?" he screamed, his face an inch from mine and his gun pointed straight at me. The bayonet was waving around some-where behind the pistol. I stared straight ahead, trying to look as innocent as possible.

"Maybe it was you, you fucking Jew-bastard!" he screamed into the face of the man behind me, who, I'm sure, also maintained a startled but innocent look. He kept up the tirade, screaming into each face in turn, and pushing the barrel of his gun within inches of our quivering noses. None of us was going to give him a clue, as he was obviously quite crazy.

He was clearly working himself up into a fit. If he didn't kill somebody, he was going to have a heart attack. "This guy is nutty as a fruitcake!" I thought to myself. Up until then, most of the Germans with whom I had come into contact had acted in a rea-sonable manner. And here was this psychotic character in a German uniform, with a New York accent, waving a bayonet and a Luger, screaming and yelling blue murder, and all of us sitting in our seats, looking straight ahead and trying to look as if noth-ing unusual was happening. By now it seemed as if he was so out of control that he was capable of shooting or stabbing the whole lot of us.

"No fucking —, —sucking son of a bitching —— [unmention-able perverted activity], Jew-loving — is going to call me a bas-tard and get away with it!" he continued to rave, and stuck his face within inches of a diminutive air gunner (whose eyes bulged with badly concealed fright), meanwhile holding the barrel of his Luger right up the poor fellow's left nostril. Nobody moved. We sat still, wondering when this lunatic would snap and shoot somebody. What a way to go! Shot up the nostril by a psychotic ex–New York taxi driver masquerading as a German corporal!

Then it was over as quickly as it started. Yankee Joe stopped screaming, pulled his gun out of the poor fellow's nose, turned around abruptly, holstering his pistol and bayonet, and tramped up the centre aisle to the guards' section.

For several minutes nobody moved, nobody spoke, half-expecting the crazy man to reappear. Gradually, we relaxed. In a few more minutes, Yankee Joe came out of his quarters and down the aisle, talking and chatting as if nothing had happened. It was my first, but not last, experience with what I later called the "screaming and yelling syndrome," an affliction of junior and senior NCOs in the German Army.

Fortunately, it was usually all show, and if the victim held his ground, the incident would generally end peacefully. Actually, Yankee Joe wasn't really all bad once you got to know him, just very ignorant. During the long train journey he told us about how he had immigrated to New York with his family, and had grown up on the East Side, finding employment in legal and semi-legal occupations. He wasn't working during the Great Depression in 1936 and 1937, when Adolf Hitler was calling on German expatriates to "come home." Struck with a fit of patriotism, he returned to Germany and joined the German Army. From the sound of it, he wasn't much better off now than when he left New York. He was, however, an out-and-out Nazi, and believed all of the German propaganda that Der Führer had been tossing about for the last few years.

The train journey was long and boring, lasting three days and two nights. We stopped at many stations and sidings to let more-important traffic through. Quite a few civilians appeared to be interested in us, peering through the windows and in the doors to see what sort of cargo would warrant so many armed guards. A few spit at us or made rude gestures on discovering from our guards that most of us were RAF bomber crews. But the worst feature of our enforced train journey was the certain knowledge that, hour by hour, we were travelling deeper into Germany and farther away from our homes, our loved ones, and all that was familiar.

The first night passed uneventfully, if uncomfortably. On the second day, the scenery began to change slightly. The towns and villages were farther apart and smaller, and the land flatter. The train stopped often at out-of-the-way sidings to let freight and troop trains pass. As night fell, Yankee Joe said that we were getting close to Ober Silesia, where our prison camp was located. Few of us realized that we were now approaching an area that until fairly recently had been part of Poland.

The train stopped many times during the night; indeed, we seemed to spend more time sitting in sidings than we spent actually moving. When dawn came, we could see that we were in a flat, bleak-looking area dotted with primitive-looking villages connected by winding dirt roads, which appeared to have little or no traffic. The country was bleak and grey. Even the snow had a greyish tinge. The sky was sombre and foreboding, and our spirits were equally dismal.

Finally, the train pulled into a small station in the middle of a featureless plain and stopped. Despite the size of the building, which, with its small platform and tiny waiting room, might have been called a "whistle stop" in Canada, there was a siding, long enough to accommodate a good-sized train. There were no other buildings nearby. On the opposite side of the train a road wound away in the distance, past some woods and toward a distant group of buildings about a mile away.

A platoon of German soldiers was standing at ease nearby. They were a scruffy bunch, mostly middle-aged by the look of them. (At nineteen years, I regarded anyone over the age of thirty as middle-aged!) Someone barked an order, and they leisurely arranged themselves in a line, parallel to our train and some distance from it. Our guards opened the doors at the end of the coach and started to get out. Yankee Joe came out of the guards' compartment and strode down the aisle.

"Okay, you guys, everybody out! Take all your stuff with you. This is the end of the line! Everybody off! Move it, you bastards!"

The guards outside were shouting now, attempting to speed up things. "Los! Schnell! Raus, ihr Schweinehunde!" yelled the *Unteroffizier* and *Feldwebel* (sergeant). We had no idea what the words meant, but the tones and gestures were unmistakeable.

Jumping out of the train with all of our kit, we were quickly lined up in five ranks, the standard German Army formation. Names were called out and checked off. As the other cars unloaded, it became apparent that there were two or three hundred prisoners of war in the group and all, so far as I could see, were in RAF blue. Down the road in the distance I could see a wisp of smoke and some buildings.

"Welcome to Stalag VIIIB, you lucky bastards!" shouted Yankee Joe. "This is where you're gonna live until we've won the war and probably for a couple of years after that! For you, the war is over!"

As we marched, or rather straggled, down the road, I thought, "So this is how it all ends for me!" Already I was thinking of escaping. "When the weather is warm," I thought, "I can live in the woods, I can walk to Switzerland, or Spain." Although I knew that I was hundreds of miles, maybe thousands, from those places, the idea gave me a lift. But when we came in sight of the main gate of the camp, my spirits fell. Nobody could escape from this place.

5

STALAG VIIIB

The camp was huge, covering perhaps ten acres. It was surrounded by two barbed-wire fences fifteen feet high, with the top six feet sloped inward to hinder potential climbers, and the ground in between filled with impenetrable rolls of razor-sharp barbed wire. There were guard towers twenty feet high at regular intervals, equipped with searchlights and machine guns. In each tower was a guard who was continuously searching the inner yard with binoculars. Ten feet inside the barbed-wire fence was a single "trip wire," marking a ten-foot strip of sand into which it was forbidden, on pain of death, to venture.

We could see, through the wire and past the main gate, that the buildings in the camp were much the same as the one we had left – that is, long wooden double barracks, each housing about 240 men, with "washrooms" in the centre, really just long horse troughs on either side of a half-wall, punctuated with about a dozen cold water taps. The camp seemed to be divided into compounds separated by roadways and surrounded by single barbed-wire fences, each compound containing four double-barrack blocks.

The column was halted just outside the main gate. A search of some type seemed to be taking place. Guards were frisking each prisoner and examining kit bags. My silk map and compass were

Stalag VIIIB (Lamsdorf) prisoner-of-war camp. A watchtower with searchlight dominates the camp as prisoners' clothing and bedding hang on the fence to air. 1942–1945.

still in between the layers of my socks, and my large jackknife was in my greatcoat pocket.

As the guard approached me, I casually put my hands in my pockets, a normal thing to do in such cold weather, wrapping my left hand around the pocket knife. He indicated for me to put my hands above my head. I threw my hands up, and as he searched all of my pockets, coat and pants, as well as my tunic and inside pockets, I could feel the knife, safely in my left hand, above my head.

When he finished, he turned his attention to the kit bag, motioning for me to put my hands down. As he went into my kit bag, I put my hands, with the knife enclosed in my left hand, back into my coat pockets. A small victory, I suppose, but it made me feel better already.

"Hey, Andy! What are you doing here?" shouted a voice from the other side of the wire. I looked at the group of prisoners across the wire but couldn't locate the voice. Somebody was waving. A blue uniform with a bearded face. "Jack Lyall!" he shouted. "Malvern!" It was one of my high school classmates who had joined the air force about the same time as me, and I hadn't seen him since.

I thought, "I'm in a prisoner-of-war camp in the middle of Germany, and the first guy I run into is an old school chum!" But that wasn't the only coincidence. As we were marched through the gate, toward what we came to know as the RAF compound, a large figure with curly dark hair in a Canadian Army uniform detached himself from the crowd and walked alongside our column.

"Hi, Andy!" he said, and I looked into the grinning face of my next-door neighbour from Toronto, George Barless. Or "Barrel Ass," as I used to call him.

"What the hell are you doing here, George?" I said. It was weird that the first two people I should meet, thousands of miles from Toronto, would be my next-door neighbour and a classmate from my local high school!

"I was captured at Dieppe," he said, "last August 19. Just about got killed – most of my friends packed it in!"

I had heard about Dieppe, of course. The news stories had been fed to the public the previous summer while I had been training in England. Now, and for the next couple of years, I was to hear the real stories of the Battle of Dieppe, where thousands of Canadian soldiers were killed, wounded, or taken prisoner. Most of those prisoners were at Stalag VIIIB, Lamsdorf.

As I was being marched down the main road of the camp, with George walking beside me, casually ignoring the armed guards, he told me a little about the camp.

There were ten separate compounds within the camp, each containing about a thousand men. Each compound was completely enclosed by a single barbed-wire fence, with one gate, which was closed each evening. During the day, the compound gates were opened, and prisoners were allowed to circulate around the camp and to visit other compounds.

"You'll be in the RAF compound," he explained as we walked along the road. "You're right across the road from our compound, where all of the Canadians are."

Just then I noticed what looked like a part of a handcuff hanging out from his overcoat pocket. "What's that?" I asked, pointing.

"Oh, that," he replied. "They're my chains. I'm supposed to wear them all day, but the Jerries don't worry too much except when there's a chain inspection." We were approaching another gate, and my column was starting to turn in. "All the Canadians, and all of the air force have to wear them," he said with a laugh. "They'll tell you all about it when you get settled in. I'll drop over and see you tomorrow. Meanwhile, here's some cigarettes and some biscuits to start you off." Grinning, he pressed them into my hands and loped off.

We were marching into the compound now, through the gate, turning right, down along a roadway of sorts in front of four

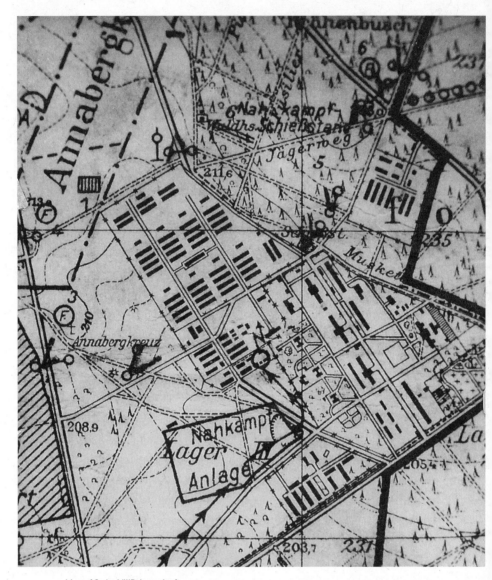

Map of Stalag VIIIB, Lamsdorf.

long barrack blocks, similar to the ones in our previous camp. We were halted and assigned our barracks. Once inside, we were each assigned to a table and a bunk. The bunks were the same as those at Dulag Luft, three tiers high, two wide, and two in length, head to head, separated only by sideboards an inch thick and ten inches high. The straw palliasses – basically a sackcloth bag full of straw – and the bodies that slept on them were each supported by about ten bed boards, two and a half feet long, six inches wide, and about an inch thick.

My crew and I were assigned to various bunks and tables in barrack block 15A, the last barrack in the row, farthest from the compound gate and next to the parade square, an area at the end of each compound where the prisoners were lined up in rows of five and counted twice a day.

So we settled in to our respective areas and had the rules explained to us. As in our previous camp, each barrack block had two parts, separated by a "washroom," each section containing about 120 men. My part of the barrack block was 15A; the back section, on the other side of the washroom, was barrack block 15B, with another 120 men.

Each table had an elected "ration king" whose job it was to divide the daily food rations equitably. A senior NCO from each barrack dealt directly with the Germans, and was the British officer in charge so far as we were concerned. There were no commissioned officers in the camp, except for a couple of British medical officers over at the hospital – referred to as the lazarette. The senior British officer in the camp was a warrant officer first class, or RSM (regimental sergeant major).

At the far side of the parade square was a concrete building called, for lack of a better name, the "shithouse," where groups of prisoners would congregate daily to pass the time of day, rumours, and yesterday's dinner. Some of the more polite, sensitive, and erudite individuals, definitely in the minority,

Up to forty prisoners at a time could use the latrine at Stalag VIIIB prisoner-of-war camp. It was rarely emptied, and conditions were extremely unsanitary. 1942–1945.

called it "the old forty-holer," for the simple reason that it had forty holes.

There were four rows of seats, each row with ten holes, the whole thing being supported by a reinforced concrete floor over a tank the size of a swimming pool and at least half full of bubbling, steaming excrement. There were no toilet seats, just forty round holes.

The best seats were the ones where you sat with your back to the wall, although from that position you were forced to observe a half dozen or more bare backsides. Here, at least, no one could see yours, a slight consolation for someone like me who had always thought of this particular bodily function as a very private matter.

At first, the smell was overpowering, but, strangely, one became accustomed to it. I suppose farmers develop immunity to some barnyard smells in the same manner. Later I was to discover that the disgusting smell had its benefits. The guards never came near the place, and a lot of contraband material was hidden beneath the seats over the years, from radio tubes to forged passports. All the same, the smell emanating from ten thousand or more gallons of raw shit was something that took some getting used to.

When we first arrived at our assigned barrack blocks, a half dozen new prisoners to each block, we were each surrounded by an interested audience of veteran *Kriegsgefangene* (German for prisoners of war, or "Kriegies") with eager questions about when we had last seen England, how we had been shot down, where and when, and literally hundreds of other questions. They were obviously starved for any kind of information about home.

From what I had learned, escaping was not all that difficult, although most escapees seemed to get caught sooner or later and were punished with minor (it seemed to me) punishments, such as a few days in the solitary confinement cells. I made up my mind to find out more about escaping, and to get out of there as soon as the warmer weather arrived.

But before even attempting to escape, I knew that I had to learn more about the camp, the local countryside, and the geography of eastern Europe, a subject that had unfortunately been practically ignored in my schooling. It was only February, and April appeared to be the earliest month that I could hope to survive in the countryside. I had a couple of months in which to prepare.

When I told my crew about my hopes of escaping, they, perhaps older and wiser, were not very enthusiastic about the prospect of joining me. I could see that I'd have to find a partner elsewhere, or go it alone.

There was an "escape committee" at the camp, but so far I hadn't met any of its members. Unlike the officers' camp at Stalag Luft III, which had a strict British military hierarchy, and where escaping could be undertaken only with the commanding officer's approval, escaping at Stalag VIIIB was the individual's affair, with the Escape Committee taking an advisory role only.

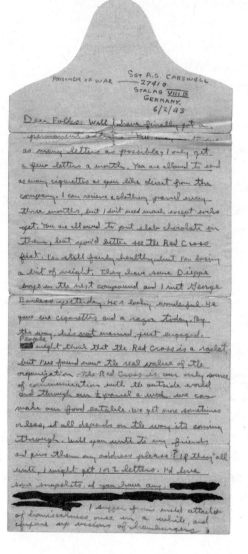

One of Andrew Carswell's letters home, written while a POW at Stalag VIIIB. February 6, 1943.

After I had made a few discreet inquiries to the senior NCO in my barrack block, the committee got wind of it and passed the word that it would contact me in due time. Meanwhile, I studied as much as I could about the camp and its routine.

It was an enormous camp, larger than I could have possibly imagined. Besides the ten thousand British prisoners of war in the camp itself, there were another fifteen thousand attached to the camp but on working parties (*Arbeitskommandos*) scattered around the surrounding countryside within, I should guess, seventy-five to a hundred miles. These men, corporals and below, lived and worked on the working parties and were only brought into the camp for reassignment, punishment, or to visit the lazarette. Sergeants and above, under the terms of the Geneva Convention, were not required to work. Most of the Canadians in the Dieppe compound were corporals or below but were not allowed to work, being considered troublemakers. Which they were.

Apparently in the early days, when some of them were sent out on working parties, machinery would mysteriously break down, tools would disappear, and things would just go wrong. The Germans could never prove anything, but there always seemed to be a Canadian nearby. So they apparently decided that all Canadians, regardless of rank, would be exempt from working parties.

The working parties consisted of groups as small as ten or fifteen, and as large as fifty or seventy-five. They worked in factories, in forest industries, in breweries, in the mines – anywhere the Germans needed them, despite the Geneva Convention, which stated clearly that no prisoner of war was to be employed in a war-related industry. In fact, many prisoners of war from Stalag VIIIB worked in war-related industries; indeed, there were few industries in Germany at that time that were not war related in one way or another.

At the front of the camp were the administration buildings and the lazarette. The compound nearest to the main gate was the working compound, where POWs of corporal rank or below awaited work assignments. This was the place where the swapping-over took place, a very necessary ingredient in the escaping game, which in the jargon of the camp, and for lack of a better name, was called the "Annual Spring Handicap," a sporting event in which a great many British prisoners of war attempted to escape each spring, and hundreds of Germans attempted to catch them.

Although most escapees were eventually caught, it was an honourable undertaking, and relatively safe, since hardly anyone ever seemed to get shot. So I decided that, since I was not destined to become a great pilot – in the near future anyway – I should try to redeem myself for having given myself up, by escaping. With a little bit of luck, I might even make it home. So far, I had been very, very lucky. I was still alive, wasn't I?

If you could have looked down at the camp from above the main gate, you would have seen two parallel roads dividing the camp into three sections. Across the front of the camp and across the middle were two connecting roads, at right angles to each other. Across the back of the camp, from left to right, were the "*Strafe* compound" (the punishment compound); the "wog" compound, which contained Indian and Arab troops; and the sports field, a football field with goal posts at either end. This was where the entire camp was assembled for "special" occasions, such as general announcements, proclamations, searches, and the like. This was where the SS colonel read Hitler's proclamation about chaining the Dieppe and RAF prisoners. This was also where we had our famous "fifty man a side" rugger match and frightened the daylights out of the Germans, who thought that a major prison riot was breaking out.

The days passed with boring monotony. Every day seemed to be a carbon copy of the previous one. At seven a.m. on the dot, "Ukraine Joe" – *Unteroffizier* Joe Kissel, so nicknamed because of his Slavic features, and the corporal in charge of the RAF compound – would stomp through the barrack block yelling, "Raus!

Alle raus!" (Out! Everybody out!), slapping each table with a resounding *thwack* with the flat of his bayonet as he strode by.

Several dozen voices would call out, from all parts of the barrack block, in a great thunderous babble, "Up your arse, you fucking square-headed bastard!" and other assorted greetings hurled about in a dozen different accents, from broad Scottish and Yorkshire dialects to London cockney, not to mention our own Clem's epithets in his broad, drawling cowboy accent, direct from western Ontario: "Ahed laak to taak that Krout sonofabitch and ..." – usually describing some colourfully obscene punishment that he would like to inflict on Ukraine Joe, which would invoke great howls of laughter from the Brits.

Of course, Ukraine Joe knew very little English, or he would have been quite upset at some of the things said to him. He probably thought that the shouting in the morning was enthusiasm. After he had associated with English-speaking prisoners for a year or more, he became very proud of his limited knowledge of English. Comprehending the import of some of the ribald verbal abuse being heaped upon him one morning, he gathered himself up in the full dignity of an *Unteroffizier* of the Third Reich, and made the following pronouncement: "I know that you people think I know fuck nothing! But you are wrong! I know fuck all!"

The roar of laughter that went up on the parade ground in the RAF compound was like a tidal wave as those who hadn't heard the original remark had it passed on to them. Within a few hours, all ten thousand men in the camp were chuckling over Ukraine Joe's contribution to the language. The phrase and the laughter went out to a hundred working parties and to other camps as well, as the story went the rounds of the POW community. A new phrase had been born into the lexicon of military profanity. Years later, the story was still being told and retold, and there are many ex-POWs to this day who will swear that it happened in their camp. But to set the record straight, it was "Ukraine Joe," Corporal Joseph

Kissel, of the German Wehrmacht, who invented, in 1943, the profanely colourful and meaningless term "fuck nothing."

Once Ukraine Joe had raced through the barrack block for the first time, it was considered expedient to leap out of your bunk, don some clothes, and get in line for the "chains parade," because the second time Joe Kissel came around, he whacked asses! And that bayonet was hard, solid steel. Although Joe never used his bayonet for cutting, or stabbing, the possibility was always there, so none of us pushed him on that score. So the second time that Joe's hooting and hollering started, the few stragglers still in bed leaped out flying, keeping as far from the slashing maniac as they could, and, half-hopping while they struggled into their pants, raced for the lineup.

Chains parade happened very quickly now, because we had learned that it was to our advantage to get it over with. The chains were carried in by four "duty carriers" chosen by roster from the barrack, accompanied by a bored guard, and were quickly snapped on. Overcoats were put on behind the bunks or some other place away from the guards' gaze: with a flip of a corned beef–tin key, one would remove the handcuffs, put on the overcoat, and then put the handcuffs back on – to the mystification of some of the newer guards, who thought that we were all a bunch of Houdinis.

Next came *Appell*, or the roll call/attendance parade. All occupants of the four double-barrack blocks, 15A and 15B to 18A and 18B, roughly a thousand RAF non-commissioned officer aircrew, all of whom had arrived in Germany by some violent means, appeared on Appell twice a day, to be counted, checked, and occasionally lectured to.

We were lined up in five rows of twenty outside each barrack block. There was no requirement to stand at attention, or indeed to maintain any particular stance. One had only to be there. Some stood at ease, with some semblance of military bearing. Others slouched, with hands in pockets, collars turned up, unshaven, and with a variety of hats, scarves, and wool mitts sent through the Red Cross or from loved ones.

One prisoner had received a pair of hand-knit wool socks from the Red Cross, with a piece of paper in the toe of one containing a woman's name and address in England. He had written to her on one of his precious quota of postcards, telling her how much he had appreciated the socks. Back came a reply, about three months later, informing him that the socks had been intended for "fighting men, not prisoners of war"!

After being counted several times by one or more of the guards, who would then report the total to Ukraine Joe, we would be dismissed and were free to wander the camp until evening Appell.

If you had saved a small slice of bread from the previous day's ration, one-seventh of a loaf of black bread, you might prepare for breakfast, as "brew up" was imminent. When "Brew up!" was called, we raced into the barracks, grabbed our tin mugs (made from a used tin can), and stood in line. At the front of the line a duty person rationed out the hot water from a container that had just been carried in by two or more men also on the duty roster. The hot water was doled out with a ladle made from a long stick attached to a tin about the size of a Campbell's soup tin.

If one had saved a bit of tea, a used tea bag, or some coffee from a Canadian Red Cross parcel, you could have a "brew" with your bread. If not, you used the hot water for shaving, for this was wintertime, the barracks were unheated, and hot water was at a premium. As a matter of fact, everything was in short supply.

Walking around the compound, or even around the entire camp (for the compound gates were unlocked during daylight hours), was a favourite pastime, but with the daily ration of food coming up around ten o'clock in the morning, most of us paced about the compound, awaiting this very important event.

The next couple of hours were taken up with talking, gossiping, rumour-mongering, and storytelling. As everyone in the

barrack and, indeed, in the camp had arrived in this particular
situation by some violent means, there was no shortage of stories.

Talking one day to Jack Lyall, my former schoolmate, I learned
he had been the pilot of a Stirling bomber, flying a mission over
Cologne, in the Ruhr valley. His aircraft had been shot up and
disabled, some of his crew had been killed, and he had bailed out
from the front escape hatch in much the same manner that I had.
As he reached for the D ring to open his parachute chest pack, he
found that his parachute was not there. Nothing on his chest but
the harness! There he was, falling straight down into a blazing city
from ten thousand or so feet, with no parachute.

He was terrified at the prospect of hitting the ground at
120 miles an hour (we all knew the terminal velocity of a falling
human body), and he was sure that he was going to die. He could
see the city coming closer and was almost resigned to his fate when
he felt a gentle bump against his head. He reached up and felt his
parachute pack, which had somehow ripped away prematurely
from his harness instead of after it opened, as it was supposed to.
Instinctively, he felt for the D ring and pulled it.

Wham! The parachute opened with a jerk, leaving him swinging in the night sky. *Crash!* A second later he bounced off a roof
and slid into a garden at the rear of a house. He crawled under a
hedge, dragging his chute behind him, and hid. An air raid siren
was blowing. Anti-aircraft guns were going off nearby. Eventually,
an air raid warden or policeman found him and turned him in.
His leg was injured, likely broken. In any case, he was lucky to be
captured by someone who would turn him in to the authorities.
Bomber crews were not very popular with civilians who had just
been bombed, in Germany or any other place.

6

Swap Over

We were expected to team up with another prisoner, called a "mucker," to share parcels, rations, etc., and to share cooking and other household chores. I "mucked in" with several different partners during my stay at Stalag viiib, changing partners, as did some of the others, out of sheer boredom, or because of different tastes in food or cooking or, as in one case, because my partner was in the "rackets." Although this gave me a higher standard of living, I didn't want to be associated with it. But the main reason for changing muckers was that I had become interested in escaping quite early in my stay, and was looking for a partner with the same idea.

I met my first escaping partner while looking for a "swapover." I had learned during my first few weeks in the camp that the only reasonably safe way of escaping was to swap over – that is, change identities with an army private or corporal who was eligible to go outside the camp on a working party, or *Arbeitskommando*.

There were two ways to escape from a camp like Stalag viiib. First, you could attempt to escape directly from the camp itself, either by constructing a tunnel, as some of the Canadians in the Dieppe compound regularly attempted to do, and regularly got caught, or going "over the wire" (actually, over, under, or through), which involved a very good chance of being shot and killed.

Second, you could get out of the camp first on an *Arbeitskommando*, where you would have a much better chance of escaping, and much less chance of being shot. Being a bit claustrophobic about tunnels and confined spaces, I chose the second method.

The problem was that senior NCOs and above were exempted from working by the Geneva Convention, and despite their brutal and sadistic treatment of Jews, Poles, and Russian prisoners of war, the Germans appeared to pay some attention to the convention. It was rumoured that the camp commandant, a colonel, had a son who was in a POW camp in Canada. It is also just possible that as members of an armed force yet undefeated in the field, and which might by some very great stretch of the German imagination even win the war, we should be treated carefully – just in case.

Despite the Germans' policy of sending all corporals and below out on working parties, Canadian soldiers from the Dieppe compound were prohibited from such assignments. When sent out to work on *Arbeitskommandos*, they had been suspected as the source of machinery breakdowns and other work stoppages, although no proof had ever been found.

That there were also spies in our midst was commonly believed, although never proved, because every Canadian tunnel-building project, and every other type of escape attempt from the camp, always seemed to be nipped in the bud just a few days before it was about to happen. So Canadian soldiers from the Dieppe compound were also prime candidates for the swapover process, if they wanted to have any chance of escaping.

Swapping over was simple, in theory anyway. All you had to do was wander about in the working compound, a compound in the northeast corner of the camp, which was full of army personnel below the rank of sergeant who were eligible to be selected for one of the many working parties within range of Stalag VIIIB, and find a suitable private or corporal who might be interested in a few months of the "soft" life in the RAF compound – and masquerading as an RAF NCO.

It helped if he was more or less the same size and shape as oneself, although the German identification photos, taken more than three years earlier, about the time of Dunkirk, never actually looked much like the individual. They usually showed a skinny fellow with a shaved head. The prisoners by then were usually much more healthy looking, and usually had a full head of hair.

In early March 1943, I was wandering about the working compound looking for a potential swapover when I met Corporal John Donaldson, a British Army corporal who had been captured three years before, in 1940, just before Dunkirk. He could speak German well, having worked on a number of working parties in various parts of Germany. He had been on a rearguard action with part of the retreating British Army in France when his unit was surrounded by German Panzers, which cut the unit to pieces before the survivors finally surrendered.

He and thousands of other bedraggled and wounded British soldiers had been marched back through France hundreds of miles, toward the German border. He told me that often they would be marched through a French town, then back around by side roads, then marched down the main street of the town again, in order to make the local populace believe that the number of prisoners captured was much greater.

He told me about the sergeant major in charge of his group who, although sick, wounded, and half-starved, as were most of the British prisoners, insisted that while marching through a town the British troops march properly and proudly, swinging their arms, heads up, eyes front, and properly in step. He didn't want the French, or even the Germans, to think that the British were beaten. Some of the French civilians along the route would weep, and press bread and cheese into the hands of the prisoners, despite the rifle butts of the guards.

The Germans were on a high in those heady days of 1940. They had not lost any battles, couldn't care less about the Geneva Convention, and did pretty much as they pleased with prisoners of war. The particular group John Donaldson was with ended up in the coal mines of Silesia, where they were worked like slaves, with unsafe conditions, long hours, and minimum rations. Quite a number fell sick and died. Some were killed in mine accidents. Compared with conditions in 1940, POWs in 1943 had it pretty soft, as John often liked to remind me, a mere rookie.

It was not surprising that most of the British prisoners captured in 1940 had lost interest in trying to escape. Having made it this far, there was no way that they were going to jeopardize their lives when the war might be over any day.

But even I, with my limited knowledge of politics and geography, knew that it might be years, if ever, that the war would be over. I knew instinctively too that the Germans and Japanese had an outside chance of winning this war. I didn't even want to think about that possibility, but it was one more good reason to attempt to escape.

John Donaldson didn't like air force people much. He liked Canadians even less. But he wanted to escape, and none of his friends and associates, survivors from 1940, was particularly interested. He had been a prisoner for three years, and while on *Arbeitskommandos,* working as an electrician, he had learned to speak German fluently. I had been in Germany only two months, could speak no German, was RAF and a Canadian to boot, but John was attracted to me because we had one powerful common need: to escape!

So I spent a lot of time in his company, getting to know the ropes. As a veteran POW, he knew the operation of the camp and, more important, the way in which the Germans conducted their affairs. We met mainly at the sports field, where hundreds of prisoners would gather to watch soccer and rugger games, and discussed our plans for escaping.

It wouldn't do, he suggested, for me to hang about in the working compound *(Arbeitslager)*, where my blue uniform might attract unwelcome attention of a guard, or worse, one of the many spies who were generally thought to be in the camp. There were no spies in the air force barracks, as we all had connections through our squadrons and our training backgrounds that were easy to check and would be hard to fake, or so we thought.

My immediate friends and associates from Table 3 were not particularly interested in escaping, nor were any of the other members of my crew, feeling quite justifiably that they had taken enough risks for a while, and were lucky to just be alive. Also, the war news was improving and every evening, when the BBC News from our secret radio receiver was read out in the barrack block, there would be cheering news about the progress of the war. The secret radios, escape committees, communications with Britain, cameras, typewriters, and other secrets were things that I knew nothing about at the time but would learn about eventually.

Meanwhile, I had to get myself a willing swapover. I discussed it with my immediate group and our block NCO, who would have to know, and they all agreed, a little reluctantly I thought, to go along with my scheme. A few days later, John brought my swapover in to meet me. His name was Dennis Reeves, a private in the British Army, currently living in the working compound awaiting orders to go to a new working party. He was willing to change identities with a Canadian Air Force sergeant pilot about whom he knew nothing.

John, of course, had told him wildly exaggerated stories of the luxurious life that Canadian Air Force sergeants lived in the RAF compound, and how all the Canadians received thousands of cigarettes in their personal parcels, compared with the smaller packets the British usually received.

The other members of my table gathered around and inspected him, deciding that he was not only an acceptable substitute for me but possibly an improvement. So he was accepted, and all that had to be decided was when and where to do the deed. He was about my size and weight, so switching uniforms and clothing would be no problem. We would have to learn a lot about each other's background so that if the Germans questioned either one of us, we could come up with a plausible background that would fit their records.

The Germans still knew nothing about me other than my name, rank, number, and home address, which I had divulged reluctantly in order to send my meagre ration of postcards home and to receive parcels. They apparently had quite a file on Dennis, including his civilian occupation, mother's maiden name, and many personal details. At the time he was captured, just prior to Dunkirk, the German interrogators either didn't know or didn't care about the Geneva Convention and extracted considerable information from their prisoners, apparently with the aid of rifle butts and boots.

So I learned that Dennis had worked in an automobile factory in Birmingham as a coach trimmer (putting upholstery fabric in the interior of cars), as well as his mother's maiden name and a lot of other personal lore, some of which I have since forgotten. But I'll never forget his face. I saw him dead, in a ditch, two years later in another part of Germany, just a few weeks before the war ended.

The big switch was made a few days later in the RAF compound, behind the bunks in 15A, in the early afternoon. There were no Germans about. Ukraine Joe didn't know me from Adam, and I had made it a point not to attract attention from any of the guards. They likely thought that all *Engländer* looked alike, anyway.

Dennis Reeves looked pretty good in my uniform, with his sergeant's stripes and pilot wings, and the "Canada" flashes on his shoulders. His army uniform didn't look too bad on me either, although it was a Red Cross issue with no regimental insignia on it. As well as this army "battledress" uniform, I had an army greatcoat, also without insignia. I didn't mind, as I had great plans for that coat.

Both of us had to remember to keep our mouths shut as much as possible when around those who spoke English. Our accents gave the lie to our uniforms. He, with his Canadian uniform, had a typical (I thought) limey accent straight from the Midlands, and I, with my British uniform, sounded like a Yank to the British. Fortunately for us, none of the Germans with whom we associated could understand English, let alone recognize accents.

John walked down with me to the working compound, my new home. He was already living there, so we became muckers, sharing our rations and Red Cross parcels. The population of this barrack block was very mobile, and most of its inhabitants were strangers to each other, an ideal situation for planting spies. Everyone here was waiting for a new assignment. Some were in for medical treatment and would be returning to the same working parties.

John suggested that I not talk to anyone unless I had to, because my Canadian accent would give me away. So I talked in grunts, mumbled, nodded, and shrugged my shoulders a lot; said "blimey," "bloody," and "foocking Jerries!" in my best limey accent; and tried to blend in as best I could. The English have a traditional tolerance for eccentricities, and considered it impolite to ask questions of strangers. I was safe for the moment.

Quite a few of the ground troops in that particular barrack were cockneys, from London's East End, and said things like, "me muvver," "me bruvver," and "me favver," and had a kind of rhyming slang in which "skin and blister" meant "sister," "trouble and strife" meant "wife," "apples and pears" meant "stairs," and so on. John helped me as much as possible to avoid the more obvious pitfalls, and reminded me again that there were probably spies in the barrack.

I had burned all my bridges. A move was imminent, according to rumours, so we began preparing our equipment for our impending escape. It was now nearing the end of March 1943, and I had been a prisoner for less than three months. April, they said, was a good month for escaping, because it was warm enough to sleep outside. How was I to know that that April in Ober Silesia was about the same as April at home? My family never opened our summer cottage in southern Ontario until the 24th of May because of the possibility of night frost.

We knew that we were likely to be searched going through the main gate, and perhaps subjected to an identity check; the Germans knew about swapping over and were always on the look-out for RAF or Canadian personnel trying to sneak out the main gate as part of a working party.

John and I had amassed a few chocolate bars, some biscuits, and some bully beef from our Red Cross parcels. It was difficult to get unopened tins except through the rackets, because the German guards punctured every tin in each Red Cross parcel when they were issued to make sure that nobody saved food for escaping. Unopened tins, however, were not too difficult to get through the search because prisoners returning from working parties often carried food items back with them in their kit bags. Knives, maps, compasses, and other items that might be useful for escaping were naturally verboten. I decided to carry my jackknife in my pocket as usual, and hold it in my hand during the body search, as I had before. John was a little nervous about the knife; he thought that the Germans might consider it a weapon.

The only argument we had during our preparations concerned vitamins. John had acquired a bottle of assorted vitamins – A, B, C, and D, I believe – insisting that they should do us for a day instead of food. I'd recently become a bit of an expert on vitamins, having just read a nine-hundred-page volume on the subject called *Hutchison's Food and Dietetics*. I had nothing else to do and, hungry most of the time, I avidly read the entire book, thus gaining an up-to-date knowledge of food and nutrition. That is, up-to-date in 1939! So I at least understood that a vitamin was not food but merely a catalyst that allowed the body to utilize certain minerals, such as calcium, or to prevent certain diseases, such as scurvy.

When I tried to explain this tactfully to John, he told me that I was crazy, that Canadians didn't know anything anyway, and that Canadian sergeants were about equal to or less in knowledge and ability than privates in the British Army. So I dropped the matter, resolving to save some real food for the day that John decided to go on vitamins.

A few days later, both our names were called out for a working party leaving the next day. It was to be Arbeitskommando E148, a graphite mine, in the Sudetenland, formerly part of Czechoslovakia and about two days' train travel from Stalag VIIIB.

According to the Geneva Convention, POWs were not to be employed in war industries, and graphite was certainly a lubricant that could be used for war purposes, as well as for making pencils. It didn't really matter much to the Germans, who decided where we went. I didn't much like the idea of working in a mine, completely enclosed by thousands of tons of rock – to me, death in an aeroplane was certainly preferable to suffocation or entombment.

That same day, I discreetly visited my former barracks and spoke with my swapover, Dennis, and with my crew and friends, telling them what I was planning and making sure that they knew my family's address in case something should go wrong. They gave me extra chocolate, food, and cigarettes to take along, and wished me luck. Cigarettes and chocolate, in those days, were worth far more than money and were the real currency of the camp. German Reichsmark, without ration coupons, were practically worthless and would buy nothing except train tickets, matches, soup, beer, and a few other items.

We spent the night in a state of excitement. The next morning after Appell, our names were called out again, and we picked up our kit bags, donned our army greatcoats, and formed up in a small group of about twenty. Three or four of us were going to E148; the rest were going to other *Arbeitskommandos* en route. We were marched out of the compound by two guards, one in front and one in the rear, along the road connecting to the main road of the camp, then made a right turn toward the main gate, where our group was halted. As each name was called out, a prisoner would come to attention and shout, "Here!" I was waiting for my name to be called.

"Reefs!" the voice shouted. "Private Reefs!"

I almost missed it! Unconsciously, despite all my preparations, I was expecting my real name. I guess I was daydreaming a little too, seeing all that open countryside beyond the main gate. In my mind I was already crossing the border into Switzerland when I suddenly realized who "Reefs" was, and that everyone was looking at me.

"Here!" I shouted, springing to attention like a good soldier. I was very sensitive about my new identity and felt everyone, particularly the German NCO, could see right through my disguise. My heart almost stopped as I saw Ukraine Joe slowly walk down the line of prisoners, hands behind his back, looking into each face. Was the panic I was feeling showing on my face? He stopped at the man next to me, studied his face for a moment, then moved on, passing me with hardly a glance.

My heart was beating so loudly that I was sure he must have heard it. He spoke briefly to the *Feldwebel* in charge, the two of them laughed at some private joke, and Joe Kissel departed, to my great relief. I wondered if he had once more been looking for Angus Dewar, former Spitfire pilot, and one of the camp's most regular, if not most unsuccessful, escapers. I grinned to myself. He's probably planning to pole-vault over the fence, or go out in the garbage truck, this very moment.

Marching out through the main gate of Stalag VIIIB, we passed through the centre of the administrative area just outside the main gate and into a small administrative building. We were halted in a large bare room where several guards awaited us. We were about to be searched.

I stood beside my open kit bag, a large bar of Canadian toilet soap sitting on the top of the folded clothing. I'd been told that if you left some soap or chocolate near the top of the kit bag, the guard might be a little less careful with his search. (Good soap was virtually non-existent in wartime Germany, and the local soap would barely dissolve, let alone clean anything.) My hands were in my overcoat pocket, my left one clutching my jackknife. The guard told me to put my hands above my head.

Up they went, the left one still hiding the knife. He didn't look up but merely searched my pockets, finding nothing of interest. He ran his hand up my legs and felt under my arms, grunted, then turned his attention to my kit bag. My hands went down and the knife back into my coat pocket. So far, so good.

He looked at the bar of soap, then smelled it. It was perfumed soap of a quality that the Germans hadn't seen for years. I looked at the ceiling. When I looked down again, the soap was gone and so was the guard.

The search was over, and the guards, having acquired soap, chocolate, and cigarettes, appeared to be satisfied. I learned later that these transactions were more dangerous for the guards than for us. If we were caught, our punishments would be nominal, but theirs could be severe, ranging from a prison sentence to serving on the Russian Front, a virtual death sentence.

All of the formalities over, we marched down the road toward the railroad station at Lamsdorf, a tiny village about a mile and a half away. It was a warm, pleasant day, and for the first time since I had been shot down, I was beginning to feel a bit hopeful about my situation. John Donaldson, marching along beside me, gave me a grin and a nudge.

The world was looking pretty good to me at that moment. The first stage of our escape had been completed, and we were well on our way toward the second. I liked these British soldiers, they had spirit and a sense of humour. Although the Germans had the upper hand physically, we had the upper hand psychologically. We refused to act like defeated men. We kept ourselves well dressed and clean-shaven, marched in step, and acted as if our guards were merely a nuisance to be tolerated.

After a fifteen-minute march, we arrived at the station out in the middle of nowhere. It consisted of a small platform with a ticket office and a tiny waiting room. From our maps and discussions with others, we knew that to the east lay Krakow, in Poland, and to the west Breslau, Dresden, and Görlitz, in east Germany. Sudetenland, our destination, lay somewhere in the mountainous country to the southwest.

The few civilians on the platform looked at us with little interest, having seen many British prisoners of war come and go. A train came puffing in from the east, whistle screaming, brakes squealing as it ground to a wheezing halt. Most German trains had compartments, accessible from the platform, like British trains, but some had coaches too. One of our guards walked along the platform and found a suitable coach with only a few civilian passengers in it. Gesticulating, shouting, and waving his rifle, he cleared the car so that we could have it to ourselves.

By now, a few more guards had materialized to take care of the various groups going to different destinations. John and I were the only two going to E148, the graphite mine. I didn't say much other than a few grunts, and settled down to enjoy the scenery.

It was a long train ride, lasting the rest of the day and part of the evening. As we proceeded west, the scenery grew more interesting, the buildings and towns improved and the countryside became hilly, even mountainous. I found myself wishing, as I had many times during my incarceration, that I had studied my European geography lessons a little more assiduously. In any case, the fact that I was heading west toward Switzerland, and toward freedom, made me feel quite happy.

Arbeitskommando E148

That evening, the train stopped in a little mountain town straight out of a picture postcard. A small river ran through the centre of the village. There was a small waterfall, beautiful old houses and buildings, and a brewery. Some of our group were to work at the brewery (lucky stiffs, we thought), and a few of us were to spend the night there – John and I, along with two others.

There were about fifteen prisoners working at the brewery in this little town, whose name I have forgotten. The prisoners' quarters were inside the brewery on the second floor in a large room, probably a former storage room.

Although the building was solid stone with cement floors and appeared virtually escape-proof, it didn't look much like a prison. The familiar double-decker bunks were tastefully arranged around two sides of the room, with neatly built wooden shelving against the wall containing Red Cross boxes and individual rations. A couple of standard wooden tables, with enough benches and stools to accommodate a dozen or more men, were in the centre of the room. Four of us were to be billeted here for the night and continue our journey the next day.

Two barred windows looking out over a stone courtyard, and a heavy oaken door leading into a stone-lined hallway were the only barriers between us and the outside.

"Does anyone ever try to escape from here?" asked John, peering through the barred windows into the darkened courtyard below.

"Don't be a bloody fool!" retorted a British sergeant. "This is the best fucking job in Germany! Why would we want to ruin everything by some silly bugger trying to escape?" He turned his attention to me. I was desperately attempting to look as innocent as possible. "You don't fool me either! I could tell you were a fucking Yank or Canadian the minute you opened your mouth! Probably a swapover, and air force at that. Don't worry, I'm not going to turn you in – but I'm not going to help you either! We've spent years getting this place organized, and we're not letting any fucking air force swapover screw up the cushiest setup we've ever had."

"Lay off him!" said John, coming to my defence. "He's an air force pilot, and he's a Canadian, but he's okay. He was shot down three months ago. We're not going to try anything here, but we're going out to E148 to work at the graphite mine, and we're going to have a try at escaping from there."

They all looked at me with considerable interest. Here was someone who had been in England recently – only a few months ago. Most of them were Dunkirk veterans, captured more than three years earlier, in 1940.

"What's it like in England now, mate?" said one in a friendlier manner. I told them what little I knew about recent events in England, the battle for North Africa, the huge buildup of arms and troops in England, and the general feeling that the Second Front would be coming soon. They, in turn, told me about their early days as prisoners, half-starved, poorly dressed for the cold winters. No wonder they were happy to serve the rest of the war in this "cushy" job.

The brewery was small but old and well established. Most of the regular workers had been conscripted for the war. A few supervisory staff, two guards, and a couple of middle-aged women were the only other workers. The fifteen to twenty British prisoners (depending on the season) were the main workers, producing a large amount of beer, all in barrels, for their main customer, the German Army.

Once the ice had been broken, our hosts turned out to be most generous. A couple of large pitchers of beer appeared. Out came the tin mugs and a few real glasses, purloined or traded for cigarettes and chocolate. Soon we were having a regular party.

"What about the guards?" I asked. "Do they know that you're stealing beer?"

"They steal more than we do!" one man laughed, "and both of them are downtown right now, screwing their girlfriends. They won't be back tonight."

"What a chance to escape," I thought, looking around this stone-walled room, but I understood them perfectly. "This is pretty good beer," I burped luxuriously, savouring my second large mugful. "I feel a little drunk!"

"We don't get to drink the special stuff," said one of our hosts, winking at the sergeant. "It goes straight to the elite troops, like the ss," and the rest of the group laughed uproariously. And so they told us how they made their "special" beer for their special friends.

In the holding bay, where the completed barrels were marked and held for delivery, the appropriate barrels were selected. Then, at an opportune moment when no civilian staff was about, one of the prisoners would knock out the bung on the top of the barrel and urinate into it, replacing the bung with a whack of his mallet: his contribution to the war effort!

We passed the night uneventfully in spare bunks made available by our hosts, using our own blankets carried with us in our kit bags. (Prisoners normally carried all of their gear, including blankets and food, whenever they were moved from one spot to another.)

In the morning, our guards appeared, the big iron door was unlocked, and our hosts went off to work, after wishing us luck on our enterprise, and no doubt feeling relieved at our departure. John and I were now assigned to one guard, who was to take us to our new working party. The others were to go on a different train to their final destinations. We ambled along with our guard to the railroad station in the centre of town, about a half mile from the brewery. He was certainly taking his time and appeared to be in a good mood. I wondered what he had been doing the night before.

After a short wait, our train arrived and we were seated in a compartment with our guard. An old man, a middle-aged woman, and a soldier came into the compartment and sat down opposite us. The soldier struck up a conversation with our guard.

"What's he saying?" I asked John.

"Not much," said John. "He's just telling him that we are a couple of English prisoners from the big camp at Lamsdorf, and that it's a really cushy job for him. He doesn't often get such an easy job. He's going to take his time going back, too. The other chap sounds a bit envious. I think he's on leave and has to go back to the war pretty soon."

The little train chugged along for a few hours, meandering through the mountainous countryside, stopping at every little town along the way. The scenery was beautiful. The sky was clear, the weather was sunny and warm, and it was hard to believe that we were prisoners of war in a foreign country. The sight of the guard sitting next to the window with his loaded rifle brought me back to reality.

Finally, the train pulled into the station. The town, like all we had passed, was another picture postcard. As we stepped out of the train, a German soldier armed with a rifle stepped up and greeted our guard. After their short conversation, we were marched up the road and out of town.

It was a long walk, two or three miles in an easterly direction, along the edge of a good-sized valley to our right, and steadily uphill. About a mile out of town, we passed a large black and dirty factory or mill. Our guard spoke to John and motioned toward the buildings.

"This is where we're going to work," said John, waving his hand toward the grimy buildings. "But we don't have to live there," he added. "According to numbnuts here, we're supposed to be billeted in a farmhouse, about a mile up the road."

I was relieved. The thought of working in that filthy black place was bad enough.

Another mile along the dirt road, past fields and woods, a farm or two, and we were there.

The farmhouse was a large two-storey house close to the edge of the road, which by now had dwindled to a track. Across the road was an outdoor toilet, a two-holer, which I was to find out later served only the Kriegies; the other occupants of the farm had their own outdoor toilet. Even the guards disdained the use of our privy, a fact which would work to our advantage later.

It was afternoon when we were marched into the farmhouse by our new guard. The train guard, having obtained a signature for the two live bodies he had delivered, left for town, soon to be joined, we discovered, by our new guard.

Just inside the front door of the farmhouse was a large room, about twenty feet square. The rear door of the room had been sealed off, and the only window was covered with barbed wire and steel bars. Inside were the now-familiar wooden bunks, tables, cupboards, and utensils, enough to serve fifteen men.

As we dropped our kit bags on the floor and looked around, we were welcomed by a British corporal. While the others sat on the edges of their bunks, watching in silence, he showed us our bunks and explained the routine. He asked me my name and where I was from.

"Dennis Reeves, from Birmingham," I said. "Dunkirk, 1940."

"Bullshit!" he said in a cockney accent. "You're a fucking Yank, and a fucking liar, if not a Jerry spy!"

John to the rescue again. "He's okay," he said. "He's a Canadian sergeant pilot. Swapped over, he did, and the two of us are going to try to escape."

All thirteen stared at us in silence. "Going to really screw up this place if you do!" said one.

"What do you mean?" said I, naively. "It's your duty to try to escape! We thought that maybe you'd help us."

Dead silence. They looked at each other.

"Well, we're not going anywhere tonight, anyway," said John, "so we can talk about it later." Then he stood up, drawing himself up to his full five feet two inches, put his hands on his hips, and stared straight into the eyes of the other corporal. "I just want to say one thing. There is still a fucking war on. We are all British. The Jerries are the enemy, not us. It is our duty to try to escape, and it is your duty to try to help us. And remember one thing, this war will be over some day, and we are going to fucking well win it. After that, there'll be a fucking reckoning!"

Thirteen faces stared at him, shocked into silence. They were clearly thinking about what he had said. There was no further comment, but from that moment on, their attitude toward us changed for the better.

The routine at Arbeitskommando E148 was very simple. At precisely eight o'clock in the morning, our guard unlocked the main door of the farmhouse and marched us down the road to the graphite mine, where we reported to our assigned jobs, some underground and some on the surface. Again my amazing dumb luck held, for John and I were assigned to surface jobs.

My job was fairly simple. The graphite was mined like coal, brought to the surface in chunks, ground into a powder, mixed with water into a sort of thick black mud, then formed into bricks, which were rolled out into the yard on steel wheeled carts and left to dry in the sun. My job was to push the heavy carts from the factory to the yard. Heavy work, but at least I was in the fresh air.

Our clothes were black by the end of a working day, as were our bodies. We were allowed to shower and change out of our working clothes at the end of each shift, so we arrived "home" reasonably clean. We soon learned to leave one set of garments in the change room and wear clean uniforms to and from work. Because of the German passion for obeying orders without question, we now enjoyed a five-hour workday.

A few years previously, the Germans had sent time-study experts to the mine to establish how much work a British POW should be able to do. Sensing what was happening, subjects of the study made sure that they accomplished as little as possible while appearing to work very hard for eight or nine hours. Being meticulous, the Germans decided that they should establish a quota of work to be completed in a day, rather than a specific number of hours.

Based on what they had observed, these experts laid down the number of tons, bags, bricks, or blocks each prisoner should produce, depending on his job. They published this data in a comprehensive list of daily requirements, had it signed by all the proper authorities – and it became law, so far as the ordinary German guard or company foreman was concerned.

The truth was that any of the prisoners could easily complete their assigned quotas by noon if they hurried, or an hour later if they took their time. And no private or corporal in the German Army was going to even suggest to his superiors that some officer has made a mistake, especially a senior officer. It was a perfect setup. Our guards were happy, they were following their orders to the letter, and we were happy, working only half days.

Each day, by one o'clock, most of us had stripped off our filthy black work clothes, showered in lukewarm water with "Jerry" soap, and put our uniforms back on. By two o'clock we were lined up by our own corporal, ready to be marched back by our guard, Herman. "Herman the German," as we called him, wasn't a bad sort of guy, if a little slow. His main interest in life was to get us locked up after supper so that he could ride his bicycle down to the village in the evening to visit his girlfriend.

For the rest of the day we were more or less free to sit outside in the sun, visit the toilet across the road, go inside to read, whittle, write, do laundry, or just loaf, as long as we stayed in sight of Herman, who counted us regularly to make sure nobody was missing.

Compared to life in the Stalag, this was not so bad. I began to see my roommates' point of view. I knew that once we escaped from this place, life would become hell for everybody. The guards would be severely punished, the prisoners would be put under harsh supervision, and the free and easy life we were now enjoying would disappear. I knew in my heart that our chances of making it all the way back to England were very, very small, and the consequences for our friends were very, very great. So I felt a sense of guilt in what we were about to do, even though I knew that we had to do it. We had better start planning, I decided, before these guys changed their minds and decided not to help us.

Each night right after supper we usually sat around and talked, or read, or played cards. Before long, Herman would come in to count us and to lock up. He would walk around the room counting, "Eins, zwei, drei ..." until he had got us all.

"Fünfzehn!" he would call out when he got to the number fifteen and then, looking around the room with an air of great satisfaction, would say, "Gute Nacht, meine Lieben" (Good night, my dears) and close the door behind him. Then we would hear the key turning in the lock and the steel bar being lowered across the outside of the steel door. With his charges safely locked up for the night, he would get on his bicycle and coast down the road toward town and his girlfriend's arms.

We weren't sure how long he stayed in town – I hoped that it was all night, for our sake. He'd never come into our quarters late at night to check up on us, assured, I suppose, by the strong bars on our only window and the steel plate, iron bar, and lock on our door, in addition to the outside door, also locked with a key.

The elderly farmer and his family lived in the rear of the house and upstairs. The family comprised an old man and woman, and a young girl of about sixteen. She was dark and good-looking, and seemed to be sweet on our corporal, who was also our official interpreter. He spent a lot of time talking to her, her family, and the guard. I wondered about his enthusiasm for our escape, and decided that we should get it over with quickly, before our little group lost their willingness to cooperate with us.

There was also a dull-looking girl of fourteen or so, below normal in intelligence, who seemed to like our "cook." He was the only member of the party who didn't work at the mine, having been officially designated as the person who cooked up the potatoes and soup, our principal German food ration.

Except for our interpreter, the corporal, the rest of the group, also captured in 1940, were ordinary blokes who had been caught up in the war in 1939 and had volunteered or been conscripted. Some of them claimed that they had enlisted only because they needed a job. Some job!

All except for "Aussie" Jones and Jimmy the Greek, whose real name was Demetrius Zogaris. Both had been captured in Crete when the German parachute troops had invaded the island and captured all the valiant, outnumbered British troops, who, having run out of ammunition, had no choice but to surrender.

Jimmy hadn't even been in the British Army. The Germans were methodically shooting everyone suspected of helping the British, so the soldiers that he was with fitted him out with a uniform before they surrendered, coaching him on what to say to the Germans, as he couldn't read or write. He was very smart, however, and did exactly as he was told. He was, as far as the Germans were concerned, an official British prisoner of war. But he received no pay or allowances, and had no connections with anyone in Britain.

He and Aussie were the first to show some enthusiasm in helping us plan our escape.

Another piece of luck! Herman the German was being transferred back to a fighting unit. He was depressed about it, and we could understand why. The possibility of being sent to the Russian Front was always there, to say nothing of having to forgo his girlfriend's charms. But his misfortune was our golden opportunity.

The next day I reminded John of the night Herman had been counting when one of the prisoners reading in bed had pulled the covers over his head in order to get to sleep. "Do you remember what Herman did as he passed the bunk?" I asked John.

"Sure," he said. "He walked over and grabbed his foot, to make sure that there was really someone under there."

"Right! And what if you and I were in bed with our heads under the covers, especially in an upper bunk; wouldn't he do the same thing?"

"Yes, I guess," John agreed, "but what's that got to do with anything?"

So I explained my idea to him. "There's a new guard coming in pretty soon."

"So?"

"Well, when he gets here, the odds are that he won't know anything about British Kriegies, right?"

"Probably not."

"So we persuade about half the guys to start going to bed before he comes in to count. He gets used to seeing about half of us sleeping with our heads under the blankets. He thinks that it's just some weird British custom. Do you see what I'm getting at?"

"Yeah," John said, "we stuff our beds and hide outside for the count. But what if he grabs our toes to see if we're really there?"

"Simple," I said. "Somebody else's toes. Aussie's and Jimmy the Greek's."

Aussie and Jimmy, John and I shared the block of four bunks in a corner of the room, built like two double beds, one above the other. There was a board down the middle of each double bunk. We'd switch beds to put Aussie and Jimmy on the outside, top and bottom. John and I on the inside, against the wall, on the top and bottom bunks. We thought that this way the guard could not possibly reach any part but the feet of the two on the inside.

We talked to the others. They were dubious but after considerable argument decided to give it a try. Our final escape plan began to evolve.

We had no civilian clothes, so we would shorten our army greatcoats to knee length to look like civilian coats in the dark. We would hide during the day and travel by night in a southwesterly direction and try to get to Switzerland. We each had packs, and considerable amounts of concentrated food such as chocolate, biscuits, and bully beef.

In about two weeks the new guard would take over, but we would start to change our sleeping habits gradually, so that Herman wouldn't notice anything different about the way we turned in. We would give the new guard a few days to get used to us, then on a good, clear night we would make up our beds to look as if they were occupied, put Aussie and Jimmy in the outside bunks, away from the wall, and have them reading in bed, with heads and both arms showing. We would then cross their feet over to the other side of the bed, and pad the blank spaces, so that the guard would have some real feet to feel, should he want to confirm that the inside bunks were occupied.

Once we had a plan, the rest of the group became quite enthusiastic. There was no longer any talk about how it was going to ruin a good thing, although some were concerned about what the Germans might do after they found us gone.

"What could they do?" I said, trying to sound confident. "After we're gone, just pull all the padding out of the bed and act surprised to find us gone in the morning. Tell them that you just woke up and we were gone!"

The new guard had never seen *Engländer* before. He had been briefed by Herman before he left, but we didn't know what was said – we hoped it included our strange sleeping habits. The first few nights he was very thorough. He pulled a couple of blankets off a couple of faces to see what was under them. The foul invective that greeted him would have grievously insulted him had he understood English. But he understood the tone and after a while desisted, although he did occasionally feel a foot here and there to satisfy himself that a bed was occupied.

The big night approached. It was about the middle of April 1943. We decided on the following Friday, a night when even the new guard could be expected to go into town. We packed our packsacks the night before and stowed them under our bunks. And we got our shortened coats ready, as the night temperatures still hovered around freezing.

8

Escape

Friday finally arrived. We came back from work at the usual time and waited for Aussie, Jimmy, and some of the others to divert the guard and get them inside so we could get our packs and equipment hidden in the bushes behind the outdoor toilet. We had to make sure that nobody from the farmer's small family was about.

Zero hour! After supper, we got Aussie and Jimmy in position in the two beds, and about half of the rest of the group got into bed, some reading, and some pretending to sleep, with their blankets pulled over their faces to keep out the light. A few were keeping the guard busy around the other side of the farmhouse with stories about their former (and mostly fictional) love lives in England.

The usual stream of men was straggling out for their late-night visits to the two-holer. John and I were the last to go out. We stayed, hidden inside the toilet, praying that the new guard wouldn't get a sudden urge, or that if he did, that he would use the farmer's privy.

Inside the privy was dark and the odour was overpowering. We sat over the open holes fully dressed, overcoats on, listening. We could hear the ordinary noises of talking and laughter from the farmhouse. In the prisoners' barracks, the sound of a harmonica. Probably Aussie. What was he doing playing the mouth organ?

He was supposed to be reading, with his feet on my side of the bed. Through cracks in the door we could see the farmhouse eerily lit by the full moon.

Finally, we heard Ludwig, the new guard, come around the side of the house, up the wooden steps, and in through the front door, slamming it shut behind him. We could hear his voice, but not well enough to tell if he was counting. Then a dead silence. Had he discovered our ruse?

My heart was pounding so loudly I was sure that John could hear it. We waited with rising fear for Ludwig to come running out of the farmhouse with his rifle cocked, ready to shoot at anything that moved. Should we run for it or just stay there and take our chances of being shot while attempting to escape?

For a few more minutes, which seemed like hours, there was not a sound from inside the house. Suddenly the door opened and Ludwig came out. He closed the door, leaned his rifle against the wall, put the bar in place, and locked the steel door. A moment later, he was on his bicycle, peddling furiously down the hill toward town, no doubt to visit the former girlfriend of his predecessor.

We waited until he was out of sight, then clapped each other on the back in silent joy and slipped silently out of the privy. We donned our packs and moved across the moonlit field, being very quiet so as not to alarm the family inside.

We were finally free! I felt a sense of exhilaration as we trudged northward, looking back occasionally at our farmhouse growing smaller in the distance. Our plan was quite simple, and in retrospect very naive. It was to travel overland at night in a generally southwesterly direction until we came to the Swiss border. We would figure out a way of crossing the border when we got there – if we got there. Neither of us had escaped before, nor had we ever studied factual accounts of other people's escapes. If we had, we probably would never have tried.

We had enough food to last us a week or so, and planned to steal the rest from farmers' fields and barns. The weather was good for mid-April. The days had been warm and sunny and the nights frosty. As we had not intended to sleep at night, the one blanket in each of our packs had seemed adequate. Both young and in perfect health, we were dressed warmly and equipped with good, solid army boots. We had warm coats, cut short enough to let us pass as civilians in the dark. If early explorers could walk across half a continent, surely we could get to Switzerland, only a few hundred miles away. Water was in good supply in the many creeks and streams that tumbled through the local hills, but we had already made one major error – we had no water container.

Reaching the woods to the north of the upper fields, we turned west, attempting to maintain our course by the North Star, plainly pointed out by the Big Dipper. We avoided settlements and roads. We trudged along in the light of the full moon, scarcely daring to talk but fully savouring that wonderful feeling of freedom. I felt that I would soon be back in England.

After a few hours of walking we seemed to be well to the west of our *Arbeitskommando*, and altered course to a more southwesterly direction. The country became rougher and more mountainous, and we could no longer skirt along the edges of the fields. We were now picking our way through dense woods in the pitch dark. It was slow going. We occasionally fell over logs or slipped into ditches and streams, but for the most part managed to maintain our course directions without any serious injuries.

By about three o'clock in the morning, it was clear that we were well away from Arbeitskommando E148, and that no one was likely to find us provided that we remained in the woods. We hurried on, keeping our eyes open for a good hiding place for the day: we couldn't risk being out in daylight in an open area.

As the first light of dawn began to illuminate the eastern sky behind us, we found a clump of bushes near the edge of a wood

Escape maps were printed on silk, rayon, and tissue paper. They could be folded to a very small size and easily concealed.

with a clear view of the fields below. There did not appear to be any buildings nearby, so we rolled up in our blankets in the thickest part of the bushes and promptly fell asleep.

I woke up to the sound of a dog barking in the distance. It was about ten in the morning and quite warm in our little nest in the bushes. We looked out between the branches and saw that we were on the upper edge of a series of fields, which were being ploughed by a farmer driving a lone ox. He was some distance away, but the little dog appeared to be a real threat. What if he sniffed us out and revealed our presence to the farmer?

Carefully, we crawled back through the bushes into the woods until we found a dense clump of young trees, where we took refuge. Unfortunately, it was full of biting and crawling insects that plagued us the rest of the day.

We slept fitfully during the afternoon and were relieved when darkness finally fell so that we could get on our way. Our first objective was to find water, since we had had nothing to drink all day. We soon located a mountain stream and drank our fill. Kicking ourselves for our great stupidity in not bringing a container, we resolved to get one as soon as possible.

By the second night the terrain was more mountainous, and the woods thicker. It reminded me of my own Canadian bush. Hour after hour we struggled in the dark over rough ground, dead trees, brambles, ditches, and streams, always maintaining a more or less southwesterly course. My large-scale silk map of Europe was next to useless. Occasionally, in a shielded position, we would light one of our hoard of matches and try to figure out where we were. All that we could tell for sure was that we were somewhere in the mountains of Sudetenland.

We stopped to rest at regular intervals, ate some of our small ration of chocolate and biscuits, and drank gratefully from the little streams that we regularly encountered. We seemed to be climbing most of the time, and occasionally got a glimpse of lights from some village in the valley. There was supposed to be a universal blackout in occupied territories, but perhaps some of the peasants in outlying areas had not heard of it or, like independent farmers the world over, just ignored the regulations.

We tired more quickly now and began to realize that travelling cross-country through mountainous, wooded terrain at night was slow, difficult, and dangerous. Several times we had slipped down the steep slope of some wooded ravine, invisible in the darkness, and avoided a serious fall by sheer luck.

After midnight, we seemed to have crossed a major ridge. We could tell we were at a high elevation by the lack of trees and general rockiness of the terrain. There was no sign of any pursuit, or indeed of any human habitation at all.

Maintaining our course by the stars, glimpsed occasionally through broken cloud, we began to descend, with many detours around and over difficult ground. Our stops were becoming more frequent, and despite our excellent physical condition, we were becoming exhausted.

Breaking suddenly out of the forest, we stumbled across a road. It was rough and narrow, little more than a trail, but it headed in the right direction. From the evidence of woodcutting in the area, it was obviously a logging road. If there were woodcutters in the area, hiding during the day might become more difficult.

It didn't take us long to decide to follow the road. In the darkness, with our short coats and hatless, we felt, or hoped, that we looked like a couple of labourers. We agreed that if we should meet anyone on the road we would just keep on walking and, as we passed them, give the standard, official, and required greeting of the day, "Heil Hitler!"

We had carefully studied the greeting practices of Germans soldiers and civilians and had noted that "Heil Hitler" was the most standard greeting, accompanied by an outstretched right arm, and was always answered in kind, except by the British Kriegies, who usually replied, "Fuck off, you square-headed bastard!" or some other equally friendly comment.

Gradually descending, we had been trudging along for two or three hours when suddenly, rounding a bend, we came upon a tiny village. Just a collection of three or four houses. No lights were shining from any of them as we passed. A dog barked. In another hour or two it would be dawn. If we met anyone now, we could only hope that person would think we were early risers.

We had just cleared the village and were rounding another bend in the road when we saw two people approaching. It was too late to leave the road and make a run for the bushes.

"Act natural," I whispered, "and give 'em the old 'ile 'eetlah' salute."

John nodded.

As the two men came closer, we could make out in the darkness that they were roughly dressed – labourers or farmhands.

They were looking at us with some curiosity, and I could feel my heart starting to pound again. They were about ten feet away when a cloud covered the moon and the road darkened. We moved to the right to let them pass. If I was acting "natural," I certainly didn't feel natural, and I felt sure that these two locals had spotted us as phonies. I imagined that everyone in the area was looking for two escaped prisoners of war.

They were about two feet away when I almost shouted in my enthusiasm, "Ile 'eetlah!" and threw up my arm in the approved Hollywood-style fascist salute. Startled, John threw out a second volley. "Ile 'eetlah! he said in a voice even louder than mine, and threw out another pukka Nazi salute.

The two farmhands almost jumped out of their skins. By the time they had recovered from their surprise, we were past them, and could hear them both muttering, "Ile 'eetlah" in reply. We kept walking at a rapid clip and were soon out of sight and earshot of the two.

"It worked!" John said. "Did you see how those fellows jumped? They must have thought we were Gestapo agents!" We had a good laugh together, the tension gone. Our confidence was improving now that the walking was easier; the future began to look rosier. Dawn was approaching, so we started to look for a place to hide. We left the road and climbed up into the woods until we found a dense thicket where even the woodcutters were unlikely to go. Rolling up in our blankets, we were soon fast asleep.

The thicket felt warm and sunny in the morning, and although we could hear the distant sound of axes chopping, no one disturbed us. We ate some more of our rations and again resolved to acquire a water container, as going all day without a drink was becoming a problem.

That night, we set out earlier than usual, partly because of our thirst, and partly because of our new feeling of confidence. We had evaded the Germans for three days now and had travelled quite a few miles. We were becoming dirty and unshaven, but having briefly glimpsed the faces of the two farmhands in the moonlight, we realized that our scruffiness was an advantage.

We travelled through two more small villages during the next two hours, and used our Nazi salute to advantage several times. Sure that we sounded as genuine as a couple of Hitler Youth, we became almost overconfident. God knows who some of the people we passed and saluted must have thought we were. A couple of Gestapo agents disguised as farm labourers?

Early in the evening we approached a large town. The paved road we'd been on now had merged with a larger road that led down to a bridge over a river and into the town. The only way we could maintain our direction was to pass over the bridge and go through the town. After a short whispered conference, we decided to act as casual labourers and simply stroll along the main road and across the bridge, which to our relief was unguarded. The town was much larger than we had thought, and quite a few people were still out on the streets. Occasional flashes of light showed up through the blackout as customers tumbled out of bars and beer halls, and we could see that quite a number of them were soldiers. Carelessly, I bumped into someone in the dark and a torrent of alcoholic Teutonic abuse came forth.

"Ile 'eetlah!" I said into his ear, in the most confident voice I could muster, shooting out my hand in my best Charlie Chaplin style.

It was like magic. "Heil Hitler!" he answered in a very subdued but still drunken voice, and stumbled away.

"Amazing," said John with a chuckle. "That sure stops them in their tracks!"

That night was our best yet. We estimated that we must have covered twenty or thirty miles so far and were well to the south-west of our starting point. Dawn was not far off, so we started looking for a hiding place. We were now in a rural area dotted with farms and not much cover. The only reasonable-looking hiding place seemed to be in a sort of tree nursery with a lot of small pine and spruce trees, almost like a Christmas tree farm. It was well off the road and surrounded by a hedge on three sides, with a railroad line running along the fourth side. We settled in a clump of bushes behind some trees, sheltered by a hedge, and in sight of the railway.

It began to rain, a cold drizzle. We had no rainwear, and the bushes and trees offered no shelter. We huddled under a tree, gradually becoming wetter and colder. A train approached, labouring up the incline. The track was headed in a southwesterly direction and was uphill for as far as we could see. It was a long freight train with many heavily loaded cars, slowly puffing up the slope at about ten or fifteen miles an hour.

John and I looked at each other with the same thought. "What about it?" I said. "It's going the right direction, anyway."

"I'm game!" John replied, throwing his pack on his back.

We peered through the bushes as the train went by, a steam locomotive with two men in the cab. They were peering straight ahead through the rain and didn't seem to notice us. The train contained boxcars, lumber cars, flat cars, tank cars, coal cars, and hay cars. The hay cars were similar to the lumber cars, flat cars with five-foot sides, loaded to a height of about ten feet and covered with heavy tarpaulins, tied down with ropes. We decided to try for one of them.

When the engine was a safe distance ahead, we ran out of the bushes and alongside the train. By running as fast as we could, we could just about equal the train's speed. I grabbed a ladder between a hay car and a boxcar and pulled myself up. I looked back to see John sprawled along the ground. He had tripped on some signalling equipment beside the tracks.

He picked himself up in an instant, sprinted along beside the train, and pulled himself up on a steel ladder at the front end of a lumber car. I dropped off, ran alongside again and picked up the ladder next to him. Both of us quickly climbed into a space at the front end of the car.

It was a flat car, its sides five feet high. Inside, and to a height two or three feet above the level of the sides, was stacked a large variety of lumber and building materials, with a tarpaulin on top that didn't quite cover all of the lumber. The tarp was tied down in several places, but by moving some of the smaller pieces of lumber and rearranging one of the piles a little, we soon had a cozy little nest under the tarp and, surrounded by lumber, completely hidden from view. We were safe until the car was unloaded.

Dawn was breaking by the time we had organized ourselves, and we peeked out from our hiding place to see where we were. The train was heading in a southerly direction, and again began to curve away to the southwest. What luck! With any breaks at all, we should be close to Switzerland by the end of the day, or so we thought.

The countryside had become rolling farmland, dotted with tiny villages, each with its own church spire. We laughed and talked in our normal tones. Nobody could hear us, even if we shouted. We ate some more of our diminishing rations, and finished a cigarette. Still no water container! With youthful optimism we put up with our thirst, sure that we would eventually find some water; we always had before.

At about noon, the train pulled into a siding, and sat for an hour or two while cars, including ours, were shunted, connected, and disconnected in a seemingly random operation. We prayed that our car was not destined to be unloaded. It wasn't.

Later in the afternoon we started moving again. The train picked up speed and was soon moving swiftly across the open countryside. I asked John how he had managed to trip as he ran alongside the train – he could have easily been killed. He had never in his life hopped a train, he told me. In contrast, I'd often hopped freights in my teens with a friend (and without my parents' knowledge), strictly for kicks. I would never have imagined when I was thirteen years old that such a talent would come in handy six years later in a situation I would never have believed possible.

The rain had stopped and the skies had cleared. Our train was steaming steadily across the countryside, sometimes southerly, sometimes northerly, but always westward. I was thirsty, as was John, and we agreed that when the train stopped at nightfall, we would leave it, at least for a short time, and try to find a stream and an old bottle to store our water in. The countryside was becoming more populated, and we began to see the signs of a large city. The parallel highway carried a considerable amount of traffic, most of it military.

It was still daylight, with a lot of people around, so we put our heads down and pulled some more lumber over our little shelter. We could see through a crack that we were pulling into a large marshalling yard in a major city. Just as the sun began to go down, the train stopped and began shunting around in the marshalling yards. It dropped off a few cars, including ours, on a section of track well off the main line.

Now we were in a quandary. We knew that railroad marshalling yards were major targets for Allied bombers and were also heavily guarded to prevent sabotage. If our freight car was to be unloaded here, we were sure to be caught, and possibly shot.

We had no idea where we were. A quick look around after it became dark showed that there was no activity around our particular section of cars, although in almost every direction we could hear or see some kind of activity not too far away. It became quite cold, and our clothing was still damp from the rain. We hesitated to take out our blankets in case we had to make a quick getaway.

The car ahead of us was loaded with hay and covered with a heavy tarp held down by four ropes, one at each corner. As the night wore on, it became colder. Our food was almost gone, and we'd had nothing to drink since the previous night. The hay wagon looked inviting and warm. After another quick discussion we decided to slip over to the hay car, burrow into the hay beneath the tarp, and at least be warm.

At about midnight, all seemed clear. There was nobody near us, and the moon was hidden behind some clouds. The marshalling yards seemed almost deserted. Quietly we donned our packs and climbed down.

Suddenly two lights appeared around the end of the line of cars, about a hundred yards ahead. Two figures were illuminated in their flashlights' dim glow, maintenance men heading straight toward us! It was too late to climb back into the lumber car.

"Get under the car!" I whispered. We were standing by the centre of the car, between the front and rear wheels. I draped myself over the front axle and pulled my feet up off the ground. I could see John doing the same thing at the back axle. I was freezing cold, but I was sweating. My heart started pounding. I wished to hell that I was braver! I was sure that everyone within fifty feet could hear my heart thumping.

I could hear the two men coming closer, talking loudly in German. I had no idea what they were saying. I resolved to ask John what they were talking about if we ever got through this. They stopped opposite the wheel closest to me. My body was still draped over the axle. I was sure that they could see my leg, which I had pulled in as far as possible.

The light was shining right on my leg. I stopped breathing. They continued talking for a few seconds, then moved on. They passed John's hiding place with scarcely a glance and continued along the side of the train until they were out of sight. I was just about to slip down from my perch over the axle when there was a crash, and the train started to move.

Christ! What to do? I could see John hanging on his axle for dear life. The train moved about fifteen feet and stopped. We both rolled clear and stood up.

"Let's get into that hay car," said John, "before we get ourselves killed."

We scrambled up under the tarp, dragging our packs, expecting to burrow into the soft hay and get warm at last. We got quite a shock: the hay was hard as a rock.

For the next two hours we worked away with my jackknife, literally cutting out a couple of grooves in the top of the hay, large enough to lie in, with our packs, under the tarp. Finally, we were lying side by side, deep enough into the hay that our outlines wouldn't show up on the tarp, our heads facing toward the front of the train. As a final touch, I cut a triangular flap in the tarp from which we could peek out from time to time to see where we were.

Although the hay car was not much warmer than the lumber car, we were now quite warm and dry from our exertions, and very thirsty. What we would not have given for some water. There was nothing to do but to tough it out and hope that the next day we'd be able to get out and find water. It was three or four in the morning when we finally fell asleep.

We were wakened with a crashing and clanking of cars as they were shunted around the yard. Our car was being added to a train. Soon, with a lot of huffing and puffing, we pulled out of the siding and, after considerable switching, ended up on the main line. As we gathered speed I peeked out the flap. We were headed in an easterly direction!

I suppose we should have been happy just to be moving again, but we were both racked with thirst. I think each of us privately blamed the other for the stupid oversight, although we said nothing.

The train thumped along the now-familiar countryside, and there was nothing to do but to wait until it stopped. We decided that if we got another opportunity in a smaller siding, we would leave the train and search for water. Our thirst was becoming so great by this time that all we could think about was water. Short of giving ourselves up, we probably would have done just about anything for a glass of water.

For the rest of the day, the train travelled at a moderate speed through rolling country. The sky had clouded over, and there was no way of telling our direction. We hoped it was southerly at least. Our natural good humour vanished, and we snapped at each other occasionally. Eventually, we lapsed into a sort of sullen silence.

Late in the afternoon, our train pulled into a large siding. A careful peek out the lookout flap showed that we were in a town of considerable size, and that our section of cars had been shunted to one side of a large building. A number of workmen were busy unloading, several cars away. But the large warehouse next to our car appeared to be empty. It stood on piles about four feet off the ground, and there was a scooped-out cellar, or basement, underneath. There was nobody about on that side of the train, so we decided to hide under the building until nightfall.

Quickly and silently, we eased ourselves out from our hiding place on the train and scurried under the building, as far back in the shadows as we could get, next to a retaining wall. We were well hidden, we thought, and it was just a matter of time before we could slip out of town in the dark and find some water.

A workman walked under the building, some distance from where we were hiding in the shadows. We could see him quite plainly. We remained motionless. He walked a few feet toward us, stopped, opened his fly, and started to urinate on the dirt floor, puffing on a cigarette as he casually sprayed the ground in front of him. He looked up toward us, saw us, and froze. With a terrified look on his face, he had started to back up slowly toward the open end of the basement when John called out, gently, in German.

The man stopped and John went a few steps closer to him. They spoke for a few seconds, and the man scuttled out like a scared cat. "What did you say to him?" I asked.

"I was hoping he was a Czech," John replied. "So I levelled

with him. I told him we were both escaped British prisoners of war and asked him not to say anything about us being under here. He was scared shitless. If he's a Czech, we're okay; if he's a Sudeten German, we're screwed!"

Ten minutes went by. I was just starting to feel a little more secure when we heard the sound of running feet, whistles blowing, and orders being shouted in German. More drumming of feet, like soldiers running. More shouted orders. A half dozen soldiers, armed with rifles and bayonets, came charging under the building.

"Don't shoot!" I said as we both put up our hands. I was getting pretty good at putting up my hands, and figured that it was a better alternative than a hole in the chest. They motioned us to get out from under the building. So we did, with our hands over our heads and feeling more than slightly apprehensive.

"Tell 'em, John!" I yelled. "Tell 'em who we are before they blow our bloody heads off!"

Surrounded by this menacing horde, all pointing their bayoneted rifles at our chests, and with thirty or more index fingers twitching on their triggers, I felt justifiably nervous. This was far worse than the little old farmer at Magdeburg with his antique rifle.

Still, there was a certain amount of humour in the situation. Like in the old joke about the circular firing squad with the victim in the middle, we were surrounded by soldiers, all pointing their rifles at us. If they were to start shooting, they would certainly hit each other.

While I was off on this fantasy, John was rattling off German as fast as he could to an unsympathetic-looking *Feldwebel,* and showing him his POW dog tag. "That's a good idea," I thought, and lowered my arms to dig out my identification tag, hung conveniently around my neck for just such an occasion. A rifle barrel was thrust in my face, German was screamed into my ear, and both my hands shot up like lightning.

I was terribly thirsty. John must have told them that we hadn't had any water in the last two days, for someone appeared with a bucket full of clean, cold water and handed it to me. I drank right out of the bucket. It was wonderful! A beautiful taste. I must have gulped down a couple of quarts when suddenly I vomited it up all over the ground. John was a little more fastidious in his drinking and managed to keep it down.

By now our captors had decided that we actually were British prisoners of war, and their attitude changed considerably. Our hands went back in our pockets as they decided what to do with us. John told me later that he had fed them all that stuff about being soldiers and having to do our duty by escaping, and went through the "you are a soldier, I am a soldier" routine. Soon they were acting in an almost friendly manner toward us.

Brno was the name of the town where we'd been captured, deep in eastern Czechoslovakia. So we'd come a fair distance in the five days that we had been on the loose. Even though we had been captured, we had learned a lot about escaping in those five days, and could probably do better next time. For now, it was just a matter of letting things take their course and trying not to be too disappointed about the way things had turned out.

9

RETURN TO CAMP

We were marched about a mile from the railroad yards to the centre of the city. A few people on the streets stared at us curiously, perhaps wondering why we had such a large armed escort. At the police station the soldiers marched off after handing us over, which left us feeling slightly abandoned. The military was a known quantity to us, but the police? The Gestapo's treatment of prisoners was well known; my stomach knotted.

Our fears were short-lived. The police, it turned out, were Czechs and, if anything, seemed to like the English better than they liked the Germans. The senior policeman was a sergeant, and two corporals were around the station most of the time. John and I were put in what looked like a combination lounge and locker room, and told to stay put. One man was left to guard us, and gave us magazines and newspapers to look at.

Other policemen came and went during the day, scarcely paying any attention to us. We were allowed to wash and shave, and to keep our cigarettes. Our food rations were practically gone. We offered some of our healthy supply of Canadian cigarettes to our guard, who was quite pleased, not ever having smoked such a high-quality cigarette.

That night they put us into a cell, almost apologetically – it was "rules" and they would get into trouble if they didn't. The cell had two bunks and was about the same style as those in the Luftwaffe guardhouse. I was becoming an expert on cells.

They gave us some bread and ersatz coffee for breakfast the next morning and again allowed us to spend the day in the policemen's lounge thumbing through the magazines and listening to music on the radio. We were given soup and sausage and were fed quite well, considering wartime shortages. This was better than camp fare, and we felt no urgency to return.

One night we were sitting in the lounge, listening to the radio before going down to our cell for the night, when the sergeant went out on some business. John motioned toward the radio and said to our corporal in German, "That is a Blaupunkt, isn't it? They are very good radios, ja?"

The guard agreed.

"Can you get England on it?"

"Jawohl" (Certainly), he said, looking around to make sure there was no one else in the station. "I'll show you." He flicked a switch, fiddled with the tuning and volume control, and suddenly we heard "This is the BBC, from London," a broadcast direct from Hollywood to London by shortwave that was being rebroadcast from London on shortwave. It was a "special" by a young rising comedian from Hollywood named Red Skelton.

The sketch was very funny, but I was the only one who seemed to understand the American humour. John didn't really get it, and the Czech spoke little or no English. But for me, it was an amazing experience to sit in a Czech police station in April 1943 and listen to a broadcast from Hollywood, with Red Skelton, via the BBC.

Just then, we heard the door open and close below, and footsteps on the stairs. The guard quickly flicked the radio to a local station, which was blaring out German patriotic marching music, and motioned to us not to say anything by putting a finger to his lips. Then he made a throat-cutting motion and rolled his eyes, as if to say, "This is what will happen to me if they find out!"

After this, three or four days passed in this almost idyllic situation, in the company of our friendly policemen, and we were beginning to enjoy ourselves. One morning, a guard came down to our cell and told us to get our things together, we were being transferred to the local prison. When we asked why, he said that they couldn't get enough food rations for us at the police station. When John asked where they had got the rations that we had been eating up until now, he told us that the policemen had been sharing their rations with us.

Escorted by two policemen, we marched a few blocks to the town prison, which occupied a whole block. Three sides were the prison proper, and the front of the building contained the living quarters of the jailor and his family. To enter the prison courtyard, you had to traverse the jailor's quarters, entering through the front door and passing through his apartment and kitchen.

Looking up, you could see three storeys of barred cell windows, all overlooking the large courtyard. It was used for exercising prisoners once a day, for the jailor's garden, and for the jailor's daughter's rabbits, caged in a big rabbit hutch.

The jailor's daughter was a beautiful, shapely, blonde girl of about eighteen, named Hildegard. The jailor himself was a good-natured, heavy-set scoundrel with a black beard, who immediately searched us and confiscated our considerable supply of cigarettes. My knife had gone, picked up by the soldiers who recaptured us at the marshalling yards. When we protested the loss of our cigarettes, he laughed uproariously and told us that cigarettes were not good for us.

He did, however, during our daily exercise visits to the yard, offer each of us one of our own cigarettes, meanwhile lighting one for himself and commenting with a wink and a leer on their excellent quality.

Our cell had two bunks stacked one over the other, a slop bucket, and a stool. It was so small that if one of us paced the floor, the other had to lie on a bunk. The bucket was emptied by one of the "trustees," who confessed he was to be hung for sabotaging parachutes in a parachute factory.

Our daily meal came about noon. It consisted of a large tin bowl of turnip soup, containing mysterious substances. Also a chunk of the ubiquitous black bread. Well, not black, really – a sort of dark brown, the colour of dirt, according to John. We speculated on how much dirt actually was in it, as well as bugs, flies, weevils, and other unmentionables. As it was relatively fresh, I presumed that all of those things would have been sterilized by the heat in the oven.

The prison routine became quite monotonous day after day, with no word on whether we would ever get out of the place. Up in the morning, pace the cell for an hour while the other lay on a bunk, then switch over and lie on a bunk while the other paced the floor. The closeness was beginning to get to us. I became quite irritated about a lot of little things that John was doing, and I could see that I irritated him also.

After a few hours of this, we would finally be let out in the courtyard for our "exercise," our big break of the day. A chance to feel the sun, to see the rabbits and watch Hildegard, the jailor's daughter. Fifteen minutes was all we got, but it was wonderful to smoke one of our own cigarettes, to laugh with the good-natured rogue who was our jailor, and to get a good look at Hildegard, who seemed to be wearing flimsier dresses every day and was forever bending over to tend her rabbits.

Then back to the cells, more pacing, then our meal, for what it was. After the daily meal, more pacing and talking, until it was time to turn in. John and I had exhausted just about every subject and seemed to disagree on everything. One day was the same as another. The food, what little there was of it, was terrible. A week or two had gone by; I had lost count. I was beginning to dislike John intensely! Not for any one particular thing, but for everything about him. He wasn't too keen on me either.

One evening, just before we were scheduled to turn in, we had switched places and John was pounding the floor. He started to expound again on his favourite subject, that a private in the British Army was roughly equivalent to a sergeant in the Canadian Air Force. I said something obscene to him, referring to his intelligence, parentage, and legitimacy with a few other crude comments, which stopped him in his tracks momentarily.

"I've got a good mind to knock your head off!" he said, stopping his pacing.

"You're not big enough!" said I, referring to the fact that he was a few inches shorter than me, albeit quite a bit broader and more muscular.

That did it. I leapt off the bunk, and he threw a punch that almost closed one of my eyes. I had a few boxing skills myself, so I returned a couple of punches that started the blood flowing from his nose. After that we were all over each other with murderous fury. I got in a dozen good shots to the face, neck, chest, and head, which should have knocked him out. He landed an equal number of punches on my head and face. The stool was knocked over, and the bucket too (thank God it was empty).

For the next few minutes we had at each other with all the fury we could muster. The stool was broken and the bucket was bent. Then the door burst open. Two guards rushed in, their rifles at the ready. We stopped, staring at them with surprise. They looked surprised too, for if I looked half as bad as John, I must have been quite a sight.

He was bleeding from several cuts to his face, his clothes and hair were dishevelled, and he was covered with dirt from where we had rolled around on the floor, punching at each other.

"Was ist los?" (What's going on?) shouted one of the guards.

"We were just exercising," said John in German. "We do this to keep fit."

The two guards looked at us, then at each other, shrugged their shoulders, and said, "Die Engländer sind alle verrückt!" (All the Englishmen are crazy!), and walked out, locking the cell door behind them. John and I stood there, looking warily at each other, each waiting for the other to start something. I was too tired to fight anymore, and so was he, so without a word we both turned in to our bunks.

It took me a long time to get to sleep, wondering what had got into me. Every bone in my body was aching. I was still angry with John, but not nearly as angry as I had been before the fight.

The next morning, I got up to a dead silence. He wasn't speaking to me, so I wasn't speaking to him. This really stupid situation went on for about three days. A guard would come in and say something to us. John would answer him, and he'd leave. "What did he say?" I'd ask, still not understanding any but a few words of German.

"Ask him yourself!" John would snap.

About the third day of our mutually silent treatment, I began to think, "What a ridiculous situation. Here we are, the only two English-speaking people within two hundred miles, and we're not talking to each other." It was so funny that I started to smile to myself. I looked up to see a trace of a smile on his face. I started to chuckle. He laughed. Then we both started laughing uncontrollably until the tears ran down our faces.

"You want to do some more 'exercise'?" he said, and I laughed again.

"It's a wonder they didn't shoot us," I replied, and we both broke up again.

"I guess I started it," I said. "I shouldn't have said those stupid things."

"No, I started it, it was my fault."

"I threw the first punch!"

"No you didn't, I did!"

We almost came to fisticuffs about whose fault it was, until we saw the humour of the situation again and agreed that it was nobody's fault.

"It's those damn square-headed bastard Jerries' fault for locking us up in such a shitty cell," he observed, and I agreed with him, happy to have someone to talk to again. He admitted that he had been a bit lonely too, and that a tiny cell like ours was no place for two grown men to sit and sulk at each other.

The next exercise period in the courtyard was a happy one. Our good-natured jailor gave us each one of our own cigarettes and informed us that they were finished. We calculated that he had stolen at least half of them. Oh well, he could have stolen all of them. The good news was that we would be leaving the next day. A guard was coming down from Lamsdorf to pick us up and take us back. Everything was looking up! Except Hildegard, who was bending down to tend her rabbits. Her father, suddenly realizing what was going on, screamed something at her, and she scuttled back into the apartment, knowing full well the impact she must have had on these sex-starved men.

The next day, we were summoned by our jailor and told to pick up our belongings and report to the courtyard. In great haste we gathered our meagre belongings into our packs, and made our way along the corridor and down the stone stairway to the courtyard below, whispering our goodbyes to the other inmates.

Stepping out into the spring sunshine, the first thing we saw was our own unmistakeable German Army guard, a short, fat little soldier in a green uniform with a big rifle. He had a big smile on his face and greeted us in German, to which John answered, translating as we went along.

"I've come to take you back to Stalag VIIIB," he told us. "I understand that you escaped. You've come a long way from Lamsdorf. How did you do it?"

John told him that we had hopped a freight train.

"That was the wrong thing to do," he said. "You should have gone on the passenger train." He then went on to tell us about his big escape from the Russians. Apparently, he had been captured briefly but had managed to get away and back to his own lines. So we had a lot in common, he said. He told us that he would give us the information to do it properly next time. It looked as if it was going to be an interesting train trip!

After all of the formalities were completed, papers signed, and receipts issued for two prisoners (I wondered if the receipt said "in good condition"), we were marched off toward the railroad station in the centre of town. The few civilians we encountered en route gave us scarcely a second glance. I suppose it was a normal state of affairs for prisoners of one type or another to be marched about the streets by armed soldiers.

After a twenty-minute walk, we came to the Brno railroad station. It was similar to other stations we had seen in Germany, with a fairly large waiting room, old-fashioned wooden benches with curved backs, and a dingy ticket office behind an illuminated wicket. An arched entrance led to the various *Bahnsteige* (tracks), above which there were large signs indicating which *Zug* (train) went on which *Bahnsteig*. A *Schnellzug*, we learned, was an express train (to be avoided, as our guard explained, because they were usually crawling with Gestapo and ss, not to mention officers, for whom he apparently had little affection).

Our train was not due for an hour or two, so we relaxed on a wooden bench while John and our guard chatted about what went wrong on our escape and what we should do to improve our technique. His name was Hubert. He agreed that every soldier's duty was to try to escape, and that every soldier was bound to do his duty. His information was invaluable, and his dislike of officers and other people in authority was quite refreshing.

"Don't take freight trains," he warned, "because the freight yards are well guarded and difficult to get out of. If you have to, jump on and off the trains outside the marshalling yards. Unfortunately, they are usually going too fast. Express trains are fast, but there are lots of checks of passengers, tickets, and passports. Short-run workers trains are better. They are usually crowded, full of ordinary workers, as well as foreign workers from all over Europe, and very seldom are there any checks done for papers or anything else."

Hubert changed the subject suddenly without missing a beat and began talking about how long it would take us to get to Lamsdorf. I saw that a few Teutonic-looking civilians had wandered over to see who or what was being guarded. One of them, a mean-looking middle-aged individual, looked us over very carefully, then turned and made a big display of spitting disdainfully on the floor, I suppose to show us what he thought of us. Hubert ignored him and decided that it was time to get over to the proper platform.

Our train finally pulled into position beside the platform and Hubert found us an empty compartment, taking a menacing position by the window – more to discourage other civilians from getting in, I thought, than to prevent us from getting out. Hubert was my kind of soldier.

For the next ten hours as our train headed north, stopping regularly at every whistle stop along the route, Hubert told us a lot about himself. As he talked with us he shared the bread and sausage he had brought along. When we stopped, he'd get us water, acting more like a friend than a guard.

It was late at night when we arrived at Lamsdorf, where another sleepy-looking guard was waiting to escort us back to the camp. We trudged back down the road, the two guards in tow, almost happy to be getting back "home" after our adventure. It was now nearly the middle of May 1943. I had been a prisoner of war for four months and already had escaped once. The next time, I promised myself, I would be more successful.

We fully expected to be marched straight to the "*Strafe* compound" – the punishment compound – where all escapees and other malcontents were housed with strict security and no privileges. For some reason never explained to us, we were taken back to the working compound from whence we'd left only a month ago and assigned bunks in one of the barracks.

Nothing was said to us, we weren't called up before any tribunal, nor were we punished. Perhaps the weeks locked up in the Czech jail and the prison were considered sufficient punishment. Or perhaps Hubert, with that devious nonconformist brain of his, helped us by fudging our documentation or by some other ruse. I wouldn't have put it past him, he was a great guy.

Back to the now-familiar routine: "Appell!" "Brew up!" "Soup up!" "Spuds up!" "Rations up!" and, occasionally, "Mail up!" and the call for Red Cross parcels, usually shared weekly, between two men. I wasn't ready to go back on an *Arbeitskommando* right away, so it seemed like a good idea to swap back to my true identity.

Things seemed pretty quiet, with no indication of any reprisals for our escape. I wandered up to the RAF compound to see my friends, and my double, Dennis Reeves. They were delighted to see me and listened eagerly to my story, letting out whoops of laughter. Dennis had been getting along famously with the RAF chaps in the barrack block and had become very popular with his table mates, who clearly regretted seeing him go. He also had been collecting all my mail – including a couple of thousand Canadian cigarettes.

Among the mail were two letters from my family, on the prescribed air mail forms. It was wonderful to hear from them, especially my father, a World War I veteran who spent four years in the trenches. He told me that everyone was delighted I was still alive after all the uncertainty, and remarked philosophically that, as a POW, I was at least out of danger and would likely survive the war.

10

LIFE AT THE CAMP

Although the most dramatic parts of the story of my years as a prisoner of war are the attempts to escape, these together occupied only a few weeks of the more than two years I was a POW. The reality of being a prisoner deep in the heart of Germany in 1943 was a long and boring existence, day after day, in the crowded and dirty confines of the camp. There was never enough to eat, never a chance to get warm in winter, and never enough privacy to make one feel like a human being. Nevertheless, by and large, we prisoners maintained our hope that someday we'd be free, and we maintained reasonable discipline. In the end, many of us did live to go home, but it was an extremely difficult time.

The winter of 1943–1944 passed very, very slowly. Although we were relatively well clothed, thanks to the Red Cross, and each receiving Red Cross food supplements of a half parcel per week, the grinding cold of that winter seemed even worse than the previous one. Perhaps it was because the winter had been partly over when I'd arrived at Lamsdorf in January 1943.

Like most of the others, I had my original blue wool serge uniform, an RAF wool greatcoat supplied by the Red Cross, sturdy army boots with wool socks, scarves, hat, and mitts, all knitted by relatives and friends and received through the Red Cross. Throughout most of December, January, and even February, the

Most prisoners preferred the outdoors to their overcrowded barracks at Stalag VIIIB (Lamsdorf) POW camp.

temperature hovered around zero degrees Fahrenheit, and sometimes much lower.

We were assigned three-decker wooden bunks in one of the barrack blocks. Each bunk was of a standard that we were to become very familiar with over the next two years, six feet long, two and a half feet wide, and about ten inches deep. The bottom supports consisted of a half dozen or more bed boards, placed across the bottom of each bunk, and supported by a ledge, or strip, about three-quarters of an inch wide. Each bunk contained a straw mattress, called a palliasse. The bunks were in stacks, three high, two wide, and head to head with another identical stack, making twelve beds in one block. This arrangement put twelve heads in fairly close proximity to each other, and twenty-four feet, often foul-smelling and dirty, as far away from the heads (and noses) as possible.

Between each block of bunks was a narrow aisle, barely wide enough for a man to walk through or hoist himself onto his own bunk. Each barrack had an open area to one side, where there were rows of tables. Each table accommodated ten men, and there were twelve tables for the 120 men in each barrack block. In between each block was a washroom consisting of two metal troughs stretching the entire width of the barrack block, one facing each way. At regular intervals along each trough were cold-water taps. On the other side of this washroom and sharing the facility was an identical barrack block, which housed another 120 prisoners.

Not that the barracks were warm – they were constructed of wood, uninsulated, and drafty, and the small amount of heat from the occasional fires provided little warmth, but the body heat from a 120 men did make a difference. With all the doors and windows closed and the cracks stuffed with paper, the temperature was definitely above freezing inside, at least during the day. During the coldest weather, we each wore our greatcoat, hat, and mitts all of the time, and with only two blankets on a straw palliasse, we often wore our clothes to bed and spread the greatcoat over the top blanket for extra warmth.

Despite the cold, there were some "fresh air fiends," like Paddy Greir. Most Englishmen seem to like to sleep with their windows open, but at Stalag VIIIB, when the temperature was twenty below zero, most of them used a little discretion. Not so Paddy. Often, at ten or eleven at night, when just about everyone was in bed, he would throw open a window near one of the tables, take deep breaths, and do his exercises. Instantly, a hundred voices would shout, "Close the fucking window, you stupid Irish bastard! You trying to freeze us all to death?"

Paddy would laugh and retort in a loud, jeering voice, "Oh shut up, you ignorant fuckers. This place smells like English pig shit and you need some fresh air!"

Then a couple of large and menacing Kriegies would lower themselves from their bunks and advance on him, threatening him with violence. Which never happened, of course, except verbally.

Paddy would back down and close the window. The hulks would go back to bed. A chorus of voices would tell Paddy what they thought of him in colourfully profane language. It was a stylized ritual – everyone played his part and said his lines. Everyone knew how it would end. It was all part of how we compensated for the boredom and the fear that we would be stuck in that place forever.

In my teens I had read a book called *No Mean City*, about the slums of Glasgow. It was a horrendous story about tough criminal gangs that fought and slashed each other with straight razors. Jock Martin, my crewmate and a former policeman, wasn't too surprised when we heard that a "Scotch razor gang" was operating out of one of the army compounds, terrorizing and robbing other prisoners. Although the RAF compound had not been hit, the "wog" (Indian and Arab troops) and other compounds had lost valuables to these gangs. The problem was finally solved when a group of Canadian provost (military police) types from the Dieppe compound posted themselves outside the gang's compound armed with iron bars from their barrack fireplaces. They stopped and searched everyone who came out, and beat the shit out of anyone who had a straight razor on him. After that, there were no more invasions from razor gangs or from anyone else.

My respect went up for the "wogs" too; they had once again proved their legendary fighting ability. According to one story, the gangs had been beaten back in the "wog" compound when the inmates chased them off with homemade knives and swords. Their compound was at the end of the camp. It was populated mainly by British-Indian troops, as well as by some Arab and Asian colonial troops. I knew nothing about them; they kept to themselves and seemed to have their own social life. They received the same rations and Red Cross parcels as any other British troops. It seemed strange that the Germans, with all of their institutionalized racial hatred and intolerance, would respect anyone in a British uniform, regardless of race or creed, as being British. This anomaly would save the life of Harry Levy, an English Jew from London's East End.

Levy was an RAF wireless operator/air gunner, the only survivor from a five-man Wellington bomber crew shot down over Belgium in 1942. He had survived a low-level parachute jump after his plane had blown up. Belgian Resistance people who saw him float down in a field just outside Brussels gave him civilian clothes, destroyed his uniform, and moved him to a hiding place. Two days later, dressed in the civilian clothes and briefed to act as a deaf-mute, he was taken by bicycle, tram, and trolley to an apartment in the heart of Brussels.

One morning as he was alone, shaving, in the apartment, his benefactors having left for their jobs, the door was broken down with a tremendous crash, and three Gestapo armed with pistols confronted him.

"I was terrified," he admitted, "standing there in my underwear shorts, with shaving soap all over my face, and those big ugly bastards pointing their pistols at me. They dragged me into the main room and told me to put on my clothes, which were lying on the couch. Meanwhile they ripped the place apart, looking for something – I don't know what.

"I didn't speak German, but I know some Yiddish, and there are some similar words. But I spoke English to them and they didn't understand. They recognized the language, though. They thought I was a spy. So they took me down to the Gestapo prison and grilled me for about three days. I told them that I was an RAF flyer – I had to tell them a lot to convince them that I wasn't a spy – and they still weren't convinced. They said I looked like a Jew."

Harry Levy was handsome, tall, and dark, with a hawk-like nose, rather like my grandmother's, and piercing dark eyes. He could have easily been Spanish, Portuguese, Greek, Lebanese, or Italian. I could well imagine the Germans comparing him to their well-published stereotypes and immediately pegging him as a member of an "inferior race."

Although suspicious of his Jewish looks, the Gestapo had still been unable to discount his claim of being a legitimate prisoner of war, and so he was temporarily spared the treatment normally meted out to Jews, Poles, Resistance workers, and other so-called enemies of the state. In order to save his life, he was forced to give his squadron name, the markings on the plane, and the names of the other crew members, the target, home base, and other information about the operation before they would admit to his claim. Up until then he was considered a potential spy, enemy agent, saboteur, or Resistance worker, and as such liable to be shot summarily. He sweated out his solitary confinement, starvation diet, and incessant interrogations for three months, until one day, with no explanation, they turned him over to an army escort and sent him by train to Stalag VIIIB at Lamsdorf.

He and I used to have wonderful talks at the end of the barrack, late at night, when we discussed philosophy, religion, sex, and just about any other subject about which I knew absolutely nothing. Harry was not interested in escaping, and I could understand why. He had spent several months in a Gestapo prison. As far as he was concerned, he had already escaped something far worse than what he was now undergoing.

Around that time we heard disquieting stories from outside the camp about the Nazi treatment of Jews. A British corporal just back from a working party near Gleiwitz had been with a small group of prisoners being escorted back to their base by a guard when they saw a larger group of prisoners being herded along by several soldiers. He said that the prisoners were so skinny they looked like walking skeletons, and that the guards kicked and beat them if they walked too slowly. He asked the guard what their crime was and was told that they were Jews, that's what their crime was. And, he said, the worst thing of all was that nobody on the street seemed to be paying any attention to them.

It was, he said, unbelievable the way they treated those prisoners.

Group photo of the group from Stalag VIIIB barrack block 15A. Last row, fourth, fifth, and sixth from left: Harry "Paddy" Hipson, Harry Levy, Andrew Carswell. Front row, third from left: Claude "Clem" Clemens.

I couldn't imagine any prisoners being treated worse than the Russians. The Russian prisoners in the camp near us had no Red Cross to look out for them and were in a constant state of starvation – the USSR had not been a signatory of the Geneva Convention. According to fairly accurate sources in our camp, the Russians were so badly off for food that when a prisoner died, he'd be propped up by his friends on Appell for several days, until he started to smell, so that he would be counted and they could get his rations.

Harry Levy was part of my early education on race relations. Growing up in an Anglo-Saxon neighbourhood, racial and religious prejudice was part of my inheritance. Protestant and Catholic schoolchildren would shout insulting jingles and couplets at each other, the local Orangemen held parades designed to annoy the Catholics in honour of long-ago battles and events about which nobody cares about anymore, and everyone went to church trusting that God was on his side and that the other side would go to hell, or at least not get the same treatment in heaven as the truly faithful.

I knew only three Jewish kids in our school, and all their parents were rich. One kid's parents owned a shoe store, and the others just seemed to have a lot of money. Some of my relatives said that Jews helped each other; that was why they were rich. Down along the beach, where most of the kids loafed during the summer, in 1937, when I was about fourteen, some political organizers were rabble-rousing among the young people and telling them that the Depression was all the fault of the Jews. They had a rubber stamp and an inkpad with a new and strange symbol on it that they stamped on any willing kid's arm. I got my arm stamped because all the other kids were doing it. It was a swastika.

When I got home, my dad grabbed my arm and asked, "What's this on your arm?"

"It's new," I said. "This guy on the beach says that the Jews are causing the Depression and they're going to get rid of them."

My dad looked grim. Without a word he marched me into the kitchen and scrubbed my arm with Old Dutch cleanser and soap until the skin almost came off. Then he sat me down and talked to me for two solid hours about politics, tolerance, religion, and war. I never forgot that lecture. He told me that if I ever did or said anything that stupid again he would take a stick to me. I told Harry Levy all this one night during one of our many late-night conversations.

"Andy," he said patiently, "what gives you the idea that Jews are rich? Where I come from, in the East End of London, there are hundreds of thousands of Jews, and they are all poor – really poor. And there are thousands of them with no work. Until this war came along, most of us couldn't find a job. There'll always be poor Jews, and a hell of a lot more than there are rich ones."

I've always remembered that. And I never asked Harry why he

didn't swap over and try to escape. Because I knew. And I wouldn't have either if I'd been in the same situation. He was just damn lucky to be alive and to be at Lamsdorf.

Another humiliation we all had to face was the "chains." Immediately after the fiasco at Dieppe, a number of German prisoners were discovered dead, their hands tied behind their backs. According to the Geneva Convention, prisoners of war were not to be tied up or mistreated in any way. A few of the Dieppe prisoners with whom we had spoken agreed that some of the German prisoners had been tied up and put on boats to be taken back out to the waiting destroyers. The Germans had lobbed mortars into the boats and sunk them, killing the German prisoners as well as the Canadians who were with them.

In any case, the bound-up bodies washed ashore, giving the Germans clear evidence of an "atrocity." Hitler had one of his tantrums and swore that he would shackle all the Canadian prisoners of war in retaliation. For good measure, he would shackle all of the RAF *Luftgangsters* at Stalag VIIIB as well, which he did.

One morning, a company of SS storm troopers, armed with machine guns and looking very grim, marched into Stalag VIIIB at Lamsdorf. The entire camp was assembled on the football field and, surrounded by the heavily armed SS troops, listened to a proclamation read by an SS colonel.

"By the order of Der Führer," he read, "and because of the terrible atrocities committed by the Canadian soldiers at Dieppe ..." He went on, listing all of the atrocities that the Canadians were supposed to have committed and all of the atrocities that the RAF *Luftgangsters* had committed, and finishing off his tirade with the statement that, as of now, and until further notice, all Canadian and RAF prisoners at Stalag VIIIB would be chained up.

The next morning, the prisoners in the RAF and Dieppe compounds were lined up after Appell and the process began. Because there were no chains in stock, and because they had to obey orders, the Germans had decided to tie the prisoners each day with rope until such time as chains and handcuffs became available. Having no suitable rope, they were forced to use the heavy string from the British Red Cross parcels.

In the RAF compound, several long lines were formed, with two guards at the head of each line, each equipped with a box of Red Cross string. The guards were somewhat sheepish about the whole operation, being a fairly decent bunch, some perhaps a little more stupid than others, but all of them more interested in getting home for dinner than tying up a bunch of Canadian and RAF prisoners with Red Cross string.

As each prisoner stepped forward, he held his hands in front of him. The guard with the box of string would hand a piece to the other guard, who would quickly tie it around the crossed wrists. As each prisoner was tied, he would walk over by the forty-holer and, making sure that none of the guards was looking, step in, slip off the strings, and throw them in one of the toilets. Then he would slip into the yard, which was still crowded with prisoners, and get on the end of one of the lines.

By the time evening Appell had come around, the lineups were just as long as ever and the guards were running out of string. Besides, after Appell they were supposed to take the ropes off. They finally gave up and went home.

The next morning they showed up with more guards, more string, and a better system, and managed to have everyone tied up by lunchtime. It was considerable work for the guards, and they hated it, especially when the prisoners made such a game of it. Of course, when *Unteroffizier* Kissel – Ukraine Joe – was about, things became more serious because Joe had a bad temper and a sharp bayonet, which he loved to wave around and whack asses with.

After a few months of tying up everyone daily with string and untying them again every night, the guards were very happy when

Prisoners attempt to drink from tins while their hands are bound with cord. The hands of prisoners at Stalag VIIIB were bound every day for a period of fourteen months, as a German reprisal for alleged Allied mistreatment of German prisoners during the Canadian raid on Dieppe. c. 1942.

the chains arrived. The "chains" were actually handcuffs, with about eighteen inches of chain in between each cuff. A batch of chains was issued to each barrack, and every morning at "handcuff parade," two guards would have the job of handcuffing all of the prisoners in a barrack block.

When it was time for morning Appell, each prisoner would retire behind his bunk or some other place out of sight of the guards, and with a quick flip of a corned beef–tin key or a klim-tin opener, would remove his handcuffs, put on his overcoat, and put his handcuffs back on. The guards could never figure out how the men were able to put on a coat or take it off without removing their handcuffs.

The next morning was my first experience wearing handcuffs and chains. My friends showed me how to flip them open, and in a few minutes I was quite adept at removing them. Although I felt a bit stupid wearing them about the camp, I soon realized that it was

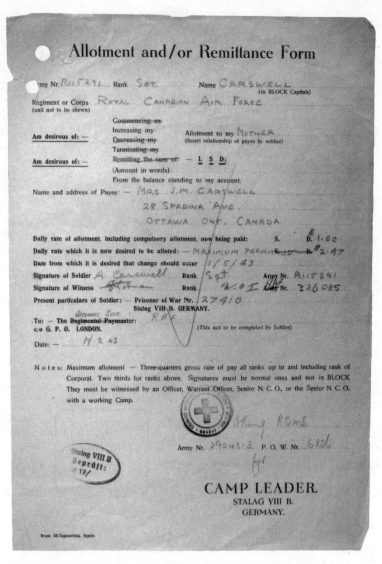

Allotment and/or Remittance Form

Army Nr. *R115291*   Rank *Sgt.*   Name *CARSWELL*
(In BLOCK Capitals)

Regiment or Corps *ROYAL CANADIAN AIR FORCE*
(unit not to be shewn)

Am desirous of: —
Commencing an
Increasing my
Decreasing my   Allotment to my *MOTHER*
Terminating my   (Insert relationship of payee to soldier)

Am desirous of: —
Remitting the sum of: — **L   S   D:**
(Amount in words)
From the balance standing to my account.

Name and address of Payee: — *MRS J.M. CARSWELL*
28 SPADINA AVE.
OTTAWA. ONT. CANADA.

Daily rate of allotment, including compulsory allotment, now being paid: S.   D. *1.00*
Daily rate which it is now desired to be alloted: — *MAXIMUM PERMITTED* — D. *2.47*
Date from which it is desired that change should occur *1/5/43*
Signature of Soldier *A. Carswell*   Rank *Sgt*   Army Nr. *R115291*
Signature of Witness *[signature]*   Rank *W.O.I*   Army Nr. *326085*
Present particulars of Soldier: — Prisoner of War Nr. *27910*
Stalag VIII B. GERMANY.
.To: — The Regimental Paymaster: *R.A.F.*
c/o G. P. O. LONDON.   (This not to be completed by Soldier)

Date: — *17.2.43*

N o t e s: Maximum allotment — Three-quarters gross rate of pay all ranks up to and including rank of Corporal. Two thirds for ranks above. Signatures must be normal ones and not in BLOCK They must be witnessed by an Officer, Warrant Officer, Senior N. C. O., or the Senior N. C. O. with a working Camp.

Acting RQMS
Army Nr. *2924313*   P. O. W. Nr. *6816*

CAMP LEADER.
STALAG VIII B.
GERMANY.

The Red Cross administered the pay allotments made by POWs at Stalag VIIIB.
Andrew allotted his maximum permissible amount to his mother. February 17, 1943.

only a formality and that most of the guards were embarrassed by the whole affair. We could remove them in seconds and usually hung them on a nail nearby when we were at the table or on our bunks.

A few weeks later, accustomed to camp routine by this time, I was playing cards at our table with a few friends when someone called "Guard in the compound!" to warn anyone who was doing anything illegal to hide the evidence. I was at the head of the table, near where the chains were hung on nails on the wall. I stood up, grabbed about six pairs of handcuffs, and was about to hand them out when I noticed that the others had become very quiet and were looking at something behind me. I turned around, the six pairs of chains in my hands, and looked into the baleful eyes of Ukraine Joe.

Caught in the act, I couldn't think of anything else to do so I just handed out the chains to the others and donned my own. The men hastily, if somewhat sheepishly, put on theirs. *Unteroffizier* Kissel stood there for a minute, looking like thunder, staring at us each in turn. We dealt out the cards and continued our game, attempting to maintain an air of innocence. After a minute or two his anger seemed to subside, and with a disgusted grunt he turned on his heel and stomped away.

I don't remember precisely when it was that the Germans let the dogs loose in the compound after hours, but I guess it was because there was too much activity going on at night between the compounds. Although prisoners were supposed to stay inside after dark, they were occasionally found in other barrack blocks and even in compounds where they didn't belong. So the Germans introduced trained Alsatian dogs to patrol the compounds. Just before sundown, when the compound gates were locked, a fierce-looking German shepherd would be released into the compound – sometimes two. They were trained to attack anyone found outside the barracks.

We weren't supposed to go out to the forty-holer after dark; a barrel stood on the porch at the end of the barrack for such emergencies. One night, one of our boys was still out in the toilets when the cry went up, "Dogs in the compound!" The poor guy sprinted from the toilets to the barracks with his pants half down, clutching his belt around his waist and doing about twenty miles an hour, two dogs in close pursuit.

The windows were flung open and the Kriegies yelled encouragement, "Come on, George! You can do it!" He leaped through the nearest window, pulled in by many helping hands amid rude laughter, with the snapping and slavering jaws of the two dogs right behind him. The dogs had been well trained and would not venture inside the windows or doors of the barracks.

Some of the Kriegies hatched a little training plan of their own. It was quite simple but involved giving up some of our scarce food. Small portions of bully beef were made up from contributions and thrown to the dogs. Developing a taste for this delicacy, the dogs came nearer and nearer to the window. The culmination of the training was when a delicious morsel of corned beef was held just inside the window. When the dog poked his head in to retrieve the meat, he was whacked on the head with a bed board – just hard enough to stun him. After a few of the dogs underwent this "training," they tended to stay away not only from our barrack block but also from our end of the compound, instead hanging about the gate until they were let out in the morning.

Food, no matter how poor in quality or how small the portion, was the high point of our day. When we heard the cry "Spuds up!" we knew our potato ration, a large wooden box of boiled potatoes, about a hundred pounds for each barrack block, had arrived. Each table had an elected "ration king" who divided up the assigned rations. We all gathered round and watched as our man brought back our daily ration of boiled potatoes, piping hot, and laid them out on the table. Would we be lucky and get some extras? There was even a roster for the scrapings from the bottom of the wooden box, as there was a roster for "seconds" at the soup line.

Our ration king, a big RAF flight sergeant, placed the box full of steaming boiled potatoes in their skins on the table, and laid out ten of the biggest in a row. Then he selected another ten, much smaller this time, and laid them one by one alongside the first row. Near the end, the second potato was getting awfully small! I looked into the box. There were still a lot of broken pieces and some potato skin, which he carefully divided up among the rows, then stood back to survey his work. Each of the ten rows contained about two and a half potatoes, some "halves" being little more than small piles of skin and broken pieces. Despite his obvious skill at dividing the ration, some portions looked slightly larger than others.

Reaching around to the shelf behind him, he picked up the "ration cards," a set of ten ordinary playing cards, each of which had one of our names on its face. My name was on the nine of spades. He shuffled the ten cards very carefully while we watched. He then placed them face down on the table and asked someone to cut them. One of the group would carefully cut the cards and hand them back to the ration king.

Then, with a great flourish, like a casino cardsharp, he would flip each card face up, at the head of each ration of potatoes. "Read 'em and weep!" he would cry as we picked up our day's ration of potatoes and carefully put them in a tin box or other homemade container. Such systems were a tribute to British sense of fair play and no doubt contributed a lot to our morale in those lean days.

Later in the morning would come the cry, "Bread carriers up!" and whichever two men in the barrack had been designated by roster for the task would take off for the cookhouse. Shortly afterward, they would be back, lugging the big wooden box with the barrack's ration of bread. The ration kings would bring back the two loaves allotted to our table of ten men and very carefully divide each loaf into five parts. The end, or heel, being rounded, was usually a little smaller but heavier, thus more attractive to some. At this particular time, the bread ration was one-fifth of a loaf of bread per day, although later it went down to one-seventh.

We stood around the table again, ten pairs of eyes watching like hawks, making sure that each loaf was cut as evenly as possible, and that every broken piece and crumb was accounted for. As with the potatoes, the ten pieces of bread were lined up in a row and any extra pieces or crumbs that had fallen off during the cutting added to portions that seemed a little smaller.

Out came the cards, and it was the luck of the draw again. "Win some and lose some!" the disappointed owner of one of the less attractive pieces might say, but basically the system was very fair. Those who didn't like the heel of the loaf could always trade with someone who had a centrepiece that, although slightly lighter, was better for making toast.

At the next call, "Soup up!" the entire barrack, 120 of us, would line up with our bowls and containers. At the head of the barrack stood a large metal container, much like a North American garbage can, which had been brought in by the carriers, four men this time, as it was heavy. Behind it stood the "soup king" with his ladle, made of a medium-sized tin can nailed to a long wooden stick.

As each man filed by, his ration of soup was plunked into his container, usually another tin, or a large tin cup. When every man in the barrack had received his allotted share, the cry "Seconds up!" was heard, and whichever table was on the roster for seconds would line up at the barrel to receive extra.

When the barrel, or *Kübel*, was quite empty, there were always the *Kübel* scrapers, who demanded the opportunity to scrape every fleck of nourishment from the bottom of the barrel. There was no roster for this, just a sort of free-for-all which most of us ignored, as it seemed a bit degrading. Besides, the soup was terrible. The scrapings from the bottom of the barrel were even worse.

The soup was called "Swede soup," a term that had nothing to do with Sweden. Its main ingredient was the Swede turnip, cut into big chunks and boiled in a kind of murky water. The other ingredients were dirt, and sometimes microscopic pieces of "mystery meat," so called because, according to local rumour, they always appeared in the soup a few days after some distant air raid. But there was no real evidence that dead horses or other accidentally killed animals were put in our soup. Actually, there was not much evidence of any kind of meat in the soup most of the time.

The soup was made in the cookhouse, a building near the north end of the camp where all the food for ten thousand prisoners was cooked. "All of the food" consisted of potatoes, bread, and Swede soup. Although the cookhouse was administered by the Germans, all of the workers were British or Irish POWs, and that was where the "rackets" originated.

The rackets were a source of income and extra food to some POWs and an evil that most of us disliked, many of us tolerated, and some took advantage of. To my mind, every loaf of bread or pound of potatoes stolen from the cookhouse was that much less for the rest of us, and for voicing such opinions, which were commonly held but unspoken, I was considered to be somewhat of a socialist, and a shit-disturber to boot.

As two of my friends, and even one of my crew, were from Belfast, they soon made connections at the cookhouse and often made mysterious references to the "rackets" and the "spud rackets." I noted too that they soon appeared to be better fed than the rest of us. To my own shame I even accepted a few gifts of potatoes and bread that they slipped my way, mainly because I was too hungry to turn them down. Now I had two things on my mind to give me deep feelings of guilt – my navigator, John Galbraith, and accepting food stolen, or at least misappropriated, from the cookhouse.

There was a sort of double standard in the camp. Although you never stole from your comrades, and personal effects, clothing, and food were quite safe when left unguarded in the barracks, quite a few, I noticed, took advantage of the rackets in one way or another. Indeed, the tough justice in the camp was such that, if any POW was unwise enough to steal from his comrades and was caught, the penalty was to be thrown bodily into one of the large tanks of sewage under the forty-holer and pushed under a few times until almost drowned. Not surprisingly, that crime was almost nonexistent.

In about August of 1943, the war in North Africa began to heat up and there was a resulting influx of army prisoners of war from

Italy. Discussions, sometimes heated, about the Siege of Tobruk and the Second Battle of El Alamein became commonplace. We were up-to-date with our war news, thanks to the banned nightly BBC broadcasts, but here were men recently transferred from Italian prisoner-of-war camps who had actually been in the battles for North Africa.

Many an argument ensued between army and air force bods about the support, or lack of it, from the RAF during the North Africa campaigns. But along with the stories and arguments about African defeats, the prisoners from the Italian camps had brought with them an amazing piece of new technology. It was called the "klim-tin blower." The impact of this invention on us in the summer of 1943 could be likened to the introduction of the microwave oven in more modern times. It revolutionized our cooking habits.

Like all great inventions, the klim-tin blower operated on a very simple principle. It was a forced-air burner, like a blacksmith's forge, in which chips of wood, bits of coal, or almost any kind of combustible material could be converted into a very hot fire, which would boil water or cook food much faster than the conventional stoves found in the camp, and use far less fuel.

It was made from a klim tin (hence the name), a square cocoa tin, a centrifugal blower made of sheet tin, and various wooden cranks and wheels, connected by a belt made from woven shoelaces or leather thongs. Turning the crank, which was attached to a large pulley, spun a small pulley, attached to the axle of the blower, at a great speed and blew air through the cocoa tin into the bottom of the klim-tin burner, feeding oxygen to the smouldering twigs, paper, or coal chips, and producing great heat, which would boil a potato or cook a glop in a very short time.

Once the daily rations had been received there wasn't much else to do but walk around with friends and acquaintances, make new friends, visit other compounds, explore the camp, and, in general, put in time.

As winter approached and the weather became increasingly colder, our greatest problem was keeping warm. Most of us by now had several layers of warm clothing, including greatcoats and warm mitts and socks, usually sent by our relatives. Every barrack had two fireplaces, each with a small firebox built into a brick chimney extending through the wood roof. These two fireplaces, situated about a third of the way from each end of the barrack, were the only source of heat for the building. By mutual agreement, the microscopic ration of coal provided was used only for cooking individual meals. The idea of using a few handfuls of coal to heat such a large and draughty building was laughable.

The standard procedure for cooking the meagre rations or warming up leftovers, usually in a klim tin, was to add your name to a roster attached to the chimney, then hang about the stove until your turn came up. We often argued about whether someone had jumped the queue or whether a particular container was occupying more than its fair share of space on the stovetop. But, by and large, the operation was carried out in a civilized fashion.

Each Canadian Red Cross parcel contained a pound of pilot biscuits, similar to common soda crackers except that they were four or five inches in diameter and a half-inch thick. These we would crush into fine crumbs, mix with raisins, sugar, and powdered milk, and then add enough water to make a sticky, gooey mess, which we called "glop." The whole mess would just about fill a klim tin. "Klim," of course, was simply "milk" spelled backwards. Klim was the only powdered milk available in 1943 and required a deft hand to arrive at anything slightly resembling milk, in taste or texture. To make the milk, you first made a paste of klim and water, eliminating all of the lumps, then slowly stirred in more water until you arrived at something that looked like milk (but didn't quite taste like it).

The Englishmen were not used to drinking milk as a beverage and added only minuscule amounts of milk for colouring their tea ("chaw"). So klim was an ideal ingredient for glop, where the disgusting taste could be submerged by the strong flavour of sugar and raisins.

Some of the more imaginative cooks attempted to make puddings rather than baking their glops in tins. Their procedure was to form the glop into a ball, wrap it in a cloth – preferably a clean one (although we had faith that boiling would remove all germs) – and boil for an hour or two, depending on how long one could get a space at the stove. The water left over from this concoction was not thrown away but drunk as a sort of beverage – not as flavoursome as tea or coffee, but certainly better than the occasional German issue of "mint" tea, which we usually used only for shaving.

To keep up morale and pass the time, we tried all kinds of things. One of my closest friends in the camp was Pete Skinner, a brilliant local humorist and philosopher whose ready wit and repartee was one of the brighter features of barrack block 15A. Pete and I collaborated on the great "Krafty Arts" show, which attracted over two thousand visitors.

The idea was born when we visited one of the British Army compounds to see a fascinating arts and crafts show, put on by the inmates of that particular compound. The exhibits were truly impressive, having been the fruit of years of careful and loving labour and craftsmanship. There were complete, delicately hand-carved chess sets made from toothbrush handles, working model steam engines made from tin cans, beautiful oil paintings and watercolours fit for an art gallery or museum, plus many other pieces of fine craftsmanship.

Pete suggested one evening that we put on an art show and I agreed. Since the war might be over before we could organize anything as good as what we had just seen, I suggested that we take a more original approach, something quick and funny that would catch people's attention. I remembered the Broadway show *Hell's a-poppin'*, a big hit before the war that had been made into a movie. It was zany, senseless, and funny.

We called it "The Krafty Arts Exhibition of 15A" and it was a roaring success. Of course, it had to be a success because everybody in the camp was bored out of their minds and anything slightly interesting was worth walking a distance to see. We advertised our show for several days by putting up publicity posters.

Pete and I made most of the exhibits, with the exception of some of the more obscene displays, like the wax vagina contributed by volunteers. (The British medical officer stationed in our camp said that the wax sculpture was extremely realistic and obviously done by someone who knew his subject well.) It was entitled "Things to Come" and was one of the most popular exhibits.

We did a lot of "paintings," really cartoons, with borrowed poster and watercolour paint, and in reasonably good taste considering the times. We had exhibits like "Toothbrush handle, made from ivory chess set" and "Tin can, made from model steam engine," as well as legitimate models and carvings, samples of knitting and embroidery, and lots and lots of drawings of nude women, which, for some reason, every budding artist thought he could draw, paint, or sketch from memory.

As for our "Hellzapoppin'" theme, we did not allow our audience, numbering over two thousand from all of the adjoining and surrounding compounds, to simply enter our exhibit through the doorway. We made them climb in a window, where a man dressed as a clown whacked them on the arse with a board as they came through. It's a measure of how bored everyone was that two thousand men, military men at that, would allow themselves to be whacked on the ass with a bed board just to see a lot of second-rate art and humour that might better have graced the walls of a lavatory.

While we're on the subject of the lavatory, this was when the big rat scare occurred. The level of the *Scheiße*, as the Germans called it, had risen to very high levels, just inches under the seats. The pool underneath was generally pumped out about once a week into horse-drawn tank-carts, called "honey wagons," operated by Russian prisoners of war accompanied by the ubiquitous guard. For some reason, no pumping out had occurred for a few weeks.

Into this situation came a British warrant officer, whom we shall call McPhee, and Corporal Smith (also not his real name). They decided to go out to the forty-holer for "a sociable shit," something every healthy Kriegie did at least once a day. Besides keeping one healthy, it kept one abreast of all the latest war news and rumours, mainly the rumours.

What McPhee didn't know was that Corporal Smith was a terrible practical joker and was plotting something fiendish and maniacal that particular day. Several dozen other Kriegies in on the plot innocently wandered about nearby. Some were even in the building, occupying nearby seats. As the two men walked across the small parade square toward the white cement building, Corporal Smith kept up a chatter about how many rats had been sighted running about across the top of the *Scheiße*, and how awful it would be if one were to be nipped in the family jewels. McPhee, being a practical man, couldn't imagine how a rat could run around on top of liquid shit, but on the other hand, he allowed that maybe a small rat, or even a mouse, might possibly support itself on the stuff.

Eventually, they seated themselves side by side on two of the seats along the wall, after ascertaining that the level of the material was well below anything that might be dangling from the hole, and began discussing the latest rumour about the Second Front. Diverting his friend's attention to something interesting on the far side of the building, Corporal Smith drew a short stick from under his greatcoat and slipped it into the hole over which he was sitting. On the end of this stick was a sharp nail, driven through at right angles.

"I think I hear a rat!" he cried, and gently tapped his friend on the testicles with the nail.

"My God! A rat's bit my balls!" screamed McPhee, his eyes bulging, and leaped up with his pants still around his knees.

He never did get his pants up in his mad dash back to the barrack block, and some of the witnesses, when they had stopped laughing, figured that he had set some kind of new record for running with one's pants down. He eventually forgave his friend for the cruel joke, but ever after he insisted on having an empty seat between them in the old forty-holer whenever they went out for a "sociable shit."

Because the Krafty Arts Exhibition had been a great success and was talked about for weeks, it put 15A on the map as one of the more creative barracks. So when the "fifty men a side" rugger match was proposed, we had more volunteers than we could handle for the sporting event, one of the most memorable ever staged in the camp.

Rugger was a great favourite because it required no special equipment other than a football and two sets of goal posts. With fifteen men on each team, the idea was to get the ball through the opposing team's goal. No pads were worn, and you didn't hang on to the ball when tackled because it was perfectly legal to kick the ball at any time, including when someone was holding it, so if one forgot this essential fact, he might get his head kicked in.

The game starts with a manoeuvre called the scrum, consisting of eight men from each team huddled into a very tight circle, all hanging on to each other. The ball is thrown underneath this pile of men, who then begin kicking at it and each other until it suddenly pops out and is grabbed by one of the smaller, faster individuals, who then runs for the opposite goal, pursued and obstructed by the opposing team.

No forward passes are allowed, so when the ball carrier is tackled, he must toss a lateral pass to one of his teammates, who then continues the operation until brought down. The ball is always in play except when the referee blows the whistle for an offside or foul or something. One may kick the ball forward at any time. As mentioned above, one hangs on to the ball when brought down only at the risk of his life, so the ball is often loose, with a screaming pack of maniacs kicking at it and trying to scoop it up all at the same time.

Pete and I decided that if we could have that much fun with fifteen men on each side, we could have five times as much fun with fifty men on each side. So we recruited two teams from our local RAF barracks and advertised the game all over the camp with posters in every compound. At least half the camp turned up at the playing field to see this amazing event, and the guards in the towers were getting visibly nervous. There was no rule about any limit to the number of Kriegies allowed on the playing field, so they could do nothing about it.

The scrum was horrendous, with dozens of men involved. When the ball was tossed in, it disappeared for a few minutes, then appeared mysteriously at one side of the crowd, where a player would pick it up and head for one of the goals, only to be tackled by someone and forced to throw the ball up in the air for another mad scramble. There was only one goal scored the entire game, and nobody knew which side scored it, so the game was declared a draw.

We had decided to put on a little show, so we briefed a couple of the players and the referee for a little skit. On cue, one of the players committed a horrendous foul, a terrific fake kick to the crotch. The referee blew his whistle and yelled at the offending player, who returned the compliment by giving him the international obscene gesture. The referee then called on a group that just happened to be standing by with a rope to string the offender up on the goal posts. Under the "hangee's" sweater was a sturdy rope, tied around his chest. The group that was to do the hanging pushed him down out of sight of the guard tower, hooked the rope under his sweater, and strung him up to the crossbar of the goal post, to the great cheering of hundreds of spectators.

One guard got so excited he fired his gun into the air and rushed to his telephone to report a riot and a lynching in the sports field. By the time a small detachment of armed soldiers arrived on the field, there was no trace of any victim, rope, referee, or even a ball. The crowd was quietly dispersing, every participant with a genuine look of vacuous innocence on his face. And so another legend of Stalag VIIIB was born, the one and only "fifty men a side" football game played at Stalag VIIIB, at Lamsdorf, in the summer of 1943.

A psychiatrist might say that insanity is a form of adjustment, an escape from a reality too hard to bear. These little bits of insanity were our adjustment, our escape from the stark reality of being locked up in a virtual cattle shed, in the middle of winter, in the middle of nowhere, and not knowing when, or even if, we would ever make it home. Paddy with his little bit of Irish insanity, and others like Eric Dunmal, a crazy Englishman who played his flute in the middle of the night, may have been eccentric characters, but they helped to ease the pain of forced confinement for the rest of us.

Things like the "fifty men a side" rugger game and the Krafty Arts Exhibition were our aberrations that helped us to remain relatively normal. It may have been part of the British tradition of the time. I'm sure that the Germans found our humour difficult to understand – for them, everything had to be black or white, good or bad. They couldn't figure out how a bunch of fractious, trouble-making, argumentative complainers could make effective, loyal, and conscientious fighting men.

It would take several books to describe all the facets of daily life in a German prisoner-of-war camp and, indeed, many such books have been written, but they all reveal that we survived by taking it one day at a time.

11

Taffy Mac's Souvenir Booklet

As part of its humanitarian efforts, the Swiss Red Cross arranged a prisoner exchange between the Germans and the British for those prisoners too sick to be of any further use in the war. My close friend "Taffy Mac" McLean was, unfortunately, one of them.

Mac was diagnosed as having tuberculosis. It was bittersweet news for him, for although TB is a serious affliction, particularly in a prisoner-of-war camp, it meant that he was eligible for repatriation on the next Red Cross prisoner exchange.

Just before Christmas 1944, Mac was shipped out, deemed unfit for any future military service. Before he left, I made this little booklet of cartoons in ink and watercolour for him to take home to England. More than sixty years later he still has it, one of his few souvenirs from those terrible times.

These are only a few of the cartoons I drew while a prisoner. The Red Cross had given each POW a hardcover book with about a hundred blank pages. I filled mine with cartoons depicting life in the camp. In 1945, during the infamous long march across Germany, I burned my book so that I could boil a few potatoes.

So it's lucky Mac saved my little souvenir booklet and sent me a copy years later, because I didn't save a damn thing except my skin!

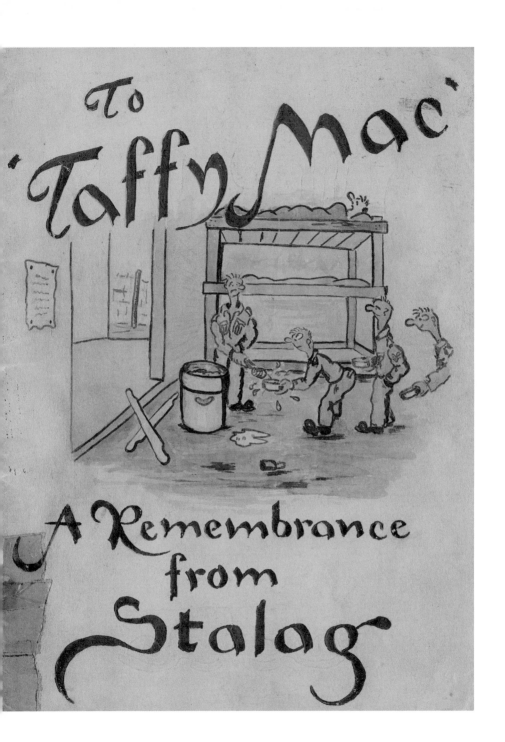

147

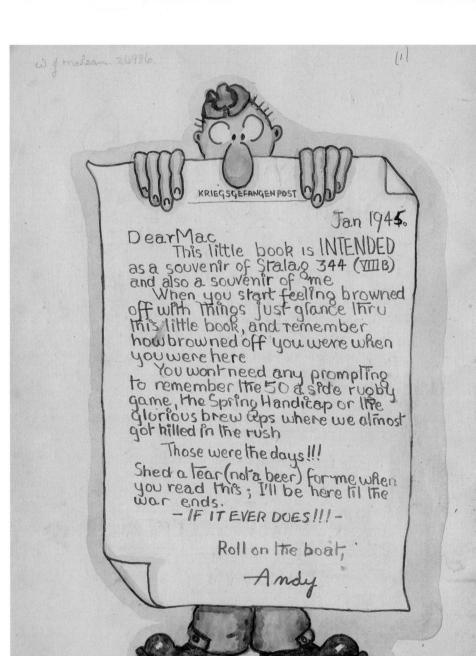

REMEMBER —

HOW WE USED TO "WATCH" THE SECTION LEADER CUTTING THE BREAD

AND THE "SPUD CARRIERS"

WHEN YOU USED TO CLAIM THAT ALL THE WEIGHT WENT ON YOUR SHOULDER

Each table of ten men had a "ration king" who divided up the bread or potatoes or whatever we had, as evenly as possible. He would shuffle and deal ten playing cards, each with a man's name on it, then flip each card face up at the head of each ration, to indicate who got which.

The spud ration worked out to about two and a half small potatoes per day, per prisoner.

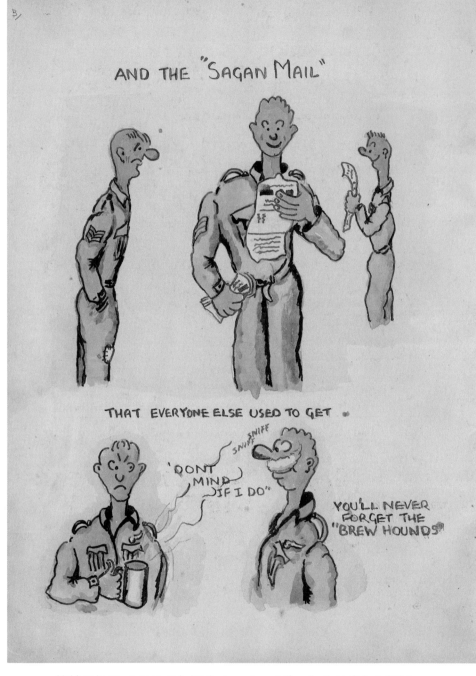

AND THE "SAGAN MAIL"

THAT EVERYONE ELSE USED TO GET

SNIFF SNIFF

'DONT MIND IF I DO"

YOU'LL NEVER FORGET THE "BREW HOUNDS"

Mail from home was sparse, and what there was came via "Sagan" – that is, Stalag Luft III, the officers' camp near Sagan, in occupied Poland, of "Great Escape" fame.

Every barrack had its own "brew hound," a moocher who always turned up when you had a cup of tea or coffee brewed.

— OR THE

BREW UP!

AND HOW WE ALMOST GOT KILLED
IN THE RUSH?

WAR'S OVER. HEARD IT FROM A A MAN WHO WORKS IN THE RED CROSS STORE

—AND THE RUMOURS
THAT NEVER CAME TRUE

Hot water was delivered in large containers and doled out a ladleful for each man. Sometimes we mixed it with tea or coffee, or cocoa. Sometimes we shaved with it.

Rumours were rampant. A good place to hear the latest ones was out in the can, the old forty-holer where prisoners went out to in groups for a sociable crap.

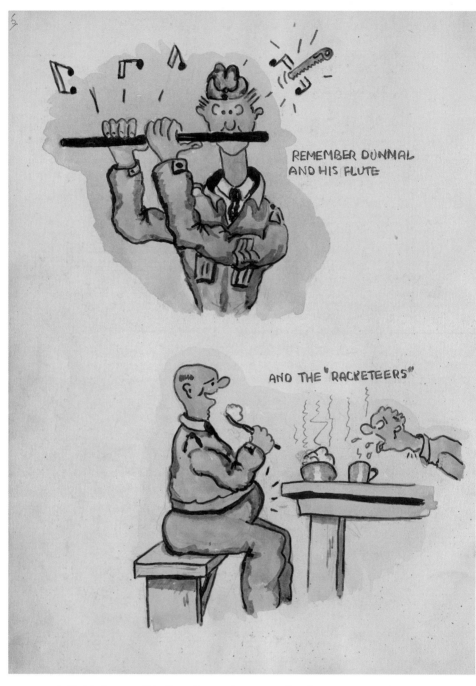

An English chap named Eric Dunmal managed to acquire a flute. He was quite a good player actually, but some of his music seemed a little weird, especially when he played it late at night.

Every compound had its racketeers, who lived by their wits and always seemed to have kit bags full of food and cigarettes. Most of them worked in the cookhouse.

Some of us were too young and naive to wheel and deal and trade our assets, or to get friendly with someone in the cookhouse or Red Cross stores.

We wolfed down our grub as soon as we got it, and kept up our spirits with plans to escape.

Crush a handful of heavy-duty soda crackers (pilot biscuits) into crumbs, add milk powder, sugar, jam, raisins, prunes, or anything else that's edible, mix everything together, put it into a tin-can oven to bake – and you have a "glop," something made only a few times a year from stored-up goodies.

The soup came in a metal barrel, carried by two or four men. After everyone got his ration, whichever table was on the roster for seconds would line up for them. And then, there was always someone who would dive in and scrape whatever was left on the bottom.

There were about ten thousand prisoners in the camp, all of whom arrived by some violent means, so there were a lot of interesting stories, not all of them necessarily true.

POWs argued on the drop of a hat – about anything. And given the difference in backgrounds between English, American, and Canadian prisoners, there were some pretty good arguments, a few even ending in fisticuffs.

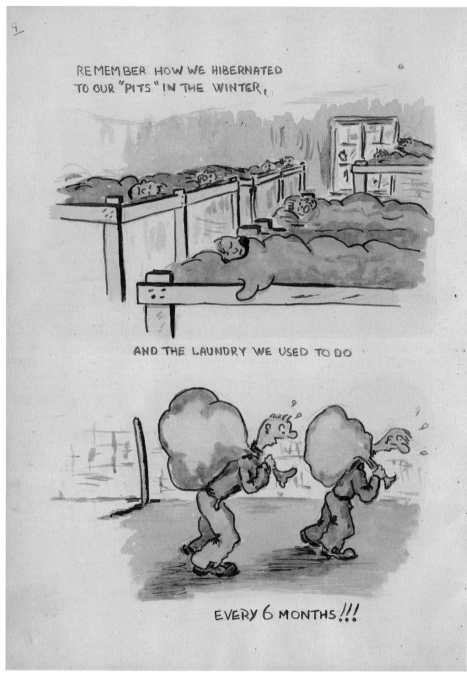

The barracks were uninsulated, unheated, and crowded, the latter probably being what saved us from freezing – our own animal heat. The sound of a hundred men snoring, all in different keys and tunes, is unforgettable.

There was no hot water in the barracks, so every six months or so we got to take our laundry down to a big building at the other end of the camp and wash it.

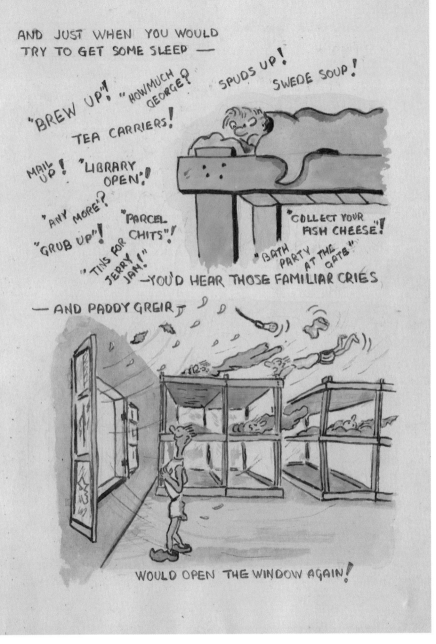

AND JUST WHEN YOU WOULD
TRY TO GET SOME SLEEP —

"BREW UP"! "HOW MUCH GEORGE?" SPUDS UP! SWEDE SOUP!

TEA CARRIERS!

MAIL UP! 'LIBRARY OPEN'!

"ANY MORE?" "PARCEL FOR CHITS"! "COLLECT YOUR FISH CHEESE"!

"GRUB UP"! "TINS FOR JERRY JAM!" "BATH PARTY AT THE GATE"

—YOU'D HEAR THOSE FAMILIAR CRIES

— AND PADDY GREIR

WOULD OPEN THE WINDOW AGAIN!

It always seemed that just when you decided to have a little snooze, there would be something important being given out that would be too good to miss.

The British always were fresh-air freaks, but in a barrack block that was full of holes and cracks anyway, it was just too much to have a fresh-air nut named Paddy Greir fling open the window on a cold wintry day or night.

157

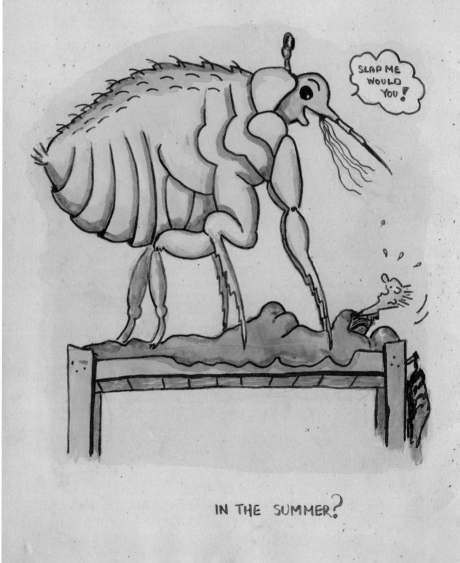

We had a lot of fleas in our beds, in part because our mattresses were straw. In spring we would sit out in the yard and pick out the fleas.

REMEMBER THE PRISONERS
THAT CAME IN FROM ITALY
IN AUGUST '43

"SPAGHETTI
FED FOR
TWO YEARS"

AND THE

"BLOWERS"

THEY BROUGHT
WITH THEM?

AND ALL THE THINGS
WE USED TO MAKE FROM TINS —

TOO BAD WE COULDN'T EAT THEM TOO!!

When the first allied POWs arrived from the Italian campaign, they brought with them the klim-tin blower, a centrifugal blower made out of tin cans and powered with a hand crank. It made it possible to cook with almost any kind of fuel.

Cooking stoves and all kinds of other utensils were made from tin cans, flattened out, cut to pattern, and held together with rivets made from the soft metal ties on barbed wire.

Most of us don't smoke now, but in those days a cigarette, or "fag," was a substitute for food and the medium of exchange.

LAST BUT NOT LEAST, REMEMBER THE "KRAFTY ARTS" EXHIBITION

WE HELD IN THE DOORWAY OF 15A BARRACK THAT DREW 2000 SPECTATORS IN A DAY

AND THE "50 A SIDE" RUGBY GAME 15A HAD

THEY SAID WE WERE "STALAG HAPPY" —

One day Pete Skinner and I saw a fantastic arts and crafts show at one of the compounds. We were so impressed, we decided to have our own exhibition in barrack block 15A. Our Krafty Arts Exhibition drew thousands of visitors. Which shows what you can do with bit of promotion.

We organized a "fifty man a side" rugby game, which got so wild that the German guards thought they had a riot on their hands – particularly when we arranged a fake hanging, and "hung" one of the players on the goal post for allegedly committing a foul.

161

Most of us had a pretty good sense of humour, which is a good old Canadian and British tradition anyway. Although sometimes certain people would go a little beyond the bounds of normal sanity – which, as any psychiatrist will tell you, is a form of escape. We called this being "Stalag happy."

12

Doing It Right

It was now June of 1943, and I was determined to escape again; but this time I'd do it properly. I knew what I had to do, but needed a lot of time and preparation. The Escape Committee could give me some help. Thanks to Hubert, our friendly escape expert, I had a good idea this time how to go about it. I had to learn a little German so that I wouldn't be completely helpless when some German yelled something at me. And I had to find someone compatible who wanted to escape with me.

Which is how I met up with Taffy Mac, alias W.J. (Bill) McLean, a short, pale, gutsy Welshman who had an irrepressible urge to escape. Mac had been a resident of barrack block 15A longer than I, having been shot down in a Halifax bomber four months before me. He was a wireless operator/air gunner who had had a very interesting career up until then.

As he told it, he had joined the RAF in 1938 when Neville Chamberlain had come back from his meeting with Hitler in Munich and said "Peace in our time," so he thought it would be a safe job. He had wanted to be a pilot, but his legs were too short. He was also short a few academic qualifications. When war broke out, he was posted to a Wellington bomber squadron, where he completed a tour of twenty-eight operations before being posted to an operational training unit as an instructor.

I asked him about the trip that brought him to Lamsdorf.

"Well, ah, we were coming back from Duisburg, on September 7, 1942. It was about three in the morning... on our way back, when suddenly we were attacked by night-fighters."

"How high were you?"

"Oh, I don't know, ten or twelve thousand, I think. There was obviously no chance of flying this one back to base because the skipper immediately said, 'Bail out!'"

"Do you know what you were attacked by?"

"One of those night-fighter fuckers."

"Fockers?"

"No, Messerschmitt 110s, you idiot, one of those fuckers!"

"Oh! And did everyone bail out?"

"So I put on my parachute," Mac went on, "and I said to the skipper, 'Are you there?' and he said, 'Yes,' and I said, 'In that case, I'm going too' – and so out I went. The rear gunner was killed, the rest of the crew survived, and the navigator is still missing.

"I landed with a parachute and I was slightly wounded in the leg, so I couldn't walk very far. I was picked up by a farm worker, a very kind person, who put me on the bar of his bike and wheeled me to a cottage, where they gave me some soup and called in the local army characters, who called in the air force [Luftwaffe] people, and they took me to Cologne at first to interrogate me, and then I went to Dulag Luft at Frankfurt-on-the-Maine. After that, I came here on the old eight *chevals* or forty *hommes* [eight horses or forty men] cattle cars."

As I told Mac all about my recent abortive escape, he listened with great interest, especially to the details about passenger trains.

"I hear that you've already been out once on the Spring Handicap," I said. "Tell me all about it."

"Not much to tell," he replied in his self-depreciating way. "I swapped over with a chap called Pearson and went out on a working party. My job was stacking lumber in a sort of lumberyard.

Then, with three other fellows, we chipped out a hole in the wall of the loo, which was on an outside wall. The hole was just big enough for us to get through. Sadly, I was the last one out, and it was pitch-black outside. I lost my companions the first night and had no food or equipment. So I went roaming around in circles in the dark and was picked up the next morning."

"So here we are," I said. "Both of us have screwed up one escape. Let's do it right this time, and get back home before the war ends." We shook on it.

I was just approaching my twentieth birthday; Mac was older, about twenty-two or twenty-three. With his skinny frame and fair complexion, he looked about sixteen, a definite asset when escaping (all men of military age in Germany were either in uniform or were foreign workers). Despite his small frame and pale visage, Mac was a real tiger. One day as I was standing beside him in the yard outside one of the barrack windows awaiting Appell, a large man about twice his size leaped out the window (a shortcut to avoid Ukraine Joe, I suppose) and landed on Mac's big toe. In a cold fury he grabbed the giant's collar, pulled his face down close to his, and said in a voice of thunder, "Do that again and I'll kill you!"

The big man, shocked by the violent reaction, mumbled, "Sorry, sir!" and scurried away with the terrified look of a man about to be attacked by a rabid jackrabbit.

While Mac and I were starting to plan our escape, other things were happening around the compound. In November 1943, the chains came off. Tired of being a laughing stock of the entire camp, the Germans decided to junk the whole idea and stop chaining up the RAF and Canadians. It was just too ridiculous. I don't know whether Hitler ordered the chains off or whether the scheme just fell into disrepute.

Days and nights went by with steady monotony, each adapting to the routine in his own way. Morning Appell, preceded by the loud thwacking on wooden tables by Joe Kissel's bayonet. Lots of epithets as sleep-drugged and partly dressed Kriegies leaped out of windows to avoid Ukraine Joe's wrath. Then the forming up in five ranks and the counting. Occasionally, we amused ourselves by shifting positions in the middle of a count from a rear line to a centre line, to put the count off. It frustrated the guards to have one too many, then one too few, in their final count.

It was self-defeating, though, for until the count was correct, nobody left the parade, and most of us had better things to do.

Such as picking fleas out of our palliasses. The flea population increased during the heat of the summer. Although we had virtually eliminated the bedbugs and lice through the German delousing programs, fleas appeared regardless of the cleanliness of the individual. So throughout the spring and summer, groups of men sunned themselves in the open areas between the barrack blocks, emptying the straw from their palliasses and arranging them in loose piles to dry in the sun.

As the straw was drying in the hot sun, it was carefully sifted in small handfuls so that any fleas that happened to be in a particular batch could be crushed between thumb and forefinger. Flea picking was also an innocent-looking diversion covering more important activities, such as planning an escape or plotting to corrupt some innocent guard.

In the summer and fall of 1943, we began to get the banned BBC News regularly. As the Allies' fortunes improved, so did our morale. Every evening after the compound had been carefully checked for guards, one of the RAF types from another barrack block would come over to our barrack and read the latest news, never more than an hour or two old. We didn't ask where the radio was located, but the rumour was that it had been manufactured from individual parts blackmailed from a guard and assembled by a former ham operator, now a WAG (wireless operator/air gunner).

As we later discovered, the procedure for obtaining illegal items was fairly straightforward. Simply put, if you could make a series of

Prisoner at Stalag VIIIB (Lamsdorf) tuning a homemade crystal radio set in an attempt to pick up news of the war.

seemingly innocent transactions with a friendly but gullible guard, you could gradually escalate the type of things asked for in return for real coffee, chocolate, sugar, etc., until the guard finally balked at risky items, such as foreign workers' passports, camera parts and film, or typewriter parts. When the guard, understandably, refused to obtain such things, he was threatened with exposure.

A dirty trick, no doubt, but very effective. If caught in such a trap, the guard would have to choose between serious punishment, such as imprisonment or military court martial, transfer to the Russian Front (a virtual death sentence), or cooperation with the prisoner. Most chose cooperation.

It was another example of how severe punishments are inevitably counterproductive. I read somewhere that in the French Army in World War I, the penalty for stealing – even a loaf of bread – was the firing squad. The result was that food theft was rampant, for no soldier, even an NCO, would likely turn in a comrade for a minor crime that would result in the death penalty. I don't know about officers, though – a lot of them were proper bastards and would probably enforce such penalties, no matter how strict.

Every few months we were given the privilege of having a shower down at the camp bathhouse. Groups of about one hundred, a complete barrack, were marched down and made to stand around outside the bathhouse for a few hours awaiting their turns. The water was not hot, nor was it cold, but a cool lukewarm. It was such a pleasure to get a complete shower. Ordinarily, we washed as best we could at the barrack trough under a cold tap, with the aid of a make-do washcloth and a bit of real soap from home. Some of us had traded off our genuine soap for bread and had to use the local German stuff. With it you could literally grind the dirt off your skin.

Summer gradually turned into fall, and the shorter days began to grow colder, until we realized that winter had almost arrived. Mac and I busied ourselves with plans for swapping over and escaping the following spring. Through our barrack NCO we contacted the Escape Committee and enlisted its help. It was a very informal organization whose loose membership included just about anyone who had any illegal or technical talents.

Mac and I had gradually formulated a plan that we thought should work. Based on my previous escape and his experience, along with advice from other escapees and members of the committee, we had decided to swap over; go out on a working party the following April (1944); acquire civilian clothes; pose as foreign workmen, whom we now knew to be very common throughout Germany; travel by a series of local passenger trains to Stettin, a Baltic port not far from Berlin; acquire passage on a neutral Swedish ship (this would be the difficult part) and finally, we hoped, end up in Sweden. There we could be airlifted back to England, courtesy of the local British Embassy. Simple.

The Escape Committee discussed our plan, decided that it had merit, and let us know that it would assist us in any way it could.

Which is how I met Ken Hyde, the "official" passport photographer for Stalag VIIIB. He was one of these talented people who had offered their services to the Escape Committee. A warrant officer navigator who had enlisted in Calgary, Alberta, in 1939, he had been shot down in 1942. Before enlistment in the RCAF, he'd operated a photographic studio in Calgary. Now he conducted business from an office in one of the other RAF barracks. As a senior warrant officer, he shared a small room at the end of a barrack block with the barrack NCO, another warrant officer.

One wintry fall day as I was sitting at our table sipping a tin mug of hot water slightly flavoured with a well-used tea bag – no milk, no sugar – the barrack NCO tapped me on the shoulder and said, "Go and see Ken Hyde in the *Stube* at 17B. It's about your plan."

I found my way to 17B, which was two barrack blocks over from mine, and tapped on the door frame. (There were no doors to the *Stuben* – rooms or offices – but for privacy they had a sort of sackcloth drape.)

"Come in!" a voice boomed in an unmistakably western Canadian accent.

"Sergeant Carswell, sir!" I said. "I was told to see you." Warrant officers were always called "sir" by lower ranks.

"Ah, yes," he said, gazing up speculatively at me through the curling smoke from his pipe. "Carswell. Pull the drape shut over there. That's right. Now put on this jacket!" He reached under a bunk and pulled out a tweedy-looking jacket about my size. "Now put on this tie." I was wearing an air force blue shirt, so I buttoned the collar and quickly knotted the tie, a somewhat gaudy and tasteless one with weird conflicting hues.

"Don't worry about the colours," he assured me. "This picture is in black and white, not Technicolor." He reached into an ordinary-looking cardboard box and pulled out a beautiful, modern, folding Kodak camera.

"Where did you get that!" I gasped, for it was clearly new.

"Don't ask," he replied. "The less you know, the better for all of us."

Years later I learned the answer. He had been using an old German camera that he had blackmailed from a guard. More than once he had complained about its shortcomings to his inner circle. One day, some time later, he was standing in a crowd on the sports field watching a soccer game when someone pushed a paper parcel into his arms and disappeared into the crowd. Back in the sanctuary of his *Stube,* he opened the parcel, and there it was. A beautiful, new Kodak camera. He never did find out who the person was who gave it to him that day. Another unsolved mystery of Stalag VIIIB!

"You don't have to smile," he said as I posed for my passport photo. "Most foreign workers don't smile much anyway, and especially not when some kraut bastard is taking their picture. So just look serious." Which wasn't hard for me to do, especially when I began to think of the implications of the picture that had just been taken. It would be affixed to a forged passport or working permit describing me as a foreign worker who had been ordered to travel to a new job in Stettin.

Mac went through the same routine a short time later. Now all we had to do was wait and plan, and save our chocolate and cigarettes to buy the necessities for escaping.

Ken Hyde was the only member of the Escape Committee whom I met. Usually I got my information second-hand, through my barrack block commander or others. It was probably a good system, for the less I knew, the more secure the system was. How would I do under torture by the Gestapo? I didn't even like to think about it. I'd probably be a complete coward and tell them anything they wanted to know. Just the idea of carrying a forged passport across Germany scared me silly.

Getting shot or even killed, however unpalatable, were finite things that I could deal with, but the idea of being tortured terrified me. I had once read a story in which a sadistic Gestapo interrogator had strapped his victim in a dentist's chair and forced his mouth open with a steel device so that he couldn't move a muscle, then methodically drilled straight into the nerve of each tooth until the victim went insane with the pain.

Later that same year I was called to see the commandant. I was marched out the main gate and into his office by two armed guards. I convinced that they had found me out – that I had swapped over with an army private and tried to escape. That must be it. I wondered what kind of punishment it would be.

The commandant was a colonel. The rumour around camp was that his son was a prisoner of war in Canada. Was that why we were treated so reasonably? A German colonel was a pretty high-ranking officer to be ordering a mere sergeant to be escorted to his office, and I was feeling very nervous as I was marched into his spacious office.

Behind the heavy oaken desk sat a middle-aged, impressive-looking German colonel, complete with Iron Cross and several medal ribbons. Behind him hung a large framed photograph of Hitler and a couple of swastika flags. On his desk were family pictures – wife and children, I imagined. The *Unteroffizier* called me to a halt, and I stood to attention in front of the camp commandant.

He regarded me with considerable interest, then picked up an object from his desk and leaned forward. "Do you recognize this?" he asked in good Oxford English, holding up my Rolex Oyster wristwatch. I immediately recognized the watch my father had given me for my eighteenth birthday, and which John Galbraith had been wearing when I last saw him in the cockpit of the burning Lancaster bomber.

"Yes, sir," I replied, somewhat excitedly, I imagine. "It certainly is my watch. Where did you get it?"

"If it is," he replied, "perhaps you can tell me what is engraved on the back."

"It says, 'R115291 LAC AG Carswell, RCAF, First Solo – 15 October 1941.'"

"Quite correct. Here, take your watch, it is yours. You are lucky to get it back. It is a very good Swiss watch. I hope you will make a note of the honesty of the German soldier."

"Thank you, sir," I said, "but may I ask a question? What happened to the man who was wearing this watch?"

"Oh, he was part of a bomber crew that was shot down on January 17 of this year, near Magdeburg. He was killed. That was the same flight that you were on, was it not?"

"Yes, but he parachuted out of the aeroplane before it hit the ground. We're sure of that. He wasn't in the wreckage, and besides, your people were looking for him and asking questions about him for several days afterward. Also, this watch hasn't been damaged in any way. So how did he get killed?"

"I'm afraid I can't answer that question," he said, a little sadly, I thought. "According to my official information, he was killed as a result of being shot down in an RAF Lancaster bomber near Magdeburg on January 17 of this year. That is all the information that I have been given. I see now that he was part of your crew. I can only pass on to you the information that I have been given. I am sorry."

"Yes, he was part of my crew, and I'm sure that he was not in the aircraft when it hit the ground."

"I can only give you the information I have," he said again, almost apologetically, "and that is the extent of my information. You are dismissed. Good luck." He stood up, indicating that the interview was over. I saluted, the watch now on my left wrist, performed a smart about-turn, and marched off, escorted by my two guards.

When I returned to the barrack block, I told Jock, Clem, and Paddy what had happened. We were determined to find out whether John was still alive. We put an inquiry through to the Red Cross in Geneva. A month later, the same information came back. Sergeant Galbraith had been killed as a result of being shot down in an RAF Lancaster bomber on January 17, 1943. No further details

Left: Andrew's father, Morrison Carswell, kept a record of all the cigarettes he sent to Andrew as a prisoner of war in Germany. Right: Morrison Carswell in England sporting his new uniform, including a swagger stick. He was sent overseas as a member of the 1st Canadian Motor Machine Gun Brigade, First Contingent. September 1914.

were available. Clearly, the only information available to the Swiss Red Cross was what the Germans were willing to give it.

Days turned into weeks. We developed our routines. Clem read his western stories, Jock honed up on bridge, Mac and I plotted our "Annual Spring Handicap of 1944," and Paddy Hipson got more involved with the Irish cookhouse racketeers. He slipped me a few potatoes from time to time, which I always felt guilty about but ate anyway. They tasted just as good, despite my qualms of conscience. I tried to justify my weakness by telling myself that if I refused the potatoes, they would just go to someone else.

For some reason, I received a lot more parcels from home than did my RAF friends, and my cigarettes came in thousand lots, rather than in two hundred lots, as did the British personal parcels. I put this extra currency to good use by sharing it with my crew and friends, and adding it to my hoard of chocolate and food for the pending escape.

13

EIKHAMMER

Soon it was March and swapover time was rapidly approaching. Mac and I had saved and scrimped all winter and had a considerable cache of food and cigarettes for our escape. The Escape Committee had slipped us our completed passports, warning us it was now our duty to make sure that they were not found at any of the irregular camp searches. I hid mine in the bottom of my kit bag, wrapped in filthy socks and underwear, with some cigarettes and soap the next layer up in case a nosey guard actually searched it.

Our "passports" were actually working and travelling permits issued to foreign workers, permitting them to travel from job to job. As train travel was virtually the only method of travel, it was normal for any train to have foreign workers travelling from one place to another.

My passport, or *Ausweis*, had a rather good photo of me in a civilian sports jacket, looking suitably serious. My name on the passport was Paul Swaboda, and I was a Czech electrician, born in and a resident of Prague, travelling to Stettin to report to the *Arbeitsbüro* (employment office) there. It was signed by the chief of police at Gleiwitz and looked very official and genuine. It was an excellent choice of nationality, as most Germans didn't speak Czech, and many Czechs didn't speak German. So we'd be able to bumble our way through Germany with our minimal German and, barring the bad luck of running into a Czech-speaking German, we would be home free.

Mac was also posing as an electrician from Prague, under orders to report to Stettin. Although his passport gave his real age, about twenty-two or twenty-three, he looked about fifteen in the picture.

It was about the middle of April 1944 when Mac and I swapped over. We had waited until there was a bit of activity in the working compound so that we wouldn't have to hang about too long and risk the chance of running across Ukraine Joe, who still snooped about a lot, trying to uncover swapovers.

We "mucked in" together for the food rations and Red Cross parcels, and with adjoining bunks, we were pretty well left to ourselves. We knew the routine by now, so we kept a low profile and waited for the call.

I tried to develop an English accent but was a dismal failure at it. Some people just never lose their accent, and I'm one of them. I became so used to hearing English accents all day long that they sounded perfectly normal to me, and it was only when I opened my own mouth that my accent sounded strange. When I arrived back in Canada after the war, the first thing I noticed was that most people, particularly the women, spoke with a strange nasal accent. When my mother and sister spoke, to me, after so many years of hearing only British accents, they sounded very strange.

Nobody paid much attention to us in the working compound; things just drifted along. Appell, rations, soup, and mail arrived in monotonous order, and even Ukraine Joe didn't show up much.

I was Private Dennis Reeves again, and Mac became Private Joe Parsons. After just a few days in our new barrack block acclimatizing ourselves to our new roles, our names were called for assignment to a working party. As usual, I had trouble with my Yankee accent and had to keep my mouth shut most of the time, letting Mac do the talking. With his Welsh accent, he attracted no attention and fitted in perfectly. The British Army was full of Welshmen, all called "Taffy," so nobody noticed him. As a matter of fact, with his boyish looks, he looked almost too young to be in the army.

The weather was becoming warmer, and new work parties were being called every day. One morning on Appell, our names were called out for a working party at a place called Eikhammer, a small village not far from the town of Oppeln. We could hardly believe our luck. Oppeln was on the railway route to Stettin, our Baltic Sea destination.

According to our map, Oppeln was on a main railroad line to Breslau, and Breslau had direct rail connections with just about anywhere we might want to go. All we had to do was find some way to get to Oppeln from Eikhammer and we were practically home.

Next morning, Mac and I were marched out the main gate, the second time for both of us. I hoped it would be the last. There was no problem with the kit bag searches; the soap and cigarettes in the tops of our bags seemed to discourage the guards from digging any deeper, for which I was profoundly grateful. When I thought of my forged passport, escape maps, and accumulated German money wrapped in dirty socks and underwear at the bottom of the bag, my imagination summoned up the prospect of various tortures. It had cost me a couple of large packs of Player's Mild cigarettes and three bars of very good Palmolive soap, but it had been a bargain. The passports would be very useful before we were finished.

We found ourselves in a group of about twenty assigned to several *Arbeitskommandos* in the area. Mac and I were the only two going to Eikhammer, a forestry centre where we would work in a woodcutting operation. I was ecstatic to find that we would be working outdoors and not in a mine or factory.

A few hours later, we stopped briefly at Eikhammer, and Mac and I were escorted from the train by our lone guard. Although the village was small, the townspeople hardly gave us a glance as we were marched through.

Our quarters were not far from town, we learned from our guard, who communicated with us in his fractured English as we responded in kind. In fact, it was on the eastern edge of the town, not more than two miles from the train station.

Our new home was to be another farmhouse, this time surrounded by a high fence. As we approached the building, I could see about a dozen British prisoners sprawled around the front of the house, sunning themselves, loafing, and clearly awaiting our arrival. They too were under the watchful eye of a guard sitting a short distance away, rifle across his knee, seemingly half-asleep. He got to his feet and helped escort us into the farmhouse.

Having dealt with the usual formalities, paperwork, and receipts for the two of us, the escorting guard saluted, shook hands with the resident guard, and took his leave. The resident guard looked us over with slight interest, then turned us over to the British corporal in charge and returned to his chair in the sun.

The corporal, who was also the official interpreter, introduced himself. The rest crowded around to get the latest news and rumours from the main camp, particularly the war news, as they knew about the daily BBC bulletins.

Mac introduced himself as Private Joe Parsons and we were all getting along splendidly until I introduced myself as Private Dennis Reeves, captured at Dunkirk, 1940, etc., etc.

"Captured at Dunkirk, my fucking arse!" laughed a big Irishman. "You're a fucking Yank, me lad. What are ye doing in that British uniform?"

"Well, actually, I'm not a 'fucking Yank,' if you must know, I'm a 'fucking Canydian', and we're both swapovers from the RAF. We're hoping that you'll help us escape."

Dead silence. They all looked at each other. I'd been through this routine before so trotted out the "it is our duty to escape" speech, and pointed out that the war would be over in a year or two, and that our side was winning, and that after the war there would be questions as to who did what and why. Mac added a few clinching arguments too, in his unmistakeably British accent. They were thinking over what he had said.

There was another silence – a very long silence. Then the corporal and three others went into an adjoining room, where we could hear them talking in low voices.

When they came back, the corporal said, "We're going to help you, but you have to cooperate with us too. This is a very cushy working party. It's taken us years to bring it up to this stage, and you have to understand that, after you go, things will become very bad for us here again."

What they were saying was true. After Donaldson and I had been returned to camp, we'd heard what happened after our escape. The guard had immediately been transferred to the Russian Front, a big investigation had taken place, and virtually all privileges had been rescinded.

As all evidence of the made-up beds had been removed, and as the count had been correct at bedtime (this was sworn to by the guard), and since none of the locks had been broken or damaged, it had seemed to the Germans that we had just disappeared into thin air. And, of course, our fellow prisoners were no help. They acted amazed that two of their comrades had disappeared right out of their beds. The chaps down at the brewery apparently had a party in our honour, and put a little extra "flavour" in their special beer for the ss.

This time, Mac and I truly appreciated any help we might get. We all knew the consequences, not only to ourselves but to the whole working party, which was well organized, on good terms with the guards and the local people, and which would probably never enjoy the same privileges again after we left. We all knew it, and accepted it, and it was never mentioned again.

Our working party was officially designated as a forestry job, although in reality it was simply a woodcutting job. Except for the "cook" and a medical orderly who worked on a nearby local farm, the rest of us were marched about two miles into the woods each day to cut our quota.

Again, the time-study experts had done their job well, and our quotas were ridiculously low. By working fairly quickly, we were able to meet our individual quotas by shortly after noon and be back to our billets by early or mid-afternoon. Each man's quota was to cut and stack a cubic metre of wood, which in practical terms meant that each two-man team had to cut down a number of trees, strip off the branches and bark, and cut the logs into metre lengths, stacking them in piles two metres long, one metre wide, and one metre high. It was invigorating work and, with my natural love of the outdoor life, it was a real taste of freedom.

The medical orderly was treated as a special case. According to the Geneva Convention, medical personnel were given special status and were not prohibited as we were from personal parole, in effect promising not to try to escape. This one seemed to have the best of everything. He worked unguarded on a nearby farm, dropped off in the morning and picked up at night by the guard. He had all his meals with the farmer and his wife, an older couple, and their daughter, who occupied a room in the back of the house. Two grown sons were fighting on the Russian Front.

The daughter was a beautiful, dark-haired girl of about seventeen or eighteen, apparently in love with the handsome young medical orderly, a serious crime for both parties in Nazi Germany.

To his credit, the orderly didn't talk much about their affair, but we knew that they showered together in the barn after their day's work, taking turns dumping buckets of water on each other's bodies. He wouldn't talk about what else they did in that barn, but our starved imaginations ran wild. We also knew that he regularly stayed overnight with her in her room.

He had an arrangement that, on certain nights after eating dinner with the family, the guard would arrive and escort him down the road. Once safely out of sight around the bend in the tree-lined road, the guard would say good night and the young orderly would quietly return to the rear of the farmhouse and tiptoe up the stairs to his lover's room.

The next morning the whole procedure would be reversed. He would quietly let himself out of the farmhouse, meet the guard past the bend in the road, and then march back to the farmhouse for breakfast with the farmer and his wife, making a big show of greeting the daughter, whose bed he had left only minutes before.

"What colossal stupidity," we thought, realizing the danger into which he put himself. Penalties were very severe for any prisoner of war caught fooling around with a woman of the "master race." When he had showed us her photograph, we saw she was indeed a beautiful young woman. The thought of sharing a shower with her was enough to make most of us decide that the risk of being shot was a small price to pay.

But the guard! What kind of bribery, or even blackmail, was involved to cause a German soldier to be party to such illegal activities? We could only imagine how many cartons of cigarettes and chocolate bars and tins of Canadian Red Cross coffee were exchanged for his participation. The penalties for this kind of behaviour in the German Army were very, very severe.

This time, the layout of the farmhouse had an important bearing on our escape plan. The main entrance to the prisoners' quarters was through a large yard on the left side of the house and adjacent to the road, which ran in an east-west direction.

The house was north of the road. The courtyard was surrounded on the north and east sides by the house itself, and on the south and west sides by a high board fence, about eight feet high, with three strands of razor-sharp barbed wire along the top. A gate in the fence, leading to the street, was left open during the day and locked each night. The guard slept in a second-floor room on the north side, overlooking the yard.

We entered our quarters through a door on the east side of the yard that led into a small anteroom, which served as a kitchen and storage area, with no windows or other access. On one side of this kitchen was a door leading to our living quarters, a large room about twenty by thirty feet, with one heavily barred window looking out into the yard.

The door from the kitchen to our quarters opened inward. It had a steel sheet bolted to its inside and two steel brackets attached on the outside. After lockup, a steel bar was dropped in place to ensure that there was no way to open the door from the inside. As an additional security measure, all boots and shoes were locked in the anteroom at night, as a guarantee that nobody would try to escape through the window.

The outside door of the anteroom, our main entrance into the yard, was locked by a key, kept in the guard's possession at all times. So the problem of escaping from this place boiled down to four points. First, we had to devise a way to open the steel-plated and barred door to our quarters. Second, we had to get through the locked door of the kitchen, which opened into the courtyard. Third, we had to get over an eight-foot-high fence topped with barbed wire without waking the guard, whose room overlooked this same courtyard and, lastly, we had to get some civilian clothes, which would be suitable for wearing on a German passenger train.

We already had quite a lot of German money, next to worthless without ration cards, but which could be used to purchase train tickets, and with our stash of food and cigarettes, we were in fairly good shape for our pending escape.

There was an Irishman in the group, Paddy O'Rourke, from Dublin. His talents and skills were many – and of the type that in wartime would warrant a medal for bravery and resourcefulness, and in peacetime probably land him in jail. He had worked at just about everything, including locksmithing, tailoring, farming, circus barking, sales, and a lot of things that were slightly beyond the pale, such as conning and smuggling. He was a colourful character, good-natured and friendly, and hated the Germans almost as much as he did the English. Mac, being a Welshman, and I a Canadian, automatically became his friends. I asked him why he had joined the British Army when he hated the English so much.

"I needed a job," he said with a shrug, "so I joined the army. How was I to know there was going to be a bloody war?"

Between the lines I somehow got the idea that he had left Ireland in a hurry, whether it was trouble with a woman or with the law I didn't ever find out. Without Paddy's unusual skills and talents, Mac and I would never have been able to escape from there.

Every day the routine went on. At eight o'clock sharp, after breakfasting on a slice of black bread and anything else we might have saved from supper, we were lined up in the yard and marched about three miles down the road and into the forest for our wood-cutting chores. I was paired up with Mac who, for all his talents, was no lumberjack. Between the two of us, we had to produce two cubic metres of cut and stripped logs.

Our tools were sharp axes and saws, and bark strippers, which looked somewhat like steel lawn edgers on the end of long handles. Once the tree was cut down, usually with a two-man saw, we attacked it with our axes and removed all the branches. Then we stripped off the bark with our razor-sharp strippers.

Finally, we sawed each log into metre lengths and stacked them in a specified area. When our assigned work was done, we could relax until the guard decided to take us home, usually about two or three in the afternoon. We then sat around outside in the courtyard until suppertime, when we were herded into our quarters.

There was a wood stove in the kitchen, where we were allowed to cook our own meals as a supplement to the German rations prepared by the cook, a title in name only, the job being an appointment to fill a position required by the German organization chart and having nothing to do with preparing meals. It merely meant that he could avoid going out to work and could clatter about the kitchen boiling up a few potatoes and some turnip soup occasionally. For any real food, such as our Red Cross fare, we cooked our own, partly because it tasted better and also because good food seemed to suffer from shrinkage when it passed through too many hands.

Early in the evening, about eight or nine o'clock, our guard would come in, call us to attention in front of our bunks, and count us. Then he would wish us "Gute Nacht," close the steel-sheathed door to our quarters, and drop the steel bar in place on the outside of the door.

What he didn't know was that every night, while someone engaged him in a most interesting conversation or offered him a drink of hot cocoa, a few more of the seventy-six bolts holding the steel plate to the inside of the door were being reversed. Now the nuts were on the inside, rather than on the outside. Then we had a key made for the front door. It was Paddy who suggested that we make a key, and it seemed like a good idea, except that we had to "borrow" it first from the guard.

Thus, one afternoon when we were returning from our woodcutting and the guard was at the rear of the group talking with our corporal, the prisoner at the front of the column yelled to the guard to throw up the key in order to open the door. He obliged and the key was caught by one of our group and passed to the man who was unlocking the door. The key was immediately returned to the guard.

Luckily, he didn't notice that the key was a bit damp, even though one of us had carefully dried it on a towel after pushing it into a piece of soft English soap to make a mould. Paddy O'Rourke now had a perfect impression of the front-door key, and soon had a duplicate filed from scrap metal. It worked perfectly.

Things were looking up. In a little more than a week we had most of the bolts reversed on the steel door, and had a key made for the front door. Paddy had tailored a well-fitting pair of grey flannel slacks for me out of an old German Army blanket, and an even better pair for Mac from a real wool Red Cross blanket. What talents that man had!

I had managed to obtain an extra battledress tunic, stripped off the army buttons and epaulets, and made a sort of windbreaker, a style favoured by many ex-soldiers and foreigners. To get away from the British Army khaki, we boiled it up with a few indelible pencils; it came out a lovely purply brown. Not very stylish, but it no longer looked like a British uniform jacket.

On another afternoon, the guard was diverted again while one of our more athletic members shinnied up a pole from the courtyard to an attic window, coming out a few seconds later with a young man's tweed jacket and a hat, stored away in the attic possibly by a member of the family now away in the army. About a size six, it fitted Mac's head perfectly, and looked quite natty. The hat was one of those Tyrolean alpine things with a feather, and looked so stupid that we all burst out laughing. He decided to take it along anyway, but removed the feather on the grounds that no self-respecting Welshman would be seen dead with a feather in his hat.

A few days later, in early May, we were working in a fairly remote section of the forest, about four miles from our camp, when an incident occurred that almost upset all our plans. Archie, a real cockney from the East End of London, seemed to me to be unusually careful in the way in which he was felling one of his trees. It was a large one. He stood back and looked at it from every possible angle, then took a few paces to one side and looked at it again before he and his partner made their first cut.

As they sawed away with the two-man saw on the tree, about thirty feet high and a good eight inches in diameter at the bottom, I thought I saw a slight grin on his face.

"Timber!" he hollered as he jumped away, and the tall tree came crashing down – not too unusual an operation where trees came crashing down all day. Then a loud scream from the guard as he spied his bicycle lying crumpled under the trunk of the tree. He started yelling epithets, and his face got redder as his voice got louder, until he had worked himself into a rage. Then he pulled out his pistol, a big Luger, and started waving it under Archie's nose.

This was serious. It looked as if Archie was about to be shot. As the guard's shouting and screaming rose to an even higher pitch, and his waving pistol looked more and more as if it was going to go off in the poor guy's face, we realized that this was a very unfunny joke that could result in Archie's death.

The guard looked up and stopped suddenly. There were about a dozen of us standing menacingly in a circle around him, each holding a razor-sharp bark stripper, each blade about three inches from his throat. He must have quickly realized that he would not be able to get off more than one shot before his throat was sliced into hamburger. He looked silently around the ominous circle, put his Luger back in its holster, and slowly walked away.

The incident was over – for the moment, anyway. Looking back at that magnificent bluff, I realized that we were probably as frightened as he, and wondered, in retrospect, if any of us actually would have had the guts to slice his throat – and what might have happened to us all if we had!

Fortunately for Mac and me, the guard for whatever reason didn't report the incident, being content, I suppose, to bask in the glory of being the John Wayne–type sheriff who single-handedly held off the bad guys.

Our plans were again back on track. The corporal held a meeting and suggested very seriously that further acts of sabotage might put a permanent crimp in our carefully laid escape plans. Archie, the culprit in all this commotion, was suitably penitent and promised to be good, at least until Mac and I had escaped.

The next week or two was occupied with the annual reforestation project. In spite of Adolf Hitler, and the radical changes that had taken place in Germany during the war, the Germans had always been very conservation conscious. We learned that all the trees cut daily had been planted, and that the law required that each tree cut down must be replaced. This had been a tradition in Germany for hundreds of years, and a mere war was not going to change things.

So now we would march out to areas that had been stripped of trees by woodcutters such as us, and accompanied by a truck-load of young trees, would start planting the future forests of the Third Reich. God knows what those forests must look like now, for we were not too careful and often deliberately sabotaged the young trees – nothing to be proud about in our later, and more mature, years.

14

DESTINATION STETTIN

The big night approached. We were ready. Our plan was well worked out. There would be a party the night we escaped, to cover the racket we'd make when we removed the steel door. Covered by loud music and other sounds of revelry, we would remove the large steel plate on the inside of the door. This would expose the nuts attached to the two bolts holding the two angle irons to the outside of the door, which in turn held the steel bar that secured the door.

When the bar and brackets fell, it would make an awful clatter, so we devised a scheme to make an even bigger clatter at the time in order to cover up the noise. There was a big risk to this, but there didn't seem to be any alternative.

Once the inner door was open, we would be able to get our boots from the anteroom-kitchen. Meanwhile, Paddy O'Rourke, our jack-of-all-trades, had volunteered to open the outside door that led into the courtyard. From there, we thought, it would be a relatively simple matter to scale the eight-foot-high fence topped with barbed wire and walk thirteen miles east to the railroad station at Oppeln.

From Oppeln, we would take the regular workers' train (we had acquired a recent timetable) and ride to Breslau, a good-sized city, about fifty miles farther east. There, we would buy a ticket to Frankfurt an der Oder, a town near Berlin, and would then travel to Stettin, a Baltic seaport, reportedly teeming with neutral Swedish merchant ships.

The Escape Committee had suggested that the best place to contact Swedish sailors or ships' officers was in the foreigners' brothels, or *Ausländerbordell*. Apparently, the Germans were very class-conscious about their brothels, restricting the best ones for their officers and troops and allowing the rest to be used by foreigners. Never having been in a brothel of any kind, I wasn't sure what to expect, but it sounded interesting.

Of course, if I had spent a little more time at my studies in school, I would have known that, from the point of view of escaping, Denmark might have been a much better bet. The Danes hated the Germans and more or less openly defied them.

Later I heard stories of prisoners who had escaped to Denmark and were wined and dined for weeks in various homes before being rowed over to Sweden in small boats. According to one report, an escaped prisoner was scared out of his wits by being taken from house to house in a village and displayed like a prize duck, and yet, miraculously, the Germans never discovered that he was in the village.

Our plan seemed like a good one, and we'd been told that the British government paid large sums of money to sailors or officers who helped prisoners escape to Sweden, as much as ten thousand pounds – in those days a fortune.

It was now about the middle of May 1944, and we had agreed that the following Wednesday night was to be the big night.

After work on that Wednesday afternoon, Mac and I gathered all our equipment and stowed it under our bunks. The other members of the working party kept the guard occupied and amused out in the courtyard. With all the tension in the air, it was a wonder that the guard didn't sense something.

Finally it was lockup time. We stood at the end of our bunks and were counted. Then the big door slammed shut, and we heard the steel bar dropping in place, then the sound of the key turning in the lock on the outside of the kitchen door leading to the courtyard. The guard left by the courtyard gate and barred it from the outside, walking around the front of the house and into the main entrance on the east side to visit with the family.

This was really it! I was terrified that something was going to go wrong. Mac and I put on our civilian clothes and checked the food and equipment in our packs. Mac had a small valise, which had been stolen by one of the group, and I had a small packsack that had been picked out of the rubbish by Paddy and meticulously repaired so that it looked almost new. We counted our money, a few hundred Reichsmark, and divided it between us. The tension was mounting. Somebody handed me a mug of coffee. I had to hold it with both hands so nobody would see my hand shaking.

Meanwhile, the corporal and some of the others were busy removing the nuts from the seventy-six door bolts, which held the steel sheet onto the inside of the door and which had been laboriously reversed over the past few weeks.

Finally, all of the nuts were off, and two of the men gently lifted off the large piece of steel, carefully setting it down against the wall. If the guard came in now, it would be game over. Now that our decision was irreversible, I felt almost calm.

Near the window, one of the group was playing a guitar, which he'd traded for God knows how many tins of coffee and bars of chocolate. Another was making a lot of noise with a harmonica. Two large nuts were now exposed on the inside of the wooden door. Paddy produced a spanner and started to take them off. Then he told us to make a lot of noise to cover the sound of the angle irons and the steel bar dropping when he took off the two nuts and pushed the bolts out through the door.

The guitar and harmonica music grew louder and faster, and someone started drumming on a tin pot. The rest of us started singing. Paddy pushed the bolts through and there was a horrific clang, even louder than all the noise we were making, as the steel bar and the two brackets fell to the kitchen floor simultaneously. Then the guard's voice – screaming and yelling and telling us that if we didn't shut up, he'd come down and shoot someone. Our corporal yelled back that we would be good and promised to quiet down, which seemed to placate the guard.

Now I was becoming a little more than nervous. If the guard rushed in and found the steel door in pieces and two prisoners in civilian clothes, he might have one of his fits and start waving his gun around again, this time shooting someone.

We cautiously opened the big door. It opened easily, without a creak, as we'd carefully oiled its hinges more than once. Mac and I crept into the anteroom in our stocking feet and retrieved our boots, putting them on silently. It was getting late, and we knew by now that the guard had turned in for the night. We doused the lights, kept the noise down, and waited for midnight. In the stillness we could hear our guard's snoring. It was a comforting sound. As long as we could hear his snoring, we were okay.

Paddy tried his key on the outside door but it didn't open. Christ! What were we going to do if we couldn't get that door open, with the inside door torn apart and no way of putting it back together?

So we lay on our bunks, fully dressed in our civilian clothes and with our boots on, trying to stay calm, listening to the guard's snoring and to Paddy's muffled curses as he fiddled with the homemade key, with no success.

Two hours went by. It was now about two o'clock in the morning. Paddy by the light of a candle was reshaping the key with a file. Finally, a click and a muffled sigh of relief. Paddy came back to tell us that the outside door was open. The guard had stopped snoring. Maybe he had just rolled over. Then the snoring started again. We decided to get out of there while the getting was good. The other thirteen Kriegies each shook our hands and wished us luck.

We whispered our apologies for causing them so much trouble, then crept out the kitchen door into the courtyard.

Now we could definitely hear the guard's snoring. The moon seemed so bright that it was almost like sunlight, or did it just seem that way because we were so scared and nervous?

We crept over to the fence to a point near the gate where we had previously decided to go over; there were bushes on the other side that would afford cover. We threw our bags over and heard them land. Mac was shorter than me, so I gave him a boost up to the fence. He pulled himself up, then seemed to be tangled in the three strands of barbed wire at the top.

"Jump!" I hissed, frightened that he would stand there all night and attract attention from someone.

He jumped with an awful clatter. It seemed to me that he had taken half the fence with him. I didn't wait to listen for snoring, or anything else. I jumped with one gargantuan leap, mainly powered by fear, chinned myself in an instant, got a toehold on the top of the fence and a handhold on one of the uprights holding the barbed wire, and vaulted over, landing in some bushes alongside of Mac.

We sat there for a minute under the bushes, hardly daring to breathe, waiting for the volley of shots that our noise would likely draw. No sound. Absolute quiet. Deadly quiet. No snoring. I imagined that crazy guard, even now, stalking us with his rifle and Luger. I grabbed Mac's head, put my mouth next to his ear, and whispered, "Let's get the hell out of here!" He nodded.

We grabbed our bags, he with his small suitcase and I with my pack, and started the long walk down the road to Oppeln. At four miles an hour, we estimated that we'd arrive there in about three hours, that is, about five o'clock in the morning. We knew that there was a train leaving for Breslau at about five-thirty. We walked faster.

As our house was on the eastern edge of Eikhammer, we were soon out in the country, briskly walking eastward on the now-deserted road. I felt a sense of elation. This time we were going to succeed, and we'd be back in England in about five days!

Some cloud cover had come up, and the night became darker, to our advantage. We walked steadily for two hours without seeing a soul. Then, at about four o'clock in the morning, a workman on a bicycle came toward us. As he passed with hardly a glance, I said, "Ile 'eetlah!" and gave him my best Nazi salute. He merely grunted. Later, when we discussed the incident, we concluded that he was probably another foreign worker who didn't like Nazis any more than we did.

As the eastern sky lightened ahead of us, more people passed us on the road in both directions, and we realized that in this part of the country a lot of people had to get up at four in the morning or earlier to get to work on time. Nobody seemed to notice us, even though I felt as if I had "escaped prisoner" written all over me. By the time we began to approach the railroad station at Oppeln, however, I was feeling more confident.

We had both been through the station at Oppeln more than once, as it wasn't too far from Lamsdorf. How strange to be clumping into a railroad station without a guard in tow. There were several people sitting about in the waiting room, and the ticket booth appeared to be open for business. Mac felt that he could speak German better than I, so we agreed that he would buy the tickets. I sat on a seat near the exit, just in case he got into trouble, and waited.

Mac walked up to the ticket seller and said in his most confident voice, "Zweimal Breslau, bitte" (Two for Breslau, please), and plunked down a couple of the larger bills.

The ticket seller, hardly glancing at Mac, pushed one of the bills back at him and handed him two tickets with some change, which Mac pocketed with barely a look. Mac returned to sit beside me on the bench, his face expressionless, although I detected a trace of a grin and a sparkle in his eyes. I was glowing too.

According to the train schedule high up on the far wall, the next train for Breslau was due at five-forty, and it was now about five-fifteen. The later train didn't leave until eight o'clock, late enough to get us caught once the hue and cry started. We were very lucky to make the early train. Mac broke a cigarette in half, and we shared a smoke. We had been told not to flash full-sized cigarettes around in public because few people other than the military could get cigarettes. Smoking butts was more usual, especially for a foreign "volunteer" labourer.

After about an hour's wait, the train pulled into the platform, and we walked through the gate as casually as possible, showing our tickets to the attendant. He too hardly glanced at us, interested only in the tickets. We climbed into a compartment that seated eight and sat down opposite one another.

We had agreed not to talk and to pretend that we were very tired if anyone looked too friendly toward us. We'd also been told not to be too polite on German trains – "Rather than give your seat to an old lady, beat her to it, even if you have to trip her." So even though some women were standing on the crowded train, we sat sullenly in our seats and acted as if we hadn't had any proper sleep for a week and were too exhausted to move.

When the train pulled out of the station and began to gather speed, I felt a sense of elation that I had never felt before. I looked at Mac occasionally, and I could see the shadow of a smile on his otherwise expressionless face. He clearly felt the same way.

The journey to Breslau passed without incident. As we travelled through the peaceful and now-familiar farmland, I thought of our Arbeitskommando E193 at Eikhammer. No doubt by now all hell had broken loose back there.

Later we learned that the Germans had become very concerned about this particular escape, assuming that it was an outside job, done with the help of the Polish underground or some other subversive organization. Our friends at Eikhammer had feigned innocence, pretending that they had awakened in the morning to find the door open and the two of us gone. The Germans had grilled them incessantly but got nothing more out of them. Besides, it obviously was an outside job because the kitchen door lock had been picked with some kind of lock-picking instrument, and the only way the steel door-plate bolts could have been removed was from the outside, of course!

All of the prisoners' privileges had been cut off, and the guard was sent to the Russian Front. I felt a little sorry for him; he wasn't such a bad guy, even if not too bright. We had certainly taken advantage of his good-natured stupidity.

I was lost in reverie, feeling sorry for the poor dumb guard – Heinrich or Rudolph, I think his name was – when Mac nudged my foot. The train was slowing down a little, passing through the outskirts of a fairly large city. More tracks appeared on either side of us, the train whistle tooted, and we continued to slow down. This must be Breslau!

I looked across at Mac and could see a slight strain in his eyes. He was either nervous or had to go to the bathroom. I was suffering from both afflictions. This was our first time in a big German city in civilian clothes. He looked quite natty, in a scruffy sort of way, in his tweed jacket cut a little too short around the bum, and his grey slacks, which had been deliberately tailored long to cover his British Army boots; shoes were the only civilian item that we had been unable to procure. His scruffy shirt and tie went well with his outfit. Even his Tyrolean hat without the feather didn't seem quite so strange anymore. A lot of the men around us were wearing clothes that looked even worse than ours. And boots were not that unusual in a level of society in which any kind of clothing and footwear was quite acceptable.

My outfit was far more outrageous than his – my light grey German Army blanket slacks tailored by Paddy O'Rourke (pleats in the front and a nice crease), my purple jacket, black boots, and blue air force shirt, decorated with a green tie – and yet nobody looked at me curiously. I could see why. Just about everyone was wearing odd or mismatched clothing. Style was not the criterion. I had no hat but didn't mind, even though my thick hair was badly in need of a cut. My simple pack and Mac's bag, little more than an oversized briefcase, gave us a look of respectability, even legitimacy.

As the train ground to a stop with puffs and wheezes of steam and steel grinding on steel, I saw the sign on the outside wall of the large station building. Breslau.

Our eyes met. Doors were flung open, whistles blew, and everyone stood up. We filed off the train wordlessly, trying to keep up the appearance of two exhausted workers. Sticking close together, we watched carefully which way the crowds were going and realized that one gate was for civilians and one was for soldiers. We were heading for the soldiers' exit!

We quickly switched course to the other exit, where a lone station guard was collecting tickets. He didn't look up as we handed him our one-way tickets from Oppeln to Breslau and walked on into the main waiting room. A few knots of people stood here and there awaiting the arrivals. Most of the train passengers, however, seemed to be workers, who headed straight for the doors to the street. Mac and I followed them. We'd been briefed that we were to go to the main train station in Breslau for the train to Frankfurt an der Oder. We were not supposed to have any difficulty finding the main railroad station, the *Hauptbahnhof,* because it was supposed to be opposite a square that contained a statue of a man on a horse.

So we wandered the streets of Breslau for an hour or two looking for a square with a statue of a man on a horse. Just about every square in Breslau had a statue of a man on a horse! Usually with some kind of military uniform, and waving a big sword. Finally, fearing that we might attract attention if we wandered about much more, Mac threw caution to the wind and asked a small schoolboy, in his fractured German, "Wo ist der Hauptbahnhof?" and waved his hands as he supposed foreign workers did.

Experts had told us, "Don't attract the attention of children. Because they are smart and curious, and they notice things that adults never see."

I was quaking in my boots, hoping that the kid wouldn't notice my RAF-issue footwear and shirt and go running to his local Nazi Youth leader to turn us in. We didn't understand much of the flood of German that the kid threw at us, but we got the general idea. The main railroad station was on the main street that we were on, about two kilometres away, on the right-hand side. We started walking quickly, and, soon, there was the *Hauptbahnhof*. It was the station where we had first arrived.

"What the hell!" said Mac. "Those silly bastards gave us the wrong information. Let's go back in and find out when the train leaves for Frankfurt."

It was probably a good thing that we'd left the train station for a while; at least we hadn't attracted any attention by hanging about. Now we looked like a couple of labourers from Breslau going to work.

We studied the large sign in the huge hall and saw that *Bahnsteige* indicated numbered tracks, and *Züge* were trains, also numbered and identified by destination. A *Schnellzug* was obviously a fast train or express. We'd been told to avoid them like the plague because they were subject to all kinds of checks by the police, Gestapo, and ss. It was the slow commuter trains for us.

We smoked another half cigarette sitting on an unoccupied bench in a corner of the waiting room and planned our strategy. We would buy two one-way tickets to Frankfurt an der Oder, get out at Frankfurt, leave the station until shortly before the next train to Stettin was due, then return and buy a ticket to Stettin. Sitting around train stations for any length of time was a dangerous game.

We found the station toilets and finally managed to relieve our aching bladders. There was a train leaving on Track 9 at eleven-fifteen and it was now about ten-fifteen. Mac, conscious of his recent success in ticket purchasing, volunteered to buy the tickets.

I watched from a safe distance as Mac approached the ticket seller, a woman of indeterminate age who looked at him indifferently as he sputtered in his Welsh-accented German, "Zweimal Frankfurt, bitte" (Two for Frankfurt, please). She said something to him, he pushed some money through the wicket, and she started yelling at him in such a fast stream of German that even a native would have had a hard time understanding.

I thought, here we go! She knows we're escaped prisoners of war. I was ready to make a dash for the door when Mac reached in his pocket and pulled out some more money and stuffed it hastily through the hole in the wicket. He had no idea what she was yelling about but figured that it must be money, and so pushed more at her to try to shut her up.

When he came back to our bench, holding the tickets and change in his hands, he looked a bit shaken. We had another half cigarette and decided to go through the entrance gate and wait for our train on the platform. Again the station guard waved us through after glancing at our tickets.

We found Track 9 without any trouble, then realized our mistake. Our train was nowhere in sight, we were almost an hour early, and the platform was crammed with German soldiers in full battle gear, obviously going somewhere, and a troop train was clearly starting to load from our platform.

We certainly didn't want to accompany these troops to the Russian Front, where they were probably heading, but we couldn't go back and pass by the guard at the gate again without attracting attention. Some of the soldiers were giving us curious, but not unfriendly, looks, possibly wondering what a couple of bums like us were doing on the same platform with Hitler's finest. We weren't going to give them the chance to find out. We moved back cautiously to a more remote corner of the platform and sat down on a bench near the back wall, hoping that no one would come over and ask us what we were doing there. We broke another cigarette and lit up – mainly, I think, to cover our nervousness. I don't know about Mac, but my idea of a nice successful escape hadn't included being mixed in with five hundred German soldiers, armed to the teeth, on their way to fight the Russians.

Fortunately, nobody paid any attention to us. We sat in that corner for about forty-five minutes, until the troop train completed loading and pulled out of the station. When another train arrived and started filling with passengers, we sighed with relief. It was about ten minutes earlier than scheduled.

"This must be our train," said Mac, grabbing his bag. I agreed, happy to be finally getting out of the place. As we walked along the platform beside the train, trying to decide whether it was the right train, whistles blew, steam hissed, wheels started turning, and the train began to move.

"Is this the train for Frankfurt?" Mac asked in his best German to a girl sitting in one of the compartments by an open window as we trotted alongside the moving train. She nodded, and we jumped into the first compartment in the next car, pulling our baggage in behind us. It was empty, with space for about twelve, six on each side.

The train whistled and squealed as it gathered speed and moved northward out of Breslau. Looking around, we realized that we were in an older carriage that had no connection between compartments except through the door to the platform. This meant that the only time you could change compartments or enter another compartment was when the train stopped at a station. We were elated. It was the first day of our escape, we were on our second train on our way to Frankfurt an der Oder, and we had the compartment all to ourselves. We could speak English, smoke Canadian cigarettes, eat some food, and generally relax, at least until the train pulled into a station.

"I think we've got it made!" I said to Mac, munching on a biscuit and cheese that he had just handed me. He agreed.

We talked and laughed, and had a good lunch, topped off with a smoke, and some bottled water. The beautiful countryside drifted by, the farms and cottages looking like dollhouses as we came into the more populated part of Germany. The train didn't stop at all, which confused us because it was supposed to be a slow train. We even loudly sang a few ribald songs in English for no other reason than that we could. We got rid of the identifiable debris of our lunch and stretched out on facing seats of our large and "private" compartment.

"This is the life," Mac sighed. "Nobody'll believe us when we tell them that we had a private compartment all to ourselves on a train going from Breslau to Frankfurt in May 1944!"

He was right. Nothing could have surprised me more than this luxurious accommodation in the middle of wartime Germany, especially when compared with the lumber car I'd shared with John Donaldson the year before. Things were going so well that I felt positive we would be successful this time. If the next train ride was to be as easy as this, then we were practically in Sweden. Of course, there was the matter of the foreigners' brothels – the *Ausländerbordell* – to figure out. Mac also had never been inside such an exotic establishment, but nothing was going to daunt our enthusiasm this beautiful day.

The sun was shining; the sky was blue with a few puffy white cumulous clouds. We opened the compartment window and the country aroma of fresh grass drifting in, mixed with all the other summer smells, gave this ride an almost dreamlike quality. We just could not believe our luck.

For the next few hours we enjoyed it to the full, breathing in the freedom, the fresh air, swapping stories and jokes, nibbling on

English biscuits, smoking Canadian cigarettes, speaking English openly, putting our feet up and watching the villages and hamlets flash by. This train was going so fast that we were beginning to wonder whether we were on the right train. No matter. As long as it didn't stop, nobody could talk to us, and that was good. Already in a reclining position on the comfortably padded bench seats, I found myself becoming a little sleepy, little wonder since neither of us had slept at all the previous night.

Suddenly I woke up. It was dark, the train had stopped, and a female train official was shaking Mac and yelling at him in words which meant, from the sound of them, that we were at the end of the line and we had to get off. I looked around. We were in a station at a darkened platform. But where?

"Ja, ja!" we both repeated several times to placate the woman and, picking up our baggage, clambered down onto the platform. We could see some lights under the covered platform down toward the head of the train. That must be where the exit is, and the ticket collector. There was no way out of the station except through that exit or down the tracks in the opposite direction to the ticket office. Obviously, we had to turn in our tickets to the guard at the exit and proceed into the main waiting room, where we would likely find the train schedule for the next leg of our trip.

"There's the exit gate!" whispered Mac as we walked toward the illuminated part of the platform. And so it was, with the now-familiar uniformed train guard standing at the gate to take our tickets.

Mac was walking slightly ahead of me and proffered his ticket first. The man looked at it, then at Mac, and began a tirade of German, waving the ticket around and pointing to a large sign on the station that said "Küstrin."

"Good God!" I thought. "We got on the wrong train." This was Küstrin, not Frankfurt, and our tickets were for Frankfurt. I could see Mac looking at me, thinking the same thing. But his Welsh gift of the gab took over, and he said to the guard in his best broken German, "Wir haben geschlafen!" – or words to that effect – meaning, "We were sleeping."

This invoked yet another tirade from the irate trainman, only parts of which we could understand, until we saw him pointing to the ticket agent who was now peering in our direction. Of the words flying about, I recognized that the German word for money – *Geld* – came most frequently, and that *Dummkopf,* the German word for idiot, were a close second. He pushed the two tickets into Mac's hand and pushed him in the direction of the ticket seller, screaming all the while about *Geld.* The message was clear. Give the bastards some more money and they might let us get out of there.

"Danke! Danke schön!" we muttered, heads down, as we shuffled toward the ticket seller, trying to act as much like confused peasants as we could. It was clear that as long as they got their money for the difference in the ticket price, they would be content.

Mac shoved the two tickets through the ticket seller's window, where the agent checked them, looked in his book, and muttered a number, "Fünfundfünfzig oder fünfundvierzig" – or something. It didn't matter. Mac shoved some more money at him, he gave a couple of the bills back, along with some of the worthless metal change, and we were on our way, walking as quickly as we could without attracting attention toward the main station exit.

Suddenly we stopped. What was it? There was something... yes! In our hurry to get out of the station, we had forgotten to find out when the next train was leaving for Stettin. Or if there *was* a train for Stettin. We had planned for Frankfurt, now we were in Küstrin! And all we knew about Küstrin was that it was somewhere in the same area as Frankfurt. We studied the large letters and numbers high up on the wall, near the roof of the building. It must be quite a chore to change those numbers, I thought with fanciful illogic, considering our predicament.

I found it. Stettin, large as life up on the board. The next train was leaving at four-thirty the next morning on Track 2. Now we could get out of there. It was about ten-thirty at night, and we had to get out of there until early the next morning. A few whispers back and forth and it was settled. We would leave the station as soon as possible and head out of town, find a place to hide, then return to the station at about four in the morning for our final trip to Stettin, which by our calculations should take about four hours, depending on where Küstrin actually was.

My silk map was of such a small scale that only major features were shown, the width of my thumb the equivalent to a hundred miles or more. Our trip from Breslau to Küstrin had taken about eight hours, when we had only figured on four or five. Whatever the length of the ride to Stettin, if we were starting at four-thirty in the morning, we would certainly reach Stettin by midday.

We walked out through the main entrance of the Frankfurt an der Oder train station with the departing passengers and were out on the street, and in the dark. German cities and towns at this stage of the war were completely blacked out. For a moment I could see nothing but the outline of dark buildings and a few stars in the sky. Then I began to notice that there were a lot of people around, all hurrying through the darkness on some errand or other, and all potential enemies. At any moment a policeman might shine his light in our faces and ask us what our business was.

"Which way?" whispered Mac, looking up and down the street and seeing, as I did, nothing but dark, shapeless human forms seemingly moving in all directions.

"How about north?" I suggested, having no idea where we were. I could see by the North Star that we were already heading more or less north, and couldn't see any reason for turning around and perhaps drawing attention to ourselves. He nodded.

So we walked north along the main street of Küstrin for what seemed like hours, until the pedestrian traffic had thinned out to practically nothing and it was clear that we had passed the built-up area of the city and were entering farming country.

The moon was climbing in the sky and I could see that it was going to be another clear, cool night. To our right we could make out the outline of haystacks in the fields, quite a few, in fact.

"Let's burrow into one of those haystacks," Mac suggested, "and try to keep warm until morning."

I remembered the problem with the hay car on the freight train with Donaldson, and how the hay had been so hard that it was almost impossible to burrow into, but I couldn't think of a better alternative.

In the moonlight we climbed over a rail fence and headed for a haystack a good distance from the road. I found a soft spot on the side farthest from the road, and we started digging. The hay wasn't as hard as I remembered from the freight cars, but it wasn't soft either. After about an hour's work with a couple of sharp sticks, we had dug a sort of cave big enough for both of us. We lay feet first beside each other, exhausted, puffing and sweating from our exertion. There were no houses nearby, so we felt fairly safe. We'd both had a long nap on the train, so were not particularly sleepy. Despite the fact that the two of us were lying so close in this narrow hole in the side of the haystack, we began to feel cold, even with our greatcoats wrapped tightly around us.

"What time is it?" Mac whispered, although there wasn't a human being around for miles.

"About quarter to one," I whispered back, caught up by the mysterious quality of our surroundings. A ground mist was beginning to form in the hollows, and the other haystacks took on a ghostly air. A shadow seemed to move across a stack on the other side of the moonlit field. The other stacks nearby were eerily illuminated by the moon drifting in and out of the clouds. A darker shadow moved across the next stack. Was it an animal, or human? Or just my imagination? Another wispy cloud obscured the moon, and mysterious shapes moved across the field. Was that a man standing over there, or just an old stump?

"Pull your head in!" hissed Mac. "Somebody might see you!" He was right, of course. No use taking chances, even though there wasn't a soul about. Or was there?

Somebody was walking outside! Definitely, somebody or something was coming closer! The police? Or the army? My heart was doing a boom-diddy-boom-diddy-boom-boom-boom routine, and Mac was lying absolutely still. He'd heard it too. Something rustled at the entrance to our cave. I almost fainted with fright. Then there was a snort and a trampling of hooves.

A cow. Or a horse. We never did get a good look at it, but something had come over to investigate the strange sounds coming out of the haystack and had been spooked by us. We looked at each other and laughed with relief. If it had been a dog, we could have been in serious trouble.

After that, we didn't sleep much, but rested in our hole in a sort of fitful doze. It seemed to take forever for the time to roll around to three-thirty, when we had decided to start back into town. It had taken about thirty to forty-five minutes to make it from the train station to our haystack. Much later, I peered at my Rolex, thinking it must have stopped; it was about three-twenty and the sky was starting to show a little light in the east. We crawled out of our hole and brushed off our clothes as best we could. Then, after taking a careful look up and down the road, we slipped back over the fence and across the road.

15

END OF THE LINE

The road back into town was empty. Not a soul appeared until we entered the outskirts of town, where we met a workman, possibly a farmhand, walking in the opposite direction. As he paid no attention to us, we ignored him too. Soon there were a few people walking along the road in the same direction that we were heading. By now it was almost four o'clock, and we could see the outline of the train station in the grey light.

Just as the clock struck four we turned into the station. It looked deserted. Then we noticed that the ticket office, where Mac had paid for last night's tickets, was open, although there was a woman at the wicket now. Fortunately for us, the shift must have changed some time after we'd left last night.

"I'll get the tickets!" Mac whispered as we hesitated just inside the entrance.

"Okay," I agreed, thankful that he was taking on this dangerous chore. I sat down on a bench not far from the exit as Mac approached the ticket agent's wicket. Then I realized that there was another person in the station, watching us closely. It was a German military policeman.

I tried to look and act as innocent as possible as I watched Mac go through his routine of buying two tickets for Stettin.

"Zweimal Stettin, bitte" (Two for Stettin, please), he said in a sort of weak falsetto conspiratorial tone. Or maybe I just imagined it was a conspiratorial tone. Anyway, it seemed awfully loud to me in my very nervous state. I was sure the military policeman was watching the exchange even more intently.

The ticket agent was a middle-aged woman in a dark blue railway uniform, with a sour face. "Bitte!" she said so loudly I almost fell off the bench.

"Jeesus Keerist!" I thought. "They'll wake up the whole town." The woman let out a stream of rapid-fire German, which I was sure Mac couldn't understand, and I certainly couldn't. Everybody in the station was looking at them – that is, me and the military policeman were. In my state of panic, that seemed to constitute a big crowd.

Mac looked at the ticket seller, then pushed some more money through the wicket and virtually yelled in a voice I thought could be heard all the way to Berlin, "Zweimal Stettin, bitte!"

There was no mistaking what he had said. Even the pigeons in the roof came fluttering out to see what all the commotion was. I thought I was going to be sick. He didn't have to scream at her, the silly bastard. Now we were going to be caught! Or maybe even shot by that big square-headed German with the coal scuttle helmet and the oversize dog tag around his neck.

Then it was over. The noise stopped, and she pushed a couple of tickets through the wicket. Mac scooped them up and walked toward me, not even looking nervous. He told me later that he had been shaking. He handed me a ticket and whispered that we should get through the gate before the big kraut decided to investigate us. I agreed, and we approached the gate in the most confident manner we could muster. The military policeman blocked our path. He was a big man, about six foot two.

"Eine Minute!" he said in a loud voice, "Habt ihr zwei eure Ausweise?" (Have you two got passports?) – or words to that effect.

Mac reached into the inside pocket of his tweed jacket and

pulled out the carefully made forgery. He handed it to the soldier, who looked at it carefully, studying the photograph, then Mac's face. He handed it back and waved him on. Now it was my turn.

I handed him my worker's passport, which said that my name was Paul Swaboda and that I was a Czech electrician, born in Prague in 1923, and that I was to report to the *Arbeitsbüro* (labour office) in Stettin for further orders. I noticed that my hand wasn't shaking and hoped my face appeared as calm and assured as it did in the photograph.

He studied the picture and the passport, then stared into my face. "Tscheche (Czech), ja?"

"Ja," I said. What a linguist I was becoming. He waved me on, and as I passed him he said something that sounded like, "Ich dachte ihr wart Russkis! (I thought you were Russians!) Ho, ho, ho!"

"Ha, ha," I muttered half-heartedly once out of earshot, and continued with Mac along the dimly lit corridor leading to the platforms.

"No wonder he thought we were bloody Russians," Mac whispered to me. "Take a look at yourself! And look at me! We look like a couple of tramps right out of some hobo jungle." He was right. Hay was sticking out from our jackets, boots, and just about every other article of clothing we wore.

We found the appropriate platform and settled down on a bench in a dark corner. While we waited for our train we cleaned up as best we could, brushing off most of the hay. It had been a smart move to get out of town overnight; hanging about in the train station from ten-thirty at night to four-thirty in the morning would have been extremely dangerous.

A few minutes later, a train backed alongside the platform and a large number of mostly shabbily dressed people began to appear. We waited until a few of them started to board the train, then shuffled up to an empty compartment and climbed in. This was no full-width compartment like the one we had luxuriated in the day before. A corridor down the far side connected all the compartments, and no doubt a conductor or some other train official would be around to check our tickets. Each compartment seemed to be built to accommodate about eight people, four on each side. There were two doors, one leading to the corridor, the other leading to the platform.

Mac and I threw our bags up on the racks and chose window seats opposite each other. I was facing forward, and he was facing the rear of the train.

Departure time was rapidly approaching, and the train was filling with working people. Mac and I pretended to be asleep. In our compartment there was standing room only. Suddenly, a woman holding a big bag began to shout at me and point to the shelf above my head. I had no idea what she was talking about but remembered my advice from the Escape Committee: Don't be too polite. Don't give your seat up. Push and shove like everyone else...

Without saying anything, I took my bag down from the rack and put it under the seat. I hoisted hers up on the rack, which seemed to shut her up, thank God. Then I sat down again, leaving her standing, and ignored her. A couple of other people crowded into the compartment, until it felt like a Toronto streetcar at rush hour. A buxom blonde girl about eighteen years old stood between Mac and me, her legs straddled over ours.

The train whistled a couple of times with a high-pitched *toot*, a sound akin to British trains. In fact, the train was very much like British trains – maybe even made in Britain. As the morning countryside started to accelerate past the window, we could see the misty fields rush by, and even glimpsed a few inviting haystacks. Mac jerked his thumb toward them and kicked me. We grinned. The last leg of our trip. Next was the port of Stettin, and a Swedish ship whisking us across the Baltic Sea to the safety of neutral Sweden.

The steady *clickety-clack* of the steel wheels and the high-pitched whistle of the train at crossings were almost soporific, and I was starting to feel sleepy, despite my high state of excitement, when I felt pressure on my foot. It was Mac's shoe touching mine, but the pressure was intermittent, like – yes, that's it, like Morse code. (Even pilots were required to read six words a minute in those days.) He was trying to send me a message! I opened my eyes and looked at him. There was a sly twinkle in his eyes and the shadow of a dirty grin on his face as he tapped out his message. The girl straddling our legs was oblivious of us, and hung onto one of the compartment's straps in a sort of stolid stupor. Under her thread-bare coat and thin dress I could see that she had a beautiful fig-ure. Her legs were like a movie star's, even though she was wearing high boots, not exactly fashionable at that time but which some-how added to her sexiness. I was sneaking looks at her through half-closed eyes when I started to decode the Morse code coming through on my boot.

"Did you ever see such a gorgeous ass?" Mac tapped out.

"No!" *(dah-dit, dah-dah-dah)* I replied with my toe, hardly daring to look at her for fear she could read my thoughts.

"And those tits!" he tapped out. "They are lovely!"

I kicked his foot away. I didn't want to hear any more; because "those tits" were hanging very close to me, so close I could almost touch them. I didn't dare look at her face for fear she'd read my mind. Mac had that puckish, sly look in his eyes that he always got when he had some wild notion. I wanted to give him a good kick for giving me such ideas.

The hours went by and the relentless *clickety-clack* of the wheels almost lulled us to sleep. Now the countryside was more roll-ing, the sun was higher. It must have been six-thirty or seven in the morning. I didn't dare look at my watch – poor foreign work-ers weren't supposed to have Rolex watches. Our sex-queen didn't look quite so sexy anymore; she just looked plain tired. The woman who had made all the fuss about my baggage had propped herself up at the other end of the compartment and was paying us no attention. I felt sorry for them both and was tempted to offer one of them my seat but thought better of it. The other people in the compartment were a collection of male workers of various ages.

During the entire trip, the train stopped only once, at a small town, taking on and letting off a few passengers. Then it gathered speed again. Were we on the wrong train? At least we were still going in the right direction, north and east, toward Stettin.

There was a soldier in our compartment at the far end of the bench opposite me, near the screaming lady. He was obviously sleeping off a big drunk and didn't appear to be much of a threat. He would be useful, though; at Stettin train station there would be more than one exit gate, and one would be reserved strictly for the military. All we had to do was to make sure not to follow our soldier through the military exit. By making sure we stayed more or less in the middle of a gaggle of civilian workers, we hoped we'd attract as little attention as possible.

The train rattled relentlessly on, apparently following a meandering river, which appeared occasionally on the right-hand side of the train. The countryside became dotted with villages, and, at the frequent road crossings, the train whistle was *tooting* incessantly. What a beautiful holiday this would be if it wasn't for the stupid war! Mac and I were immersed in our own thoughts. I don't know what he was thinking, but I was already imagining being hustled aboard some neutral freighter and hidden under the floorboards in the captain's cabin or some other equally dramatic hiding place.

I had heard about a New Zealand corporal from Stalag VIIIB who had got to Stettin from a working party and was smuggled aboard a Swedish freighter in a wooden box about the size of a coffin. An air hose was attached to the box to pump air in to him. The box was put in the bottom of the hold and covered with a hundred tons of coal. He got to Sweden and eventually home. That idea didn't appeal to me. I could think of better ways to die than to suffocate under a hundred tons of coal.

A couple of urgent taps on my foot brought me back to reality. I looked up at Mac and he motioned outside with his eyes. We were entering railway yards on the outskirts of a city. The people in our compartment were moving and checking their baggage. This must be Stettin. My heart was pounding again. The end of the line – one way or the other! Now the tough part was about to start. We had to get off the train, out of the station, and out of the town until after dark. Wandering about in a port city like Stettin, full of troops, police, and security people, would be an invitation to disaster. The train wheezed to a stop beside a platform some distance from the station proper. A large sign read "Stettin." This was it.

The door was opened from the outside, and the standing passengers started to push forward. Finally it was our turn. I hoisted my bag down from the rack, and with a glance at Mac stepped out onto the platform, level with the compartment floor. Mac was right behind me. Nobody paid the slightest attention to us; all appeared occupied with problems of their own. We stopped for a moment and gazed around.

We were on a long, open platform stretching for several hundred yards behind us and about a hundred yards ahead, into the covered part of the station. There were several platforms like the one we were on, separated from each other by tracks, and all leading to the main station. Quite a few soldiers from our train were heading toward one particular gate, just under the overhang of the station roof. The civilians seemed to be heading for another exit. We looked at each other and headed down the platform, mingling with the crowd.

Partway along, I reached into my pocket for a handkerchief to wipe my nose. It wasn't particularly clean, which was good, because a labourer with a fancy white handkerchief might be somewhat suspect. Besides, most workmen simply blew their noses with one finger in the age-old gross way which I won't bother to describe.

There was a *clink* as something metallic flipped out of my pocket and landed on the pavement. It was my POW identification tag. There it was, lying face up for everyone to see. These tags were made in two identical parts, attached to each other by tabs, and made of some indefinable alloy, mainly lead and tin I imagine. The idea was that if the owner of the tag died, the tag could be broken in two parts, with one part remaining to identify the body, and the other part sent to the next-of-kin.

Mac and I both stopped in our tracks, turned around, and made a grab for it. I picked it up. As I straightened up, I saw two British prisoners of war behind us, smartly dressed as usual, being escorted along the platform by a rifle-toting guard. He apparently hadn't noticed anything, except perhaps a couple of scruffy foreign workers scrabbling for something on the ground. Perhaps a cigarette butt. But the two soldiers had seen it all. They looked at us as they walked by with their guard, and as they passed, one of them whispered to me in English, "Good luck, mate!"

If this were fiction, I wouldn't dare include a scene like that, for it's too unbelievable. But it's true, and truth is sometimes stranger than fiction. It felt good to know that in this large city, full of our enemies, there were two people who were at least thinking about us, and wishing us well.

I put my identity tag back in my pocket and without a word Mac and I started again toward the civilian exit gate. Would we have to show our passports? Would there be security checks? Would they ask questions? Up ahead of us, we could see departing passengers handing their tickets to a bored-looking train guard, who glanced at them, then dumped them unceremoniously in a box. Nobody seemed to be showing passports, so we kept ours in our pockets and went along with the crowd.

Aerial photograph taken during a night raid on the Baltic seaport of Stettin, showing the snow-covered city centre from eighteen thousand feet, lit by a photoflash bomb. The patches of light in the upper-right corner are from reconnaissance flares and target indicators dropped by Pathfinder aircraft. January 5–6, 1944.

It was so easy it was almost anticlimactic. We just walked through, handed our tickets to the guard, and kept on walking. Soon we were out of the station and on the street. Turning left, we walked up the road toward an intersection, from where we could see the harbour. It seemed to be full of ships, military and civilian. Many of them, about a third, had the big diagonal cross of the Swedish flag painted on their sides, as well as flying the flag of Sweden. Although they obviously didn't want to be targets of Allied bombers, I couldn't imagine how one of our bombers could discern the difference at night from twenty thousand feet.

What to do now? To the north were dockyards and indus-try, from the look of it. To the west the city spread out, and to the east, below us, was the harbour. That left south. There was a fairly wide road, almost a boulevard, paralleling the harbour. From our vantage point high up over the water, it seemed to go south indefinitely, toward the country. A whispered consultation and it was decided. We would walk out of town by the south road and then come back in after dark to try to find our contacts.

In our naivety, all we knew was that we might find some Swedish sailors, or even officers, at the foreigners' brothel, the *Ausländerbordell*. After that, it was up to us to convince one of them that they should hide us on one of their ships, a serious crime in Nazi Germany, even for a sailor of a neutral country. The sleazy area of town seemed to be just north of where we were.

There were people coming and going up and down the streets. I looked at my watch now that it was safe to do so and saw that it was about nine-thirty in the morning. We had a lot of time to kill until we returned after dark.

As we walked southward along the river road, Mac carrying his briefcase in one hand and I with my kit bag over my shoulder, we must have looked like an odd pair, but nobody looked at us. We were relieved, and even spoke English to each other in a low voice when nobody was within earshot.

We had been walking for an hour or two when it was evident that the road was turning away from the river. Eventually we came to a large park to the left of the road. There was an open gate, and as nobody was around, we decided to walk through the park. It was well-wooded, paved roadways and paths winding through a well-kept forest, with many varieties of trees, and flower gardens. This seemed an ideal spot to sit and rest; there wasn't a soul around to bother us. We turned into a cul-de-sac with a small circular road leading nowhere and sat down on a bench.

"This is a perfect place to eat," I suggested. We seemed to be completely isolated. How were we to know that in May 1944, in Hitler's Germany, it was unthinkable for two working men to be sitting in a park on a weekday, a working day, eating a sandwich. In Canada, or even in Cardiff, Wales, a bum sitting in a park was not an unusual sight.

"What'll we do with our passports?" I asked. "They're not much good to us now that we're off the trains, and we wouldn't want the Gestapo to get them."

Mac agreed. I don't think he liked the idea of having information beaten out of him, either.

So we ripped them into very small pieces and dropped them in a garbage receptacle. We were finishing up some biscuits and cheese when we noticed a policeman, an ordinary civilian policeman, standing about a hundred yards away, where the circular road abutted our little area.

"Pretend you don't notice him!" whispered Mac as he munched on his biscuits, his head down.

When we looked up again, the policeman was gone. We decided to give him a couple of minutes to get out of the area, then leave the park and get back on the road as quickly as we could. It began to dawn on me that maybe a public park wasn't the best spot for us. After a few minutes we picked up our bags and headed for the park entrance. Halfway there, the policeman stepped out of the bushes, his hand on his pistol, and confronted us. We stopped.

He asked a lot of questions, none of which we answered because neither of us could understand his rapid German. We tried to tell him that we were foreign workers, but that didn't cut any ice. We later found out that our crime was in not being at a place of work during working hours. All the passports and permits in the world wouldn't have helped. Later, we were relieved that we had no incriminating evidence on us.

Finally, he marched us over to a police car, in which sat another policeman. After a short discussion they decided to take us to the police station. He motioned us into the back of the car and unholstered his pistol, indicating that he would be happy to use it on us if we didn't cooperate. I was all for cooperating; I didn't really want a hole in the chest, particularly under someone else's name.

At the police station they sat us down on a bench and started discussing what to do with us.

"They're not about to let us go," I whispered. "Let's just tell them we're Kriegies, then they'll send us over to the army."

"Okay," Mac agreed. "They've got us, so we might as well admit we're escaped prisoners of war, and go through the old you're a soldier, I'm a soldier, it's my duty to escape routine, and then they'll send us back to Lamsdorf."

So we stood up almost simultaneously, took our dog tags from our pockets, and approached the desk.

"Wir sind Engländer" (We are Englishmen), I said in a confident voice, "englische Kriegsgefangene" (English prisoners of war), and put my German dog tag down on the desk in front of him.

"Ich auch!" (Me too!), said Mac, plunking his dog tag down alongside mine. Then, "Wir sind Kriegsgefangene vom Stalag Acht B!" (We are prisoners of war from Stalag VIIIB!), trying to outdo my clumsy German.

The result was startling. The policeman pulled out his gun and pointed it at us, motioning for us to put our hands up, which we did. He called for help and several other cops appeared within seconds. We were searched, our bags dumped out, and all the English and Canadian cigarettes and food examined. It seems that we had now graduated from the status of ignorant foreign worker to dangerous British escapee, or worse, enemy agent. After all, we had been caught in civilian clothes and were obviously British.

Another policeman, clearly the senior one, picked up the phone and started dialling. One of the others asked him something, perhaps whom he was calling, and the one word I understood chilled me: "Gestapo." I didn't need to know the context. The rest of the call was academic. From the few words that we recognized, the looks and gestures, we could be pretty sure that we were being turned over to the Gestapo for interrogation. Visions of that sadistic dentist loomed.

"Don't worry," said Mac in as confident a voice as he could muster. "They can't do anything to us. We're British prisoners of war!" I tried to feel reassured.

We sat down on the bench against the wall of the waiting room with our captor sitting opposite us on a wooden chair, his Luger balanced across his knee, his finger on the trigger. He must have seen some even wilder propaganda movies than I had, only in his we were the bad guys. No wonder he was nervous. If he was expecting some heroics on our part, he was out of luck. All I cared about was getting back to camp in one piece, as I'm sure did Mac. He was looking as serious as I felt.

16

"Achtung Schweinehunde!"

The door burst open and in swaggered two ugly bruisers in black uniforms. ss! We'd heard about these thugs and weren't about to antagonize them. They spoke to the *Feldwebel* in charge, looked at our dog tags, signed some documents, and turned around to face us.

"Achtung Schweinehunde!" (Attention pig-dogs!), one yelled. We didn't know all the words, but we knew exactly what he was saying. We stood up.

"Raus! Schnell, ihr englische Schweinehunde!" (Move it! Fast, you English pig-dogs!), he yelled, along with a lot of other German invective that we had heard many times before. We were prodded into a fast walk out of the building and pushed unceremoniously into the backseat of a large black Mercedes, with yet another Luger trained on us.

Who do these guys think we are? I wondered. They were acting as if they had just captured Al Capone and his second-in-command. The Mercedes drove about ten city blocks before stopping outside a building that could have been a duplicate of one of the large insurance buildings on University Avenue in Toronto. We were marched through the huge main entrance, which was festooned with Nazi flags. Inside was a large ballroom-like foyer, with a desk at the bottom of a winding marble staircase.

The staircase led up to a balcony that gave access to the upper halls and offices. The ceiling was three storeys high. A huge picture of Adolf Hitler, about twenty feet square, dominated the foyer, where swastika flags were displayed in every possible position. The top and bottom of the winding staircase were guarded by two large, mean-looking ss types in immaculate black uniforms and high black boots. They were armed with Schmeisser machine pistols ("paper cutters" our troops called them because they fired so fast they could cut a man in half) and razor-sharp daggers hung from their belts. I was looking at a scene that even Hollywood, with its excesses, couldn't have imagined.

Up the marble stairs we marched. Along the balcony and down a long central hall. What was this building used for before the Nazis took it over? Every twenty feet along the corridor another mean-looking ss guard was posted.

"They must have scoured the slums for every bully and rough-neck they could find to build a force like this," I thought. I'd read somewhere about "character training" in ss training schools. Each cadet was given a police dog to train and, as might be expected, some of them became quite attached to their dogs after months of training together. In some cases, when a cadet reported to his leader with his dog for the final test, the leader would say, "Kill the dog!" The cadet would then have to pull out his bayonet and unquestioningly kill the dog. In a society that revered blind obedi-ence above all and rewarded children for informing on their par-ents and siblings, this was considered to be good training.

They halted us outside an office door, came to attention, and knocked. The door opened and we were marched inside. I couldn't believe the size of the office. Behind a raised desk sat a small-ish, dark man with the ubiquitous Charlie Chaplin moustache, which we had all come to associate with Hitler. Directly behind his desk was another huge – at least ten feet square – portrait of Adolf Hitler, with swastika flags draped on either side. Beside the desk were two more swastika flags. In fact, there were swastika flags hung all over the room. Ten feet in front of the desk, the two ss guards halted, standing rigidly at attention. The little man came out from behind his desk and stood directly in front of us, looking for all the world like Charlie Chaplin.

I was getting a little nervous with all this formality and knew that as British prisoners of war they couldn't do much to us. So I reached into my inside jacket pocket and pulled out a package of Sweet Caporal cigarettes.

"Would you like a cigarette?" I asked in my most polite manner, hoping to break the ice with this minor official. How was I to know that he was the Gestapo chief for the entire Stettin area?

"Schweinehund Engländer!" he screamed, belting me on the side of the head and knocking me and the cigarettes to the floor. I tried to pick them up (cigarettes were valuable), but one of the guards stamped on my hand with his boot. So I gave that up. I picked myself up off the floor to hear Mac whisper, "Silly bastard!" He was right. When a twenty-year-old kid from Toronto tries to bribe a Gestapo chief with a couple of cigarettes, that is really not very smart.

I stood beside Mac and tried to remain expressionless while this little guy yelled and screamed at me for five or ten minutes. The two ss types could have been lampposts. I suppose if he had urinated on them they wouldn't have moved a muscle. Finally, he ran out of steam and calmed down. He began the questioning.

All we could reply was, "Wir verstehen kein Deutsch, wir sind englische Kriegsgefangene" (We don't understand German, we are English prisoners of war).

Eventually, he brought in a German girl from another office who was supposed to be able to speak English. But her English was almost as bad as our German, though maybe not quite. We tried to cooperate with her and not let her boss know that her English was not really that good.

"Where did you come from?"

"Stalag VIIIB in Lamsdorf, Ober Silesia."

"How did you travel here?"

"On the train."

"Where did you get the money?"

"Our officers in the officers' camp sent it to us for Christmas."

"Did you have any passports or papers?"

"No, of course not. Where would we get such things?" That Gestapo dentist resurfaced in my mind. My teeth tingled.

"Were there any checks of passengers on your train?"

"No." I thought about Angus Dewar from Toronto, who in one of his successful escapes over the wire (he was too tall to swap over) was stopped by an ss man on his second day, questioned, and let go. When he finally was caught a week later, he reported the ss man for inefficiency, which resulted in the man being punished. I wasn't planning on anything like that. I was going to be as diplomatic as possible with this girl, and perhaps she'd convince her boss that we really were British POWs and he'd send us "home" to Lamsdorf.

At last the questioning was finished, and the Gestapo chief seemed satisfied. What I couldn't figure out was his interest in my possible criminal activities in Britain. One of the questions, when he found out that I was an Englishman named Dennis Reeves from Coventry, was whether I had ever been arrested for any crime in England.

Then Mac and I were led into an adjoining office, where we were fingerprinted. The fingerprint experts were another couple of thugs. The way they held each of my fingers to roll in the ink was designed to be as painful as possible.

Suddenly, it was all over. We were turned about and marched out through a door at the rear of the office. We walked between the guards down another long hall. Whether the guards posted at almost every door were to keep people out or in, I never did find out. We stopped in front of a small steel door about five feet high and about two and a half feet wide. Our guard knocked with the hilt of his bayonet, the reverberations clanging up and down the hall.

The door was opened by a ferret of a man, also in ss uniform. What a contrast to the grand scene on the other side of the door. Then we were in a narrow corridor, lit by bare electric bulbs, very bright. This was a prison! We could see barred cell doors on all sides.

"Los! Schnell! Schweinehunde!" shouted the guard.

"Don't run!" I whispered to Mac as they yelled at us to get moving. "Just walk! They can't do anything to us. We're British prisoners." So we continued walking at a normal pace.

Wham! I was face down on the floor with a boot in my back. Mac was on the floor too. We dragged ourselves up.

"These guys can't do this to us!" I whispered. "Don't they know about the Geneva Convention? Let's act like soldiers, and they'll treat us like soldiers." We started marching down the corridor at a good clip.

"Los! Schnell!" screamed the guard, and we walked a little faster, but not much. I had a lot of faith in the Geneva Convention.

Thud! A black boot kicked me in the small of my back and I was down on the floor again, stunned, feeling bruised and battered, even for a healthy kid.

"Okay!" said Mac, dragging himself up from the floor. "We'd better run or we'll never get out of here alive!"

I agreed. But I felt like I could hardly walk by then, let alone run. I struggled to my feet as quickly as I could, and we started to run at a slow trot that seemed to satisfy our guards – at least they stopped kicking us.

Outside a small office, papers were exchanged and presumably we were signed in. They searched us again and took our cigarettes and my Rolex. The clerk in the office made an entry in the ledger and put my watch in a drawer, after examining it closely. Rolex was a well-known Swiss watch. I hoped I'd get it back.

Then, "Schnell! Los!" and we were off down the hall again at a fast trot. Then "Halt!" and we were stopped beside a group of about twenty men standing in two lines against the wall, facing outward. I was on the end, in the front row. Mac was behind me. A rough shove on the shoulder with the broad side of a rifle showed me I wasn't standing close enough to the next prisoner. I moved.

Another shouted order. I don't know what was said, but everyone stiffened to attention. A man with Slavic features standing beside me in the front row leaned forward and looked down the line of prisoners as if to see if someone he knew was there. *Crack!* A rifle butt to the jaw and he crumpled up on the floor, blood streaming from his face. A stream of invective from the guard and more blows from the rifle butt as the poor fellow pulled himself up and tried to stand at attention.

"This is for real!" I thought. "These guys can kill us and nobody would know or care. More orders barked out, and the other prisoners began to take off their clothes, piling them neatly on the floor in front of them. Mac and I quickly undressed, realizing by now that any show of insolence would only get us a broken face, or worse.

"Why are we taking our clothes off?" I wondered, remembering wild rumours back at Lamsdorf of concentration camps. In a few minutes we were all standing shivering in the long passageway, naked. Many of the men had bruises on their bodies. Mac and I put our dog tags on top of our clothes. Maybe they were just delousing the clothes.

Twenty or so naked men marched down the corridor, left down another corridor, up some stairs, and into a large room about twenty feet square, with a large pipe coming out of the ceiling.

"Christ!" I muttered to myself. "What's this?" It didn't look too promising: a bunch of naked prisoners being marched into a bare room with a big pipe hanging from the middle of the ceiling. I was starting to get very nervous, and Mac wasn't looking too happy, either. Then I noticed that the window on the far wall was slightly open, and I could feel a cold draught. And there was a drain in the middle of the floor. A shower! That was it! They were going to delouse us! I nudged Mac and rolled my eyes toward the window and the drain. He looked relieved.

Somebody turned a tap and a stream of ice-cold water came pouring out of the pipe, splashing on those of us in the front row. The ss guards yelled at us to get in and whacked a few men in the back row with their rifle butts. We stood under the pipe until we were soaked. Did they expect the lice to freeze and fall off? The water was shut off when they decided we were clean enough. Then they opened the windows wide, allowing an icy breeze to dry us off and chill us to the bone.

We stood about, naked and freezing, teeth chattering, until finally we were herded into a small holding cell, about ten feet wide and about twenty feet long, with no windows. There was one light bulb, about twenty-five watts, casting a dim light, and an uncovered bucket stood at one end. No toilet paper, of course.

The cell was bare, so we either stood or sat on the cold concrete floor, still naked. Mac and I chose to stand, at least for the first few hours. Afterward, fatigue forced us to squat on the floor like most of the others. The cell stunk of humanity, despite the shower we'd all had. The waste bucket at the far end was given a wide berth by all, despite our crowded state. I looked at the mass of men jammed into that small cell and suddenly realized that whatever a man looks like – European, American, or anything else – it's usually the cut of his clothes or the style of his hair, not his face or body, that makes him look like a foreigner to others.

Here we were, twenty odd men of perhaps a half-dozen differ-ent nationalities, with no clothes, all bruised and bedraggled. It seemed remarkable to me that we all looked the same, Mac and me included. Mac was skinny and not very healthy-looking. Later we were to learn that he was not very well at all, sick enough, in fact, to be invalided home on a prisoner exchange.

In passable German or my high school French, we talked with many of the other prisoners. There were Poles, Frenchmen, Belgians, Hungarians, Dutchmen, Italians, and even Germans. When one man asked us what we were, I replied "Engländer." They asked Mac what he was. He also said, "Engländer." They all shook their heads and laughed. Nobody believed us.

Then we went through a big routine with broken French and German, finally convincing them that we were really escaped prisoners of war. Now we were heroes! Even the Germans wanted to talk to us. They told us they were in prison for listening to the BBC. The others were in for various minor crimes like petty thievery, black marketeering, and not being loyal enough Nazis.

Around suppertime, some trays with metal bowls of hot soup were passed into the cell. It was Swede soup (turnip), already quite familiar to us, and boiling hot, so hot, in fact, that it burned our lips when we tried to drink it from the metal bowls. While I was waiting for mine to cool, the guard came back and collected all the trays and bowls, including those that were still too hot to drink. So I didn't get any soup that night. A hard lesson.

We spent the whole night in that cell, cold, naked, aching, hungry, and discouraged. Later, a bucket of water with a tin ladle was put on the floor. We all drank from it.

We spent most of the next day in that crowded cell trying to talk to each other in five or six different languages and waiting for whatever was going to happen next. I was afraid that I might never get out, or that I might even die there.

The idea of being shot in the back of the head, in the basement of some prison, under a false name, even though it would likely be a painless death, really terrified me. Today when I read about people "disappearing" under oppressive regimes, I feel a little of that sick terror that I know they must be feeling. There cannot be a more helplessly lost feeling than to know that you are under the total power of someone who does not have to answer for your death and who will not be called to account.

The idea of dying scared the hell out of me, of course, but what really frightened me was the idea of dying under someone else's name. If I died, I wanted at least my parents, friends, and relatives to know what had happened to me.

Later that day, after the boiling hot soup – which I learned to cool and consume quickly by blowing vigorously on the liquid at the edge of the bowl to cool the surface, then sipping quickly before it heated up again – we were moved out en masse to the original corridor where I'd stripped. There, in neat piles, were our clothes and belongings, wrinkled but sterile. One of the other prisoners, in a combination of pidgin French and German, told us that they'd been cooked in an oven to destroy the lice and fleas.

We were marched up to the next level, to the cells, accompanied by blows and kicks for those who were not moving fast enough. Mac and I had caught on to the routine by now, and jogged or loped whenever shouted at, in an effort to avoid any more kicks and blows.

Stopping in front of a cell door, one of the ss guards unbolted it and viciously shoved Mac and me into the cell. As we stumbled against the far wall, the door clanged shut behind us.

"Fucking bastards!" grunted Mac, rubbing his bruises. "They must take special courses in how to be rotten, fucking, miserable, bastards – and this bloke probably topped his fucking course!"

Mac had expressed it perfectly, if not poetically. These guards were certainly a different breed of men from those we had met at Stalag VIIIB and on the working parties. They weren't on the same planet as Hubert, the guard who gave us such valuable tips on escaping.

We looked about our cell. It was six feet wide and eight feet long – no window, but a sort of slit, or air vent, opposite the steel door. It had the usual covered peephole to allow the guards to observe the prisoners and to prevent the prisoners from looking out. There was one bunk, complete with straw palliasse, folded up against the wall and locked in that position. In the corner was a covered bucket for a toilet.

Suddenly the door was flung open and an ss guard stomped in. Yes, stomped, that's the only way I can describe it. Everything these guys did was with a lot of banging, stomping, and yelling.

"Achtung Schweinehunde!" he screamed, and we pulled ourselves to attention. He screamed in a volley of rapid-fire German for a few minutes, some of which we were able to understand. The bunk was only allowed to be down at night, being locked up against the wall during the day. We were not allowed to sit on the floor, but must stand all day. We could lie down at night, one on the bunk and one on the floor. We must keep the toilet bucket clean, the outside, that is.

He stopped. We had absorbed most of his speech. "Ich verstehe kein Deutsch," I said. "Wir sind Engländer." He looked at Mac.

"Ich verstehe nichts!" said Mac, shrugging his shoulders and spreading his hands like an Italian or Frenchman, "Ich bin auch Engländer. Wir sind Kriegsgefangene!"

The ss man took a step forward in a menacing way, raised his rifle butt, then changed his mind. "Achtung!" he yelled, and we stiffened to attention as he let himself out the door.

We stayed in that cell for a couple of weeks. The routine never changed. Some boiling hot soup and a piece of bread about midday and that was our meal for the day. An exercise period mid-morning when, on cue, cell doors opened and we lined up in the corridor with the other inmates. On order, we all turned and marched down a flight of stairs, along another corridor, down more stairs, and into a small courtyard completely enclosed by the rest of the prison.

About a hundred of us were packed into this small area no more than forty feet across. An ss guard with a long, leather-covered stick stood in the centre of the courtyard on a small podium, looking not unlike a lion tamer at a circus.

"Los! Schnell! Schweinehunde!" (Hurry up! Go, you pig-dogs!) he would scream, and we would all start jogging around the courtyard. Anyone who lagged or appeared to be going too slowly would be attacked by this man, who would leap off his podium, rush through the crowd, and pound the poor soul on the head and shoulders with his stick. Mac and I, being fairly young and athletic, avoided this treatment by staying as far away as possible from the centre, and jogging fairly quickly.

When our overseer became bored with the running and jogging performance, he would shout another order, and everyone would get down on their hands and knees. I never learned the exact German for what he said, but roughly translated it meant, "Down on your knees, you foreign bastard pig-dogs, and I'll kill anyone who lags behind!"

So we would do a few laps on our hands and knees, to the great merriment of our ss tormentor, who reminded me in many ways of the local bully when I was a kid in Toronto. He used to set fire to cats and torment all the little kids in the neighbourhood, as long as they weren't more than half his size.

Unfortunately for me, my beautiful tailored slacks, made from a German Army blanket, were starting to come apart at the seams. Mac's fared a little better because his pants were made from a Red Cross blanket, from good British wool. Fortunately, I was wearing British desert army shorts under my trousers, so my family jewels did not start to hang out when my pants disintegrated. My underwear was long gone.

At the end of our "exercise" period, which seemed to be just another excuse for our captors to torment us, we were marched back upstairs to our cells. On the way up we usually passed women being marched down to the same courtyard for their "exercise." According to one of the other prisoners who had been at the prison before, their exercise was different. As most of them were foreign women, they were made to march around the yard singing German patriotic songs. We often heard them from our cells. Whether or not they were hit with sticks or otherwise tormented I don't know, but I know at least some of them were mistreated in their cells, as Mac and I regularly heard the sounds of beatings going on in other cells, and screaming, both male and female.

Regularly, we would hear the sound of two or more men marching down the corridor, then stopping. Then we would hear a cell door open and close. Then male voices yelling in German. Then thumps and thuds, and cries, sometimes male and sometimes female. More yelling and screaming in German, more thuds and thumps, and more cries of anguish and pain. Then silence. Mac and I would look at each other. "Fucking bastards!" he'd mutter.

Standing up all day in our cell became too wearying, so we developed a routine. We took turns, one sitting down on the floor, the other acting as a lookout, stretched out on the floor with his eye to the crack under the door. We discovered that guards could not approach from either direction without casting a shadow. So the lookout watched for the shadow while the other relaxed in a sitting position on the cement floor.

I would be lying on the floor, taking my turn at lookout, when a shadow would appear. I'd leap to my feet, as would Mac, without a word, and we'd stand, leaning against our bunk with as neutral a look as we could muster on our faces. There would be a slight scraping noise as the peephole cover was moved over, and a beady eye would appear at the hole. More than once the idea passed through my mind that it would be nice to poke that eye out.

We never got caught lying or sitting down, or we would also have been severely beaten. Our cell was inspected daily for cleanliness, and we were yelled at for every real or imagined infraction.

We pretended that we couldn't understand any German, although we did understand a good deal. By now the Germans must have confirmed that we were in fact escaped prisoners of war and not desperate saboteurs or spies. Perhaps our military status saved us from some of the severe beatings we heard going on around us. I've often wondered what happened to the Pole standing beside me that first day, whose jaw was broken with a rifle butt.

The days dragged on into weeks. The routine never varied. My knees were bruised from crawling, and my beautiful grey pants were a mess. Mac wasn't in any better shape. He was dirty, dishevelled, and unshaven.

I began to despair. The prospect of spending years in this cell seemed unbearable. Our conversation was mainly speculation on when our camp would send for us. Getting back to Lamsdorf almost seemed like going home! At least we had friends there, people who knew us. Here, in a strange prison cell, with fake identities, we felt nameless, homeless. But at least Mac and I weren't fighting. My episode with Donaldson had taught me something.

One day, about three weeks later, I was lying on the floor with my eye to the crack under the door when I saw the familiar shadow. The "eye" was coming. I quietly leapt to my feet and joined an equally silent Mac, assuming our usual positions. The exercise had become almost routine by now. But the peephole didn't open. Instead, there was the rattle of the door bolt, and the door opened. An ss guard stood framed in the doorway.

17

Back at VIIIB

"Raus, ihre englische Schweinehunde! Kommt mit!" (Out, you English pig-dogs! Come with me!) the guard said.

Along a hall, down the stairs, then down another hall. This was an ominously different route. We weren't going to the exercise yard. I began to feel fear again. Please, God, don't let it end here! I wasn't a particularly religious person, having attended church more to please my parents and for its social life than from any deep conviction. Yet, I was somehow hoping that God would intervene on my behalf in this terrifying situation.

There were no windows in the passageway. No way to tell if we were above or below ground. We walked along in silence, the ss man with his machine-gun a couple of paces behind us.

Rounding a corner, I suddenly saw him, about fifty feet away, leaning on his rifle. What a beautiful sight! An ordinary German soldier. A bit short and fat, with a uniform that didn't fit too well, but a beautiful sight for our eyes. He'd come to rescue us! Finally we were going to get out of the clutches of these ss bastards.

The soldier looked at us with some surprise, checking us out from head to toe. "Soldaten?" he said in a tone of disbelief. The ss guard fired a volley of very fast German at him, which seemed to take him aback a little. He looked at us with great interest.

I suddenly realized why. I only had to look at Mac to realize that my looks must have mirrored his. He was a mess. Tattered, dirty clothing, with his pants ripped open at the knees, filthy ripped shirt and jacket, ragged hair, unshaven, dirty and probably smelly.

We were at the counter of the office where we had been signed in some weeks before. The same clerk was on duty. He checked some papers and had our soldier sign them. He waved us on, but I stopped. Both guards looked at me.

"My watch!" I said. "Meine Uhr, it's in there!" and I pointed to the drawer where I had seen him place my watch. I pantomimed with my wrist, indicating that it was a wristwatch. Our army guard began to argue with the clerk. The ss guard stood impassively watching. Finally, the soldier from Lamsdorf seemed to have made his point. The clerk opened the drawer, pulled out my Rolex, and pushed a form in front of me to sign.

I had no idea what it said, but I signed it. Thinking about the incident later, I realized that our German Army soldier had become our passport to safety. The minute he was on the scene, the ss guard's attitude seemed to soften. I suppose he realized that we were in fact prisoners of war and now came under different rules. Without our soldier my jaw may have been broken with a rifle butt for daring to step out of line.

Finally, it looked as if we were on our way out, when the ss man stopped us again. He said something to our guard and went around behind the counter. We waited. He returned with a set of handcuffs, grabbed me roughly by the left hand, and clicked the steel circlet around my wrist. He clipped the other end to Mac's right wrist. Then he went through a long spiel with our guard in which we understood him to say that we were dangerous criminals and were to remain shackled until we arrived back at Stalag viiib at Lamsdorf.

At last, we were out on the street, our plump little soldier marching us along at a leisurely pace toward the railroad station.

When we got to the train station, Mac and the guard got into a bit of an argument about the route back to Lamsdorf. Just then, our guard realized that our train was pulling away from the platform. All three of us tried to jump into a coach moving beside us at about five miles an hour and accelerating. Thanks to the handcuffs, Mac got into the train instead of under it, being dragged in by one end of the handcuff. The three of us sat down on facing seats at the rear of the coach.

The train conductor was a woman. Apparently, with the shortage of men, most train personnel other than engineers were women. This one was a fairly good-looking woman in her thirties, quite chic in her dark uniform. She was wearing a skirt, and had fantastic legs. But in the dismal state we were in, she could have been Rita Hayworth dancing stark naked in front of us and neither our interest or anything else would have been aroused.

She sat down beside our guard, opposite us, and began to ask questions about us in an animated way. He must have told us some pretty tall tales about our exploits because she began to look at us with even more interest. I could understand a small part of the conversation, and she seemed to be asking how long we had been prisoners.

My swapover identity, Dennis Reeves, had been captured in 1940, as had Mac's. When the conductor heard that we had been prisoners for four years, she seemed shocked. "They have not had any women for four years!" she exclaimed to him in German, looking at us with renewed curiosity. "How do they manage without women?" The incredulous look on her face suggested that she could not imagine any man enduring such a prolonged abstinence.

Our guard laughed and said something unintelligible, then made obscene motions with his hand in the vicinity of his crotch, which no one could mistake, no matter their language. The two of them laughed uproariously, he slapping his knees and she holding her stomach and shaking with laughter.

"Stupid bitch!" muttered Mac. "I'd like to kick her little ass!"

It had been afternoon when we boarded the train at Stettin's main station. We travelled all night and the rest of the next day, changing trains at least twice. Our guard hadn't been impressed by Mac's arguments, so his route was much more complicated than ours had been, and took longer.

Finally we arrived at Breslau. After a two-hour wait in the station, still chained together, we boarded the train for Oppeln and Lamsdorf. This was a train that was very familiar to British prisoners of war; they had all travelled on it, many of them more than once. As we climbed aboard our coach and threaded our way down to the back of the car, we passed a group of six British prisoners, accompanied by a guard, and playing cards on a makeshift board set up on their knees.

"Look at those two poor bastards!" exclaimed one in a cockney accent. "I wonder what they done to be in that kind of shape. And look, they're handcuffed together, too!"

"Must be a couple of dangerous criminals," said another. "The big one is a mean-looking bugger. Looks like he hasn't washed in years."

"Maybe they're Jews!" said a third. "I hear they treat them pretty bad in them concentration camps."

Mac and I looked at one another but said nothing. The guard, not understanding English, was oblivious to the comments. We parked ourselves in facing seats at the rear of the coach. The British Kriegies were about halfway up the car, on the other side.

"Eure Kameraden?" (Your comrades?) whispered our guard with a smile, gesturing toward the British prisoners with his thumb.

"Ja, ja," we agreed. "Können wir mit den Engländern sprechen?" (Can we speak to the Englishmen?) we asked.

He agreed to let us speak to our "comrades." He remained seated in the rear seat, his rifle across his knees and a big grin on his face. We made our way up the centre aisle. A few of the passengers looked up, then looked away, not knowing what to make of us. It was dangerous in 1944 to be too curious.

I stopped opposite the card players, Mac attached to my left wrist. "Any of you guys got a spare cigarette?" I asked.

"Jesus H. Christ!" exclaimed one of the men. "Where the hell did you learn to speak English?"

"Same place as you, I guess," I replied. "At home. It's the only language I know."

"What are you, then?" he persisted. "Spies, saboteurs, or what? Why the handcuffs?"

"We're British prisoners, same as you!" Mac interjected in his lilting Welsh accent, more pronounced than usual. "And we haven't had a fag for weeks. How about it?"

Cigarettes were proffered, and between luxurious drags we told them our story, occasionally glancing back at our guard, who seemed to be quite happy about our new-found friends.

The six were going back to Lamsdorf from a working party for various reasons, administrative and medical. They promised to get our story back to the RAF compound in case we were incarcerated in the "*Strafe* compound" (the punishment compound) or in the "cooler" (solitary confinement).

Our guard motioned for us to return. We said goodbye to our new friends and, with a few cigarettes apiece, returned to the rear of the coach, again raising eyebrows as we passed. We slipped our guard a few English cigarettes when we sat down, for which he seemed inordinately grateful.

It was still afternoon when we arrived at Lamsdorf Station. Our six new friends were taken off the train, and when we last saw them, were marching briskly down the road toward camp. Our guard had some paperwork to do with the station agent, so our friends arrived at camp about fifteen minutes before we did. The news of our arrival had obviously preceded us. Several hundred

Kriegies just inside the fence were there to welcome us, including some of our buddies from the RAF compound. A cheer went up as we entered the main gate.

Although we were brought back to the camp shackled together like common criminals, no doubt considered a humiliating punishment by the Germans, it was really quite an honour. It proved publicly that we had actually escaped, and given them a run for their money. And, after all, wasn't that the spirit of the Annual Spring Handicap? The more prisoners who tried to escape, the more we screwed up the German war effort and, in some small way, perhaps made a difference to the Allied war effort. Besides, there was always the chance, however small, that some of us might actually make it all the way home.

Our guard was told to take us to Compound S-1, the *Strafe* compound. As we ambled down the road, he asked us where S-1 was. Without hesitation, Mac pointed toward F-1, the working compound. The guard promptly marched us in and turned us over to a very surprised British warrant officer, who assigned us two empty bunks in one of the barrack blocks. Our handcuffs removed, we bid goodbye to our very weary guard and climbed onto our bunks.

We had fully expected to be punished with a week or two in the *Strafe* compound or in the cooler, but nothing happened to us.

The following day we were issued new army uniforms and other items of clothing from Red Cross stores and a Red Cross food parcel apiece. After a good wash and a shave, clean clothes, and some food in our bellies, we were unrecognizable as the dirty, unshaven, ragged, decrepit prisoners who had come through the gate handcuffed together.

A few days later, after we had convinced ourselves that no one was still awaiting our arrival at S-1, we returned to the RAF compound and resumed our own identities. Both of our swapovers were happy to go back to their original identities, well rested and richer by a few thousand cigarettes. Mac and I soon got back to camp routine, and I put all thoughts of further escapes out of my mind for the time being.

Not so with Mac. Our near success had gone to his head. Within two weeks he had swapped over again and was out on another working party. A month later he was back again, in the *Strafe* compound, for an attempted escape. When he finally got back to the RAF compound, he told me his story.

"I was going to try it alone this time," he said, "since you didn't seem too interested. But my flight engineer, a chap called Milligan, who could speak no French and no German, asked if he could come with me. Anyway, this time we went to a working party, where we were working at a printing press – I managed to break some rolls of paper, so they gave me a job just wheeling a wheelbarrow.

"About ten o'clock at night, some New Zealanders cut the wire for us, and Milligan and I went through. We were in a sort of field, with a fence running down the side of it, and just then we heard German guards coming to change shifts, so Milligan and I threw ourselves on the ground and pretended we were a couple making love.

"The German soldiers must have actually seen us because they made some obviously lewd comments and started laughing. And then they just passed us by.

"Well, eventually Milligan and I got to Oppeln and Breslau and followed pretty well the same route that you and I followed. From Breslau we went more or less straight to Stettin. In the evening we slept in a cemetery, under some bushes. The following day we went to a foreigners' brothel where the Madame came out in a bit of a panic and said, 'We're not open until two o'clock!' When I explained who we were, she said, 'Sorry, I can't help you, the Gestapo come and inspect us every day. But,' she said, 'if you go down to the café, you'll find some French workers who'll help you there.' Anyway, there, there were all these French workers enjoying a meal, and there was a couple of German soldiers too – so I waited until one of the Frenchmen went out, and I went after him, explained who we were, and he started panicking a bit. But he said, 'Wait until Pierre comes along – he'll know what to do.'

"Finally, this character comes along and decided to take us back to their barracks, where we stayed the night. The next night they took us down to the docks area in Stettin, where we were trying to find someone to take us to Sweden. We were offered a trip to Finland, but we declined. After a very pleasant evening touring the pubs, we went home to the Frenchmen's barracks.

"The third night that we were with the Frenchmen, we were getting ready for bed when a Frenchman rushed in and said that the police had arrived. Milligan and I rushed out back and hid ourselves, but the Germans found us, arrested us, and took us to the Gestapo prison. On the way back to prison, the Gestapo chap in charge told us that one of the Frenchmen had given us away because he was due to go on leave back to France the following week and he was afraid that it might be cancelled!"

"What sort of jail did you go to?" I asked.

"It was the same one that you and I went to. The trouble was that I was there under a different name. When we got to the Gestapo jail, the Gestapo checked my fingerprints and found that they matched the man I had swapped over with previously. They couldn't understand this, and as I just played dumb, they gave up in the end. After about five days, Milligan and I were returned here and they gave us six days' solitary."

Later, in the fall of 1944, Mac was sent to the lazarette on some minor medical ailment. When he came back, he told us that he had been given a very thorough medical examination and had been diagnosed as having TB. It was bittersweet news for him, for although TB is a serious affliction, particularly in a prisoner-of-war camp, it meant that he would be eligible for repatriation on the next prisoner exchange arranged by the Red Cross.

In a few weeks he was moved to the repat compound, and just before Christmas 1944 he was shipped home on a prisoner exchange, deemed unfit for any future military service. Before he left, I made him up a little booklet of cartoons about life at Stalag VIIIB. Sixty years later, he still has it, one of his few souvenirs from those terrible times.

18

March to Fallingbostel

The summer and fall of 1944 dragged on. The war news was growing more encouraging with every week that passed. The Russian
Front was crumbling, the Allies were smashing forward in Italy
and on the Western Front. Every night we were cheered by a new
advance or victory. It was just a matter of time and the war would
be over and we could all go home.

The guards became a little friendlier. More Red Cross rations
were getting through, and the thought of escaping was the last
thing on my mind. Why risk my life on an escape attempt when all
I had to do was sit and wait for the war to end? Or so I thought.

Besides, the authorities had put up a new proclamation in every
barrack block that said in large letters and in very plain English,
"Attention! All prisoners of war! Escaping is no longer a sport!"
It then went on in explicit detail to point out that being caught in
civilian clothing or in a restricted area such as a railroad siding, or
being almost anyplace one should not be, would likely result in the
escapee being shot on the spot. I decided then and there that with
the war in its final stages, another attempt at escaping would not be
worth the increased risk.

For Christmas most of us had saved up a few raisins and biscuits from previous parcels for our glops. We booked space on the
communal stove to cook them and our "roasts" (meat loaves made

from corned beef and bread and other ingredients). We ate our pathetic little Christmas dinners, along with the regular rations of Swede soup, German bread, and *Kartoffeln* (potatoes), in groups of two or three, and talked about Christmases past, present, and future, all certain that we'd be celebrating the next Christmas in our homes. But none of us knew then the ordeal that we were shortly to face, and that some of us would not survive.

The night before Christmas, I had been playing Christmas carols on my harmonica, one my dad had sent me in a personal parcel, and it had occurred to me that many of those tunes were the same in German. Earlier, Dennis Reeves had dropped by the RAF compound to see me, and to wish me a merry Christmas. We talked about the approaching end of the war, and what we would do when it was all over. For him, it was going to be a great reunion with his family. He had been in the camps for almost five years now.

New Year's Eve came and went as just another day – except for one thing. In the quiet of the night you could hear the sound of distant guns. Some thought it was the Russians. Others swore that it was just another Allied bombing raid. The next few nights were windy and cold, and we heard nothing.

Then, around the middle of the month, at about ten o'clock at night, someone out in the vestibule shouted, "Shut up in there, and you can hear the guns!" Most of us were in our bunks by then, but we all were instantly still. The silence was deafening. Then, through the thin wooden walls of the hut, we could hear them, the Russian guns! According to those who knew about such things, the Russians must be close, maybe twenty or thirty miles.

The barrack was buzzing with speculation. The Russians were breaking through! Would we be liberated by the Russians – or would they just leave us in the camps? We had heard that they didn't think much of prisoners of war, considering them to be cowards and traitors – patriots should fight to the death and never be taken prisoner. So my feelings of exhilaration and joy were tempered with some apprehension.

On January 21, 1945, Warrant Officer Currie, the senior British officer in the RAF compound, was called to an emergency meeting by the German commandant and given two hours' notice to prepare all RAF personnel to evacuate the camp. We could take only what we could carry on our backs.

I didn't own much, so it was just a matter of sewing some straps on my kit bag so I could sling it over my back. I wasn't sorry for some of the racketeers, who had so much loot they couldn't carry it all. Most of the combines (pairs of muckers), like my own, divided up the food and cigarettes and decided what to take and what to leave. We were each issued a complete Red Cross food parcel, which cleaned out the Red Cross stores.

Later in the afternoon we were lined up outside the barrack blocks, ready to move off. The guards searched each barrack to make sure that nobody attempted to stay behind, then marched us out the main gate of the camp.

There were about a thousand of us moving down the road in a line extending so far ahead of and behind me that I could not see the beginning or end. Every hundred feet on either side were the armed guards, looking almost as unhappy as we felt. The sky was overcast and threatening. It was extremely cold, about twenty below zero Fahrenheit. The snow was falling lightly, adding to the five or six inches already on the road, which was quickly being packed down into a dirty, grey ice. Darkness was approaching fast.

Our route wound along an unpaved secondary road, likely planned to keep us off the main routes, reserved for German troops and armour rushing to the front lines in a last-ditch attempt to stave off the Russian juggernaut – not too far behind us, judging from the sound of heavy gunfire in the distance.

I was wearing a British Army greatcoat over an army battledress uniform, the best I had been able to acquire since my most recent escape, a blue air force shirt, two pairs of wool socks, and a stout pair of army boots. I also had an air force blue wool sweater, which had been sent to me by my mother. I was fit and tanned, and fairly well equipped for a long hike.

The first few hours were almost fun. We marched westward on the well-packed snow, chatting with friends and acquaintances, joking about the war ending, which even the guards seemed to have accepted. Now we almost felt sorry for them, all older men who were heavily burdened down with regulation packs and rifles. Some of them looked as if they were having a difficult time keeping up.

We had no particular thought of escaping, although it probably would have been easy. But where could one go? I didn't want to get caught in a vicious firefight between the ss Panzer divisions and the Russian Army. And we were heading west, toward the Americans and the British, who were but a few hundred miles away. Last, but certainly not least to consider, there was safety in our numbers.

By nightfall the novelty had worn thin, and most of us were feeling tired, despite the regular ten-minute rest-stops every hour or so. Sitting down in the roadway to eat a piece of German bread and Red Cross bully beef, I suddenly realized that it was damn cold. It was a relief to get moving again. Nobody told us our destination for the day; we assumed the Germans knew what they were doing. The rumour, passed up and down the column, was that we would be billeted in another POW camp down the road for the night. Like most rumours, this proved to be false.

The evening wore on and we were still shuffling along, the snow steadily falling, freezing in the sub-zero temperatures, and no word on any destination. A lot of grumbling was going on, with all sorts of rumours circulating. Nobody knew anything, least of all the guards, who by now had deteriorated into pathetic old men, doing their best to keep up. At least one group with a sled let an older guard put his pack on it to help lighten his load.

Everything I owned was in one RAF kit bag, slung across my back. Besides a blanket, some extra clothing, and a Canadian Red Cross food parcel, I'd also saved up a sizable chunk of black German bread and a half dozen potatoes, along with a homemade tin-can pot and a tin-can drinking mug. A spoon and a recently acquired pocket knife completed the load.

The moon broke out from behind the ragged snow clouds, illuminating our endless column of miserable men, still shuffling along, putting one foot ahead of the other. My hands were freezing cold, even in my pockets, and my feet were icy, despite my heavy socks and boots.

Eventually, we left the road, stumbling along a furrowed cart track. A light glimmered up ahead and a huge barn loomed behind. Word came back that this barn was where we would stop for what was left of the night. Later I learned that the nearest village was Friedewald, and that several thousand British prisoners had been put into about a dozen barns in the area.

The temperature was still well below zero, and the minute we stopped marching we began to feel the deadly, penetrating cold. A few hardy individuals attempted to light small cooking fires, despite the guards' admonitions against fires near the barn. A few klim-tin blowers were started up to brew tea. Most of us moved into the barn to try to lay claim to a warm spot. Eventually, about eight hundred to a thousand men ended up in the barn I was in.

I staked out my spot in the centre, surrounded by a mass of humanity on all sides. I kept my eye on the main door, by now closed and guarded. The potential fire hazard of a thousand POWs – many were smoking – in a crowded barn with hay strewn over the floor and in the loft made me keenly aware of the most direct path to the door. I worked my way a little closer to it, deciding that I would rather be shot than burned alive, and that if some careless smoker set the barn on fire, I'd be one of the first out the door.

It was not as cold now in the barn. The frigid air, warmed by the body heat of a thousand closely packed men, was now almost up to the freezing mark and felt almost warm to me, huddled on the barn floor with my blanket wrapped around my shoulders. Fortunately, most of us had relieved ourselves alongside the roadway. The guards allowed no one outside the barn for any reason, which meant that anyone who had to urinate, or worse, had a bit of diarrhea, would have to find a remote corner of the barn. Some just let go where they sat and allowed it to soak into the ground. The smells were sickening.

After a fitful night at Friedewald, the barn doors were opened and we were allowed out. Word was passed that we'd leave in an hour. No rations had been arranged by the Germans and we were expected to eat our own food. Squatting in the barnyard with hundreds of others, I ate some black bread and some biscuits with a bit of bully beef, washing it down with water from my water bottle. (I had learned my lesson well on my escape with John Donaldson.)

Soon the German guards were barking orders, and the column began to move out. I was with a complete group of strangers now, all RAF but from other barrack blocks. I wasn't sure whether my group was ahead of me or behind me. No matter. We were all going in the same direction and to the same destination, wherever that was.

Day two was a repeat of the first day, only worse. Bitter cold, endless marching, infrequent stops, and hollow threats by the guards to the stragglers. We occasionally saw a German officer or two passing by in either direction, possibly checking up on the guards, or perhaps estimating the numbers of occupants for the next barn.

I was becoming very tired. After two years of confinement, punctuated by two all-too-brief escapes, marching twenty-five or thirty miles a day seemed to be too strenuous an exercise. I wasn't as fit as I thought I was. My feet were in good shape though; I had changed my socks for a fresh pair that very morning. The damp pair was tucked inside my pants, next to my bare stomach, to dry out – a trick I'd learned from an old army sweat who had served in the British Army in China in the 1930s.

According to him, two pairs of socks would last virtually forever on a march if you dried out one pair against your body while wearing the other. Using that system, my two pairs lasted me until the end of the war without being washed.

It had stopped snowing, the temperature was still around zero, and it was just starting to get dark on this second day of the march when the word came down that we were going to stop shortly. Sure enough, we turned off the main road near a village and joined about a thousand prisoners in a large, deserted brickworks. Guards were posted around the various exits, and we were left to make ourselves comfortable for the night.

No fire hazard here. The problem was finding something to burn. A few of us found some scrap wood and started a little fire that about a dozen of us sat around. There was a water tap some distance away and a couple of crude privies nearby, soon filled to overflowing.

The next morning a German Army truck came in and issued a cup of Swede soup per man and about a fifth of a loaf of bread apiece. Our morale rose considerably. By seven o'clock we were on the road again. It was still very cold, but a little warmer than the previous days, and the sun was shining. We were still heading west, our column filing from the other barns and factories in the Priborn area. I marvelled at the numbers of people on the roads. Not only were there tens of thousands of British prisoners of war, but there were many civilian refugees from the battle area pushing carts and baby carriages full of household effects ahead of them. They were too dazed to pay us much attention. But I found myself wondering, what would I feel like if I had seen my home destroyed and was fleeing from an invading army?

One group of about fifty women, all ages, poorly dressed in flimsy garb and clearly prisoners of some sort, were escorted by two armed guards. They were sitting by the side of the road as we went by and looked at us unseeingly. One young woman about my age looked, expressionless, straight into my eyes. I looked at her face and saw that she must have been very beautiful at one time. Our eyes met for a moment and we both glanced away. I felt a twinge of guilt, as if somehow I was responsible for her predicament, as if I should be doing something to help her. But I kept going. I still have visions of her face on occasion, looking at me.

The third day ended much like the first. After slugging all day with a few short breaks, and covering twenty or thirty miles, we finally arrived at another barn, this time at a place called Gross Greignitz. Some of the villagers had got together and made soup for the prisoners, brought it in on a farm cart in several large containers, and rationed it out the usual way. I think I appreciated it more because it was a gift from local civilians rather than because it tasted so good.

The next few days were a procession of barns, at the end of twenty- to thirty-mile hikes, through the towns of Rogan, Rosenau, Domanze, and Damsdorf. Quite a few of the prisoners were beginning to get dysentery. It was a common sight during the march to see dozens of men at the roadside squatting with their pants around their knees, letting go. Modesty was thrown to the wind, as nearly everybody had the same problem. One man had it so badly that he couldn't hold it and soiled his pants. A friend helped him clean himself up as best he could with wads of straw and got his pants back on in a hurry before he froze. The smells were horrific, although most of us had stopped noticing.

By now the relentless marching had become a nightmare. My mind was numbed with the enormity of what was happening, and there was nothing I could do but keep going. One footstep blurred into a thousand, one mile into a dozen, and I trudged on. I remember that there was a thaw after the fourth or fifth day, which should have made us a lot warmer but just caused more problems. The roads became a morass of mud, and our feet were soaking wet at the end of a day's march. I changed my socks regularly, drying out the wet ones against my belly and hoping that my wet boots would dry out with the heat of walking.

On the seventh day, we slept in the sheep pens at Alte Jauer. Sheep shit, I discovered, smells worse than cow shit. And the smell of sheep shit mixed with the human variety is indeed a very disgusting smell. Fortunately, my nose by then had been numbed to all strong odours, and still is to a degree.

By now the Germans were almost completely disorganized, and although the officers responsible were doing their best to get us to wherever we were going, the entire country was in a shambles, and supplies seemed to be almost nonexistent.

During the next four days, the nightmare became worse. The temperature remained mild during the day but plummeted at night to well below freezing. Our clothes were soaked and muddy. Our boots were completely wet, and it was impossible to take them off at night or we wouldn't have been able to put them on, frozen, in the morning. We were a great mass of dirty, dishevelled, smelly, sick, and demoralized humanity, putting one foot in front of the other, with no apparent destination. The guards appeared completely demoralized and hobbled along beside us, unwilling prisoners of their own circumstances.

Many prisoners died during the march of pneumonia, pleurisy, and just plain dehydration from dysentery. One that I remember only as "Mac" – McGinnis, I think – whom we all thought of as an "older man" (he was about thirty), had been in barrack block 15A. He succumbed to pleurisy about two weeks into the march. He had been a public school teacher, a fund of knowledge, and editor of *The Stimmt,* a more or less weekly wall newspaper in the RAF compound. I can still remember him, slightly bald, with a quizzical look on his face and a reeking pipe, discussing some esoteric subject with some of us less well-educated types. He was a joy to be around. An RAF navigator, he was just a nice guy. He died one night in one of the barns.

Jock Martin, my flight engineer, who was fastidious about keeping accounts and records, kept a diary going for about thirty days, then suddenly stopped after a terse entry: "27/2 Sick Cart to Stadtroda." The rest of the story I got from him long after the war. On February 26, 1945, after more than thirty days of sleeping in barns, sheep pens, brick factories, and even a state farm, he had ended up in a barn "seven kilos past Eisenberg." The following day, he and about a dozen others were too weak to get up and were left for a "rest." The next day, they still couldn't move, and one of the German officers arranged for some "sick carts," horse-drawn carts that would hold about eight men each.

The following day about sixty very sick prisoners, most of whom were in the last stages of dysentery, were taken in sick carts to a "hospital" in a town called Stadtroda, where they were laid out on the floor and fed the standard German ration of Swede soup – with nothing else. Not that it was the Germans' fault – there was very little food for anyone.

As Jock told it to me, he was lying on a dirty blanket on the floor beside his good friend Jock McKinley, unable to move, in their own filth. He said to his friend, "Jock, if we don't get up pretty soon, we're going to die," and his friend agreed.

The orderlies could do little but inspect them regularly and take away the dead. Besides the Swede soup, they had a little medicine, anti-diarrhea pills, which had little effect. While Jock was there, the orderlies carried away about thirty bodies. He kept trying to get up but only managed to stay standing for a moment or two, then would fall back to the floor.

Finally, after several days of watching the corpses of his comrades being carried out, he started to get better. He told me that he knew he was getting better when the stuff coming out of his rear end began to get lumpy. When he managed to stay on his feet for a few hours, with meagre strength, he began to nurse his friend back to health and clean both of them up. By the time the Americans arrived at Stadtroda, about half the prisoners there had died.

I didn't have as orderly a mind as Jock and had better things to do (I thought) than keep a diary. So I remember the rest of the march as a horrible mishmash, a kaleidoscope of nightmarish events that I can only recount as impressions of a bad dream.

There was a succession of barns, I remember, all the way to Stalag viiiA at Görlitz, a deserted POW camp where we "rested" and got some semblance of organization going again. We found wooden bunks, without the straw palliasses, which had long since gone for fuel, but at least we had some sort of shelter. There was a daily ration of turnip soup and every few days a loaf of black bread shared among seven men. The toilets were holes in the floor of the "shithouses," the wooden seats having also long gone for heating. Unfortunately, nobody had pumped out the reservoirs under the toilets and the stuff was piled up above each hole. It was impossible to stand over the hole as you were supposed to; the best you could do was to squat as near as possible to the smallest pile you could find.

Years later, reading about the exodus of Kurds from Iraq after the Gulf War in 1991, my heart went out to them when I read of whole families coming down with dysentery. Few newspaper readers or television viewers could have any idea of the enormity of having diarrhea in conditions where the most basic of sanitary conveniences were nonexistent. I wonder if the reporters, going back to their tents or comfortable hotel rooms, would have had any idea of the enormous suffering that was going on.

After a few days' "rest" at Görlitz, we were on the road again. Another succession of long daily marches in snow and slush, with stops in places with names like Reichenbach, Weissenberg,

Aerial view of the devastation caused in Dresden, Germany, following RAF Bomber Command and US Army Air Forces raids on the city in February 1945.

Bautzen, and Komanze. On one of those days we passed through a little village south of Dresden a few days after it had been virtually wiped out by British and Americans saturation bombing. It had been full of refugees, and prisoners of war like ourselves, who apparently died in the thousands. Some of the people along the sides of the road, seeing the RAF blue uniforms, threw stones at us. A natural reaction, I would think, although at the time we had no idea of what was going on.

One day, in a corner of a barn, some of us found sacks of something that looked and smelled like food. About the consistency of corn flakes, it tasted slightly sweet. Unfortunately, there was a bitter aftertaste that offset the sweetness. It was sugar beet residue, left over from the sugar-making process, and used as animal feed. It gave me a severe case of indigestion and more of the runs. Another day, we ran across some wheat grain in bags. We all filled our pockets and put handfuls in our packs. But we found it almost impossible to cook or eat it, even after hammering it between two stones. Another time, I found a couple of half-rotten potatoes under some straw and decided to cook them the following evening.

There was no fuel anywhere, not even a stick. I had a book of cartoons that I had drawn while at Stalag VIIIB, the hardcover book of blank pages having been a gift from the Red Cross. I borrowed a klim-tin blower from one of the others, and, carefully feeding in pages from my cartoon book, I managed to cook those two potatoes. The book is completely gone now, and the only record of any of my prisoner-of-war cartoons may be in other prisoners' log books, and the small book of cartoons that I made for Mac when he was shipped home on a prisoner exchange. I still don't regret that decision; those two potatoes helped me get through another day.

It must have been near the end of February, although I had no idea what day it was or how long we had been shuffling through the snow and mud in this freezing hell. I felt as if I had been marching through the snow forever. One foot ahead of the other, all day long, I didn't look up, just kept track of the shuffling feet ahead of me. I had not changed my clothes or washed for a month. None of us had. We were weak and starving, given the irregular and pitifully small rations of turnip soup and bread issued by the Germans. The Red Cross rations were but a pleasant memory. We lived from day to day, like animals, waiting for the food ration and too weak to do more than drag ourselves slowly westward along the snow-covered roads, and hoping that the night's accommodation would not be worse or colder than the previous one.

There was amazing cooperation among us considering that we were all in the first stages of starvation; nobody fought over the rations, which were usually divided up fairly.

Somewhere along the line, I became sick. I had already had dysentery, but in a much milder form than some of the others. One morning I woke up vomiting into the straw beside me. I was shaking with alternating chills and fever. I was barely able to stand. I examined my face with a small steel mirror borrowed from a companion. I could hardly believe what I saw.

As well as the dirt, the beard – scraggly as it was for a twenty year old – and the bloodshot eyes, my whole face had turned yellow. Even the whites of my eyes were yellow, the bloodshot veins standing out as a sort of brownish-orange. I looked like something out of a horror movie. I put my blanket back in the kit bag, changed my wet socks for my damp ones, put the wet ones against my belly, and joined the column.

After a few hours marching, I could no longer keep up and so sat down by the side of the road. A guard came by, looked at me, and kept going. Other men were falling out, many in much worse condition than I. Another guard came back along the column and looked at the group of us sitting and lying beside the road, shook his head, and continued on. A non-commissioned officer came by for yet another look, and told us to stay where we were. He told us that he would try to arrange some transportation. By now, I didn't care much what happened, for I had (as I discovered later) a serious case of hepatitis, as well as dysentery, influenza, and food poisoning. A German NCO came by and told us that if we could walk a few miles to the nearest railroad siding, he would try to get us on a couple of freight cars and hook us onto a train.

By now our miserable group of sick men must have totalled more than two hundred. I was too sick and cold to notice what was going on. Somehow we made our way, escorted by several guards, to a railroad siding about three miles away. How I got there, I don't know. I had to stop to vomit or squat down by the side of the road to relieve myself every few minutes.

A few hours later, I found myself lying in some dirty straw in a freight car with about thirty or forty others who were too sick to walk. We lay there for several hours, with no food or water, wondering what was next. Shunting and crashing noises told us that we were being hitched to a train, and soon we were moving – somewhere. For the rest of the day the train moved steadily westward, stopping for long periods at sidings to allow more important trains by or to accommodate traffic going in the opposite direction. At some of the stops we were given water, which was very welcome in our parched state. I vomited most of my ration up, but enough stayed down to keep me alive. There was no food, but most of us were too sick to care. Later that evening, we pulled into a siding and spent the night in the car, miserable and freezing.

The next morning, after some water and a small bit of bread, which I was able to keep down, the car was hooked up to a freight train and we started moving again. For the rest of the morning we moved slowly westward, jerking to a stop at every siding along the route. Finally, at about two in the afternoon, the train pulled into a siding at a place called Halberstadt and stopped. That name I can never forget.

An air raid siren in the town started up and the sound of diving aircraft and cannon fire filled the air. We all sat up. Sick or not, none of us wanted to be on that train, on an open siding, during an air raid. We dived for the door, and in seconds the car was cleared. The adjoining field was full of running men, looking for cover. There wasn't a guard to be seen; they already had taken cover. I saw a shallow ditch in front of me, the only cover around, and dived into it.

To my right in the distance I saw them, six RAF Mustang fighters, peeling off into a dive and coming straight at me. When I saw little white puffs appearing out of the front of the wings, I pushed my head down into the ground. Then the sound of cannon fire and the pinging of bullets hitting metal, like breaking piano wire. As the last aircraft went overhead with a roar, the locomotive blew up with a tremendous explosion, scattering debris for thousands of yards in all directions. I could hear bits and pieces of metal falling around me. I glanced up to see the RAF roundels on the side of the departing fighter banking in a climbing turn to rejoin his formation.

There wasn't a German aircraft to be seen. The Mustangs left as suddenly as they had appeared, and all was quiet, except for the hissing steam from the wreckage of the badly damaged locomotive.

Bodies were lying in the field after the raid, all of them British prisoners of war – about two dozen, according to the Germans. One British Army corporal was jumping up and down, beside himself with rage and cursing the RAF, saying that the pilots should have been able to see that we were British prisoners. I allowed myself a wry smile thinking about those pilots up there, worried mainly about their own skins and concentrating only on destroying a German train. Those little bugs scurrying about on the ground were no concern of theirs.

The guards didn't appear too worried about any of us trying to escape, for they knew, as we did, that the train was our only source of transportation, and that none of us was in any kind of shape to get back out on the road again. The Germans organized stretcher bearers for the wounded from among those of us who were healthy enough to carry anything, and we commenced picking up those who were still alive. I walked across the field to look at a corpse lying on its back not far from one of the other cars. It was Dennis Reeves, my first swapover.

There he was, his sightless eyes staring unblinkingly at the sun now emerging from behind the clouds; his face the yellow, drained colour of death; a jagged hole in his belly the size of a bowling ball; that familiar, unmistakable smell of death.

I felt suddenly sick in a different way from all the other sicknesses that had become part of me. Here was a man whom I had known well, who had been a prisoner of war for almost five years, killed by one of our own aircraft only a few months before the war must surely end. I thought my nose was running, but it was tears that were running down my face, mixing with the dirt. Most men in my generation were brought up to hide their emotions. My father had always said that it was okay for women to cry but not men, so I had usually held my emotions in check, no matter how strong. Still, a time comes in every man's life when some immense sadness overwhelms him and the unbidden tears overflow. This was one of those times.

They put us back in the freight cars and posted a guard. A party of volunteers helped to bury the dead – someone told us – in the local cemetery. I have often wondered if Dennis is in that grave-yard, and what it says on the marker, if there is one. It should have said, "Life is not fair!"

The next day, the Germans managed to find another train to hook us up to, and we were on our way again, steadily heading west, with long stops at sidings along the way. We were lucky that no more air attacks came our way, and we eventually arrived at our destination, Stalag XIB at Fallingbostel.

Fallingbostel was almost a carbon copy of Lamsdorf except that it was older. It had originally been used for French prison-ers of war who were later released to work in the civilian work-force. It was southeast of Bremen and north of Hanover, about equidistant, deep in northwest Germany, and well away, at this time, from advancing British and American forces. The camp was organized in much the same manner as the one we had left. There was cold water in between the barrack blocks, and a forty-holer in each compound. Compared to the hardships that we had just been through, it was luxury.

Unfortunately, there were no Red Cross parcels, and very little food. The daily ration consisted of a cup of watery turnip soup and a small piece of bread. It was hard to fault the Germans: they had little food for themselves.

There were daily and nightly air raids on nearby cities – the Luftwaffe seemed to be nonexistent. Later, we realized that the few Luftwaffe units left were busy trying to stem the relentless British

Red Cross map of British and Dominion POW camps in Europe, c. 1944. Areas pertaining to Andrew's initial mission to Germany and time spent as a POW are highlighted in bold.

and American advance and to keep themselves from being completely destroyed.

My health started to improve, as did most of the others', despite the poor rations; we had our bunks and straw palliasses, dry blankets, and decent shelter from the elements. We managed to rinse out – without soap – and dry our filthy clothes, and I unearthed an old razor blade, and several of us had a shave. It was now well into March, the weather was becoming milder and more spring-like, and the war news was good. Recently captured prisoners, mainly RAF and US Air Force, were telling tales about such huge numbers of men and tanks and aircraft involved in the Second Front that we found them almost impossible to believe. The Dunkirk veterans were astounded by the enormity of the Allied effort. Some change from their dismal defeat!

Day and night, Allied bombers and fighters flew overhead, and the concussion of distant explosions could be heard and felt almost all of the time. We began to see short-range aircraft skimming the treetops on their way to and from strafing runs. The Germans were becoming desperate. It must have been unendurable for any intelligent German to see the destruction of his or her homeland continuing while Hitler raved like a lunatic about secret weapons.

Outside the fence, in the other compound, were the Russian workers, technically prisoners, but in fact allowed to roam relatively freely. These men carried on an active trade in barter through the fence almost every day. Anything valuable could be traded for food. One day when I was particularly hungry, I noticed that one of the Russians had two loaves of bread that he was trying to sell. They were big loaves, round like cartwheels and weighing about two kilos each.

He pointed to my watch, my beautiful Rolex Oyster, the one John Galbraith had been wearing when he disappeared. My only valuable possession. He held up one loaf. I shook my head. He held up the two loaves, close to the fence. I could smell them; they had just been freshly baked. I took off my watch, handed it to him, and grabbed the two loaves. All the men at my table ate well that night. I put the second loaf away for my mucker and me to eat later.

That bread lasted us another week, and I never regretted the transaction. Looking back now, I'd do it again. Food you must have; you can always buy another watch.

In this camp, like every other camp, there were the racketeers, most of whom worked in the soup kitchen and distributed the bread. This time it was the Poles. They ate gourmet dinners with wine, and threw more food in their trash tins than we got in our daily rations from the Germans. I don't know how they managed it, but they had been in the camp for a long time, probably four years or more.

Some of the British prisoners would go over and dig through their garbage, picking up little tidbits of discarded food. I saw one poor army type digging through a trash can looking for morsels while a couple of watching Poles laughed at him. If I'd had a gun, I would have blown their heads off.

19

GOING HOME

By April, everyone in the RAF and British Army group had gotten rid of anything tradable in return for food, and we were all in a uniform state of semi-starvation. The most popular subject at our table while dividing up or eating our meagre rations was when the war was going to end. Some said weeks, and some months.

It was clear that it had to end fairly soon, but those of us who had been in the "bag" for a few years were still cynical. We had gone through Second Front rumours for two years before it had actually happened. When D-Day really arrived, it was almost an anticlimax. We had virtually packed our bags so many times that we could hardly believe it when it actually happened. That was almost a year earlier, and the war still went on. Some days I was so discouraged I wondered if the war would ever end.

There was more German armoured-vehicle activity in our vicinity than usual, and it was not uncommon to see their tanks and armoured cars in the distance. The sky was full of Allied planes, including a lot of short-range aircraft.

One night, about nine in the evening, just after dark, we were sitting around the table playing cards when one of the British soldiers said, "Listen, I hear a Sten gun!" Everybody in the barrack stopped what they were doing and listened. The windows were open and there was no wind. There it was. *Tacka tacka tacka tacka*

– the unmistakeable sound of the Sten. Then another sound –
Brrrrrp! Brrrrrp! Brrrrrp! – the sound of the German Schmeisser, the
"burp gun," which fired so fast it could cut a man in half.

We looked at each other, hardly daring to express what we were
thinking. If that was a Sten gun, which it clearly was, then there
must be British troops somewhere near. We listened for more, but
a breeze had sprung up and we heard no more shooting. We all
went to bed that night wondering if tomorrow would be the day.

The next morning some of us were sitting around our table
waiting for the rations to arrive when one of the army types rushed
in and said breathlessly, "I just saw a Churchill tank!"

We all laughed. "Bullshit!" said one. "That's a German Tiger
tank. There's lots of them around."

"Come and see for yourself," he replied. "I've been in the army
long enough to tell a Churchill from a Tiger!"

We all rushed out and lined up inside the wire to have a look.
Strange – there were no guards in the guard towers, and there was
not a German to be seen. Something was coming up from our left.
There it was, in a shallow defile running parallel to the camp fence
and about twenty or thirty feet outside the wire: a tank!

It was unmistakably British, and it was followed by another,
and another. And there were more behind. As it came closer, we
could see the tank commander's head and shoulders sticking out
of the turret. He wasn't looking at us but at the wooded area two
miles ahead, through binoculars. The tank stopped, the gun swung
a few degrees, then fired. There was a resulting explosion in the
woods. The tank moved on. The prisoners inside the fence cheered
wildly.

Several more tanks moved by, their crews in smart and crisp
uniforms, their faces healthy and clean-shaven, and looking so
very, very, young. But they were grim-faced and serious about their
job, and it was only the fourth or fifth tank that actually stopped
and the crew talked to us. The rest kept moving along.

Liberated POWs at Stalag XIB near Fallingbostel, Germany. April 16, 1945.

There was some small-arms fire from a wood only half a mile away, and a Bren gun carrier went racing over to investigate. Then a lot of firing, followed by silence, and the gun carrier reappeared.

Inside the fence there was bedlam. Wire cutters appeared, from where I'll never know, and the fence virtually disappeared in minutes. Men were cheering and yelling and laughing and crying and hugging the embarrassed soldiers who jumped off the tanks. All of the tanks going by now were throwing off boxes of rations, chocolate bars, and cigarettes.

But there was still a war going on. More small-arms fire came from the nearby woods, and a Jeep-load of troops raced over to investigate. There were bullets flying around in all directions, and here were we, jumping around like idiots, right in the line of fire.

I couldn't really believe it. After all this time, the war was really over for me, I was still alive, and I was going home. I stood back quietly and watched the revelry, and listened to the screaming and shouting. Occasionally one of my friends, my barrack mates, would run up and shake my hand. I was laughing and crying at the same time. As the tears ran down my face, I saw with my mind's eye Dennis Reeves' crumpled body lying in the field at Halberstadt. As I thought of him again, an overpowering wave of sadness came over me again. But for a one-in-a-million fluke, a rotten piece of bad luck, he could have been here with me today.

For the next few hours we stood around in little groups, talking and laughing, and waiting for the British Army to arrive. For it was the British Army, the British Second Army, the "Desert Rats" under General Montgomery, who liberated us, as we were informed by a very young-looking lieutenant who came into our camp shortly after the tanks had gone by, looking for the "senior" officer at the camp. Unfortunately, all of the recently captured aircrews and other officers had been evacuated from the camp by the Germans before they had pulled out.

The best we could do for him was a warrant officer Class 1, of which we had plenty, including me, having gone painlessly from sergeant to warrant officer Class 1 in automatic promotions while in the camps. Unable to find any real senior officer, he advised us to stay inside the camp for our own safety until arrangements were made to evacuate us. He warned us that there was a real war going on outside the camp, and that at a place called Celle, not too far away, a battalion of ss storm troopers was putting up a fierce battle. We could hear the sound of heavy firing from that direction as he spoke.

I, for one, decided to follow his advice and not let any stupid battle get me killed in the last few days of the war. He also told us that food would be sent in as soon as possible – a comment that was greeted with great cheers.

About two hours later, a huge army truck drove up and stopped in the middle of our compound. It was loaded with bread – fresh white bread, still hot from the oven. Each of us was handed a loaf. A *whole loaf* for one man! I couldn't believe it. We hadn't seen white bread for over two years, and even in England it hadn't really been white bread. This stuff was like Italian bread, soft and fluffy on the inside, with a thick, golden crust. It melted in my mouth. Without butter, jam, or cheese, just by itself, it was by far the best meal I have ever had in my entire life.

Later in the afternoon, a friend suggested we take a walk down by the village since the camp gate was wide open and there were no guards, German or British, to stop us. Remembering the officer's warning, I agreed but suggested we be careful. He admitted that it would be silly to be shot by a stray bullet so close to our release.

Strolling down the road toward the village, we were luxuriating in our freedom when we met a couple of heavily armed British soldiers patrolling in a Jeep. It was easy for them to guess we were from the camp, and when they heard us speak, they were satisfied we were friendly. I told them we were just wandering about, checking out the countryside, when one of them suggested a strange thing.

"Why don't you break into one of the houses and pick up some souvenirs?"

"I couldn't do that," I said, remembering the farm people who had brought over soup and water to the barns during our forced march.

"It's easy," he said. "All you have to do is kick down the door and walk in. If they've got anything valuable around, just take it. They won't give you any trouble, they're too scared!" Then he proceeded to tell us about a farmhouse he had looted, where the whole family sat numbly by as he loaded clocks and precious ornaments from the mantelpiece into a duffle bag. "They were scared shitless," he laughed. "They thought I was going to shoot them all."

I felt a little sick. Here were my liberators talking about looting and intimidating some poor farmer and his family. I thought about the farmhouse near Zerbst, where I had taken shelter in the winter of 1943, and what decent people they had seemed to be. Maybe I was still young and naive, with little experience of the real world, but what he had said disgusted me.

"Sorry," I said, "we're not really interested in looting. Besides, I thought that kind of stuff was illegal. I didn't know our side did that."

"Sure it's illegal, but who's to find out?" the soldier replied as his buddy looked on, a trifle uncomfortably, I thought. "And who's going to report us?" he asked with a touch of menace in his voice as he shifted his automatic weapon from hand to hand.

With that remark, the other soldier put the Jeep in gear and they sped off without a word. We walked back to the camp, our appetite for further exploration dampened for the moment.

The next couple of days were anticlimactic as we awaited the promised transportation home. We were to be airlifted, they said, but it had to be organized. Meanwhile, we filled up on the copious

Field Marshal Montgomery crosses the thousandth Bailey bridge to be constructed in northwest Europe, near Recke, Germany. April 13, 1945.

rations supplied by the British Second Army, and waited. The next day we were invited to listen to a talk by General Montgomery himself at a theatre in the nearby town.

About a thousand of us filed into the old building to hear the general. He was an impressive man. When he came on stage, the theatre was hushed. We could hear every word he said in his clipped English accent without benefit of a microphone. He welcomed us and congratulated us on finally being free, and promised to try to get us out of there as soon as possible. Then he started to tell us about the progress of the war.

At that moment, a rotten section of the theatre floor collapsed, several rows of seating along with the occupants crashing through to the ground a mere three feet below. There was considerable laughter and commotion but no one was hurt. All through the hubbub, General Montgomery continued his talk as if nothing had happened. His reputation as being unflappable was preserved for all of us.

The third day, April 19, a convoy of British Army trucks appeared at the camp, and we were told to climb aboard for a trip to a nearby aerodrome for our flight back to England. A couple of hours later, we were unloaded at an airport nearby. There were several long queues stretching out onto the tarmac. I joined the one that seemed a little shorter than the others.

How strange to be standing in line in Germany awaiting an aircraft back to England. Literally thousands of men were lined up, with their pitiful belongings in shabby kit bags and packsacks – dirty, unshaven, unkempt, but happy.

Squadrons of four-engine Lancasters, Halifaxes, and Stirlings, and even the old twin-engine Wellington bombers, were being used for this massive airlift, including several squadrons of RAF Dakotas (DC3s), which were then the latest passenger aircraft, used by many airlines. We were lucky in that Dakotas were using this particular aerodrome and that at least we would get a seat of sorts.

As I gradually moved up in the long line, I watched the planes, like buses, land, taxi over to the waiting lines, fill up with passengers without shutting down, then taxi out and take off. I was getting up near the front; it was late afternoon when I heard they were going to cut off the operation when night fell, so I was becoming agitated.

I was, finally, nineteenth in line when an empty RAF Dakota pulled up and the crewman announced that this was the last flight. I knew that the aircraft would hold at least twenty-five men. I would be back in England that night!

I climbed aboard and found a seat on the starboard (right-hand) side near the back. The canvas, bench-type bucket seats ran down each side of the aircraft, and were the same type paratroopers used when jumping into battle. The cable connector for the static release lines was still in place. Maybe this was the last thing some of those paratroopers ever saw. There was a little compartment in the rear with a chemical toilet, an Elsan, which I was happy that I wouldn't have to use. I buckled on my seatbelt and waited.

A young RAF pilot officer came down to inspect the passengers. Noticing the pilot wings crudely sewn on my army uniform jacket and my warrant officer badges, also crudely sewn on, he stopped.

"You're a pilot?" he asked.

"Was," I replied. "I haven't flown for over two years."

"How would you like to sit in the co-pilot's seat?" he asked. "I can fix it with the captain."

I was overjoyed. He told me to wait until after the takeoff, then he would come back and take my seat, and I could have his.

He was as good as his word. Right after takeoff, he strolled back and indicated that I was to go up front. Followed by envious glances, I walked up to the flight deck and was welcomed warmly by the entire crew. The captain was a flying officer, as was the navigator, and the wireless operator was a flight sergeant. When they heard that I had been a Lancaster pilot, they seemed impressed, and made me feel like a real human being for the first time in a very long time.

We landed at Brussels for fifteen minutes to refuel, then took off again for England. I remained in the co-pilot's seat. When he discovered that we used only one pilot on the four-engine Lancaster bomber, the captain seemed determined to show me that one pilot could do everything required on the DC3. It was one of the most pleasant flights I have ever made. The crew plied me with chocolate bars and cigarettes and treated me like an experienced pilot, which I was not.

We were flying at about eight thousand feet as we approached the English Channel and the sun was just disappearing below the horizon. Shortly, we would see the cliffs of Dover ahead. At the captain's invitation, I was wearing the headphones.

"Listen to this," he said, flicking a switch. Music was playing from a BBC station. The wireless op was doing a good job!

We were about half way across the channel. The cliffs were silhouetted in the last vestiges of a beautiful red sunset reflecting from a bank of cloud in the distance. Lights were starting to flicker on in the English countryside. He noticed my surprise.

"The blackout's over," he said. "We don't need it anymore." Just then, by some peculiar accident of fate, the radio began to play a then-popular song, "When the Lights Come on Again All Over the World." I was so filled with emotion that I had to look away, and I was glad it was growing dark so that he wouldn't see the happiness running down my face. I was so happy that I wanted this moment to go on forever.

When I had left England, twenty-seven months before, almost to the hour, I had been climbing out, eastbound, over the North Sea, at the controls of a Lancaster heavy bomber, heading for Berlin. A lot had happened since then. Now I was heading back, in the co-pilot's seat of another aircraft thanks to the generosity and understanding of another pilot who must have known, in his heart of hearts, how much his gesture had meant to me.

It was now pitch-dark outside, and the pilot informed me that he would need the co-pilot to operate the radios and gear for landing. I thanked him for his generosity and went back to my seat, telling the co-pilot that the captain required his services, and thanking him for giving me such a wonderful trip.

The airport we were heading for was called Wing Airport, and was apparently not far from Oxford. We would be met there, the pilot told me, by a reception committee and looked after. Which turned out to be the understatement of all time.

The Dakota circled the field, dropped its wheels and flaps, and finally touched down, smoothly and professionally. I assumed that there would be nobody there to meet me. I didn't know anyone in England anymore and certainly nobody knew I was coming. After my emotional high over the English Channel, I prepared myself for a dull time with typical British officialdom.

The aircraft taxied in past the blue lights marking the taxiways and finally stopped at a brightly lit area. There were a lot of people outside, but it was difficult to see out the windows, as they were fogged by the steam from the sweat of the returning prisoners.

Finally, my turn came to step out onto the passenger steps. I saw a big, open, lighted hangar with decorated tables, and a lot of people sitting and standing around. A carnival atmosphere was in the air, with music playing from a loudspeaker and the smell of food. When I reached the bottom of the steps, a young woman took both my hands in hers and said, "I'm really happy to have you back. Come over here with me to one of these tables, and I'll get you some tea and cakes." She sounded as if she really meant it.

She was about eighteen, pretty, with brown hair and a figure you couldn't ignore. She was a WAAF (Women's Auxiliary Air Force), and her WAAF uniform fitted her like a tight glove. To me, virtually not having been near or having seen any women for years, she was a vision, a goddess.

I'd cleaned up as much as possible in the camp that morning but still felt unkempt in my ill-fitting army uniform with wings and rank insignia roughly sewn on, army boots, and no hat. I needed a shave, and probably a good wash too. I felt out of place with this marvellous creature and couldn't figure out why she had singled me out for this special treatment. I said as much, and she explained.

The RAF had prepared very carefully for the returning prisoners of war, and had been operating these reception depots for some time. The WAAFs had been trained to act as hostesses for the returning POWs and to make them feel at home. She really was happy, she told me, to be welcoming returning prisoners home and would rather be doing this than any other job.

She sat me down at one of the tables and almost immediately reappeared with cakes and a cup of tea. While I devoured these and secretly admired her, she explained that the incoming procedures would take a little time, and it was her job to help make the time pass as pleasantly as possible.

Whoever had designed these reception procedures had done

Volunteers from the Women's Auxiliary Air Force greet liberated British prisoners of war as they arrive back in England. May 12, 1945.

a marvellous job. Each returning prisoner had a young woman assigned to look after him and to make sure the documentation and delousing procedures were as painless and efficient as possible. I had to visit a little booth, where an orderly squirted delousing powder under my clothes, and then another booth where an orderly wrote down all the particulars of my captivity, service number, home address, etc., before sending me back to my table goddess.

Finally, the WAAF picked up a slip of paper with my name on it and told me that I would be given a room in the sergeants' mess for the night. In the morning, after breakfast, I and others would be put on a train for London, to be re-kitted, and then on to Bournemouth, where all the Canadian ex-POWs would be processed for returning to Canada. I was sorry to leave her. For those all-too-brief few moments, I was in love with this wonderful girl who had made me – a scruffy, dirty, and probably smelly stranger – feel as if I were her long-lost brother.

She called over a young leading aircraftsman (LAC) and told him where to take me in the sergeants' mess. Then she took both my hands in hers, told me how much she had enjoyed meeting me, and kissed my unshaven cheek. At that moment I would have done anything for her. She was an angel. I left her reluctantly. I can't even remember her name now. She's probably a beautiful grandmother, with a lot of beautiful grandchildren.

The young LAC walked me over to the sergeants' mess and showed me my room. I had forgotten that a warrant officer is a pretty big wheel around a sergeants' mess. I had a whole room to myself. And a chest of drawers. And a mirror. I looked in the mirror and saw myself for the first time in a long time. A haggard young man, quite thin, with a slightly yellowish complexion, and several days' growth of beard. There was a real washroom down the hall, with clean white toilets, tubs, washbasins, and showers. I sat on the bed and examined the white sheets.

There were towels on the washbasin, soap – real soap – a razor, and a pair of clean RAF-issue pyjamas at the end of the bed. I showered and shaved and made myself squeaky-clean. Then I put on the clean pyjamas. Tomorrow I would be completely re-outfitted with a new uniform. I would throw all my old clothing away except for my German dog tag, which I would keep as a souvenir.

I turned out the light and sat on the bed in my new pyjamas, looking out the window, marvelling at the lights of the camp and the twinkling lights of the town in the distance. There was no blackout. The war was practically over, for all intents and purposes, although many more people would be killed before it was really over. But for me, on April 19, 1945, exactly two years, three months, and two days after I was shot down, the war was really over.

I didn't sleep at all that night, I wanted to enjoy every minute of my new-found freedom. And I did. And I still am.

THIS IS TO CERTIFY THAT—

No. R115291 Rank WOI

CARSWELL, ANDREW GORDON

(insert full name in capital letters and underline surname)
whose personal description, photograph and
signature appear hereon, is serving in the

ROYAL CANADIAN AIR FORCE

Changes in rank or appointment to commissioned
rank are to be indicated below. All entries must be
made in ink by an officer. Signatures or initials are
not required.

New Rank	Effective Date	Reference of official authority for change in rank and date of authority
P/O	23-4-45	

Personal description of holder

Height 5' 10½" Build SLIM

Colour of eyes HAZEL Colour of hair D. BROWN

Date of birth 29/MAY/1923

CARD No. 1954191

Signature of holder ....

Signature of Issuing Officer ....

Rank .... Date 17/5/45

Andrew's RCAF ID card, issued May 17, 1945.

273

Epilogue

I finished writing this book in 1990, a couple of years after I retired from Transport Canada as the regional aviation safety manager for Ontario.

I kept in touch with most of my surviving crew and friends from the POW camp. I attended POW reunions in London, Calgary, and Toronto, and still make it to the functions in Toronto, although our ranks are thinning as we age. I push wheelchairs once a week at Sunnybrook, the local veterans' hospital, and consider myself lucky to still be able to do it. Dorothy, my wife of sixty-three years, is still looking after me, and that is the luckiest break of all!

Shortly before the war in Europe ended, I was commissioned and sent back to Canada, and, a few months later, discharged by the RCAF. I returned to school and obtained my Grade 13, then was admitted to the School of Architecture at the University of Toronto.

I met and married a beautiful woman named Dorothy McCreadie. To support myself, my wife, and my baby daughter, I took a job working as a labourer for a Toronto house builder. One summer afternoon, I was on the roof of a house hammering in shingles when I heard a familiar drone and glanced up. An RCAF Lancaster was making a low pass over Toronto, and I watched it with more than a little interest. Mr. Northy, the house builder, never one to tolerate slacking off on the job, asked me what I was

Dorothy and Andrew Carswell on their wedding day,
Old Mill, Toronto. December 27, 1947.

looking at. "I used to fly those," I said. "Sure, sonny" was his skeptical response.

I was happier with my second job as a flying instructor at the Toronto Island Airport, working for Tom and Bob Wong, former RCAF flying instructors who had started a flying school called Central Airways. I had by then acquired a commercial pilot's licence and also an instructor's rating.

In 1947, the RCAF was given the task of surveying and photographing all of northern and Arctic Canada. I re-enlisted in the RCAF as an "experienced" pilot, quitting my job as instructor at the Toronto Island Airport and leaving the School of Architecture in my second year.

I was posted to Ottawa, to RCAF Station Rockcliffe. I spent the first summer flying as second pilot on Operation Magnetic, a survey operation designed to locate and investigate the movements of the North Magnetic Pole. At the end of the short arctic summer season, we returned to Ottawa and I was posted to the flying boat school at RCAF Station Sea Island, near Vancouver, where I was to learn to fly the Canso on and off water, in all conditions.

At the end of the course, I graduated as a fully qualified Canso captain, and the following season I was given a similar operation to perform, with the same scientific crew. Unfortunately, while pulling away from our camping spot on an uncharted lake, the Canso scraped over a rock and began to fill. Unable to get it off the water, I headed for the nearest island; the Canso sunk a hundred feet from shore. We got everyone, plus the emergency equipment, onto shore, and then radioed the base in Edmonton. A Dakota flew over the next morning and reported ten survivors. As there were only nine of us, we thought that perhaps a bear had stood up on the beach as the plane went overhead. The next morning, one of our own Cansos came over, landed, and took us back to Winnipeg, where after a short investigation we were flown back to Ottawa, given a few days leave, a new Canso, and told to go back and finish the job – which we did.

In 1951, after a third tour in the Arctic, based at Yellowknife, I was transferred to RCAF Station Sea Island, to a search and rescue unit, again to fly Cansos. There we spent most of our time searching for lost aircraft, sometimes lost ships, and occasionally lost people. The challenging ocean, coastline, and mountains of British Columbia meant lost aircraft or ships were more frequent there than in the eastern provinces. So I was pretty busy for the next six years piling up time on the Canso and, during the winter months, instructing at the flying boat school, the only amphibious flying boat school in the RCAF. I also did some flying time on Dakotas (DC3s), Expeditors, Norsemen, Otters, and even the Lancaster, my first aircraft love. I learned to love the Canso, slow that it was, because it was so reliable. Whenever I asked for an overseas posting, or training on jets, I was told that I was needed to help train Canso pilots.

GOVERNMENT HOUSE
OTTAWA

27th May 1959.

The Governor-General is commanded
by The Queen to invite you to an Investiture
which Her Majesty is holding at Government
House on Wednesday, July 1st, 1959, at which
time you will be invested with the Air Force
Cross, the award of which was promulgated in
the Canada Gazette of March 15th, 1958.
A memorandum is attached giving you
detailed instructions.

Squadron Leader Andrew Gordon Carswell, AFC, CD.

Left: Squadron Leader Carswell accepting the Air Force Cross from Her Majesty Queen Elizabeth II,
Government House, Ottawa. July 1, 1959. Right: Invitation from the Governor General to an investiture
being held by Queen Elizabeth II at Government House, Ottawa, where Flight Lieutenant Andrew Carswell
was awarded the Air Force Cross. July 1, 1959.

In 1957 I was posted to a recruiting unit on St. Clair Avenue
in Toronto for my administrative tour. After a couple of years
there, I was promoted to squadron leader and posted to Goose Bay,
Labrador, to be the chief operations officer.

While at the recruiting unit, I was awarded the AFC (Air Force
Cross) for my search and rescue work. I was told that it was to be
presented at Government House in Ottawa by the Queen, who, in
1959, was visiting Ottawa. So my wife and I went to Ottawa, where
I actually got to shake hands with Queen Elizabeth II. I am usually
quite a big talker, but when she asked me, "What did you do to get
this?" I was tongue-tied and could only murmur, "I rescued some
people" – or words to that effect.

From Goose Bay I went to Staff College, and from there we
went to RCAF Headquarters and then to Trenton to get checked
out on the Caribou aircraft preparatory to going to El-Arish, in

Andrew and Dorothy's fiftieth wedding anniversary, 1997, Old Mill, Toronto.

the Middle East. I flew for the United Nations to Lebanon, Egypt, and around the Sinai Peninsula. After three months, the establishment for my rank changed and I became redundant. As there was a Caribou aircraft needing a major overhaul, I was asked to fly it back to Canada. It was a pretty interesting trip, back over Europe and then Greenland – where the ice cap rose in height to almost the altitude of our unpressurized Caribou.

After Trenton, I moved back to Toronto, into Dorothy's and my house in Scarborough, until the commanding officer ordered me into Married Quarters on the grounds that I was his chief operations officer and so he wanted me to live on the base. I was posted again, this time as an instructor at the staff school at Avenue Road, in Toronto, and finally, a few years later, again back to Downsview, as senior air services officer. I retired in 1970 at age forty-seven, the compulsory retirement age for majors at that time.

My family and I moved into a house in north Toronto that we had bought, and I got a job as an aviation inspector with Transport

Canada (then called the Department of Transportation). I worked at that job for eighteen years, before retiring again at age sixty-five, in 1988. Dorothy and I have five children, ten grandchildren, and two great-grandchildren. We lived in Washago (north of Orillia, Ontario, in the Muskoka district) for thirteen years in a lovely house on the Severn River before moving back to Toronto nine years ago.

As well as a little bit about myself, I thought I would provide a postscript with postwar biographies of my surviving crew members and the central figures from my life as a POW.

Claude "Clem" Clemens

Clem Clemens, our rear gunner, came from Sarnia, Ontario. After the war he moved back to his Sarnia home. He worked briefly as a customs officer, then for an oil company. We saw him regularly at POW reunions and other functions. He passed away a few years ago.

Joe de Silva

Joe de Silva, the eldest member of the crew, occupied the Lancaster's mid-upper machine gun turret. He was married, with two children. After we were captured, the Germans told us that his body was found in a field near the town of Zerbst, with his unopened parachute still strapped on. Why it had not opened, we will never know.

Some time in the 1970s, after I had retired from the RCAF, Joe's son contacted me. He had never believed the story about Joe's parachute not opening and wrote a letter asking me for the real story. I wrote him back explaining that the parachute story was, in fact, true. He never replied.

Years later, in 2003, I read a story written by Joe's son that had been posted on a BBC online archive called "ww2 People's War." I found it quite moving:

THE LAST GOODBYE:
A PILOT FROM RAF WADDINGTON, LINCS

On a bitterly cold morning of 16 January 1943, with snow more than a foot deep in places, my mother took me and my baby sister on a bus ride from Lincoln to the main gate of RAF Waddington.

She had spoken to my Dad on the phone and arranged to meet him purely because she missed him so much since he had voluntarily joined the RAF. He had joined up after watching an aerial dog fight over Clapham Common, London.

I remember my Dad cycling down the drive on an old bicycle, wearing his flying suit, having been or about to be briefed for that night's operation. He seemed to have a heated conversation with a Sergeant at the Guardhouse before coming to us for about fifteen minutes.

Because I was so cold he put his flying jacket around my shoulders (I still have the jacket as my most valuable possession). It was a tearful goodbye when he left.

Returning to Monson St., Lincoln, we had tea, and in the twilight, my Uncle and Aunt, Mother and I, stood in the little garden as the crescendo of aircraft engines increased overhead. One of the Lancasters flew directly above us and the wings dipped slightly, left and right. "Andy always does that on the way out, if he can. They are off to Berlin now," my Uncle told me. He worked for the GPO and always seemed to know what was going on.

Lancaster W4379, 5 Group, 9 Squadron, failed to return from Berlin that night. Sergeants A.G. Carswell, RCAF (Pilot); C.E. Clemens, RCAF, (R/AG; J.W. Martin, RAF (F/Eng); H.C. Hipson, RAF (Bm/A); E.J. Phillips, RAF, (WT/OP) survived the POW camps and forced march from Poland to Germany as the war ended.

Sergeants J.E. Galbraith, RCAF (Nav) and JHW de Silva, RAF (MU/AG), my father, died and are buried close to each other in Berlin.

My mother spent over twenty-five years in a psychiatric hospital after receiving the telegram informing her my father was missing and presumed killed. My sister and I were raised by loving grandparents.

I have many memories of WW2, this is the one that stands out foremost.

Article A1996482, by Berlin9Squadron, contributed November 9, 2003, to WW2 People's War, an online archive of wartime memories contributed by members of the public and gathered by the BBC. The archive can be found at bbc.co.uk/ww2peopleswar.

Headstones for Joe de Silva (left) and John Galbraith (right). Berlin 1939–1945 War Cemetery, Germany.

John Donaldson

I was never able to find out what happened to John Donaldson, my first escape partner. He went out on another working party after our first escape, and I never heard from him again. After the war I made some inquiries but got no answers. I sincerely hope he survived the war. If anyone could escape successfully, it would be John.

John Galbraith

After my crew mates and I were captured and put on the train for the interrogation camp, the Germans were still looking for the seventh member of our crew, John Galbraith. None of us knew what had become of John, until later, when the commandant of Stalag VIIIB at Lamsdorf, a German colonel, summoned me to his office and showed me a Rolex watch, the one I had loaned to John to assist in his navigation. My name was engraved on the back, and I immediately identified it. When I asked the commandant about the person who had been wearing it, he told me that Sergeant Galbraith had been "shot down" on January 17, and that there were no other details.

My crew mates and I made further inquiries through the Red Cross and finally received a letter from the Red Cross in Geneva on March 28, 1944, saying that John's body had been found and was buried in a cemetery for Russian POWs.

Many years later, in February 1984, I was contacted by John's mother and through her learned why John had liked his privacy and been loathe to join in on our many crew pub crawls: John had fallen in love with a nurse at RCAF Station, Winnipeg. Unfortunately, she was an officer and he was an NCO, and military regulations of that time did not allow officers to marry other ranks.

Bryan Wannop, John's brother, who was only four years old when his older brother was killed, gives this account:

"Jack made a trip home to Calgary, where his mother was living, in late 1941 before he had finished his training with the RCAF, which I believe was in Winnipeg. At that time he told Mom about the love of his life, Margot Parker, who was a nurse in the RCAF – also, I believe, in Winnipeg. I do not know if at that point he had planned his marriage before he went overseas, but it was their intention to marry at some point.

"I was told that Jack and Margot were married the night before he went overseas. Margot told me, only a few years before she died in 1999, that Jack had written her daily, sometimes twice a day, from the day he went overseas. When his plane was shot down, the only notification my mother received was that he was missing in action and that went, on, I believe, until 1946 or 1947, when he was officially declared dead.

"My mother indicated that Margot was convinced that he was still alive, either imprisoned or injured, and she arranged at once to be transferred overseas to London, where I understand she spent more than six months checking hospitals looking for him, believing that he might have been so seriously injured or suffered a loss of memory so that he could not make himself known.

"When her father died, Margot moved with her mother to Victoria and looked after her until her mother passed away in the 1970s. During my 1995 visit, she was still filled with her love for Jack (or John, as she called him – the only one in the family to do so), talking as though the fifty-odd years since he was killed were yesterday. She never remarried."

Harry "Paddy" Hipson

Harry Hipson, our Irish bombardier, stayed in the RAF for a while and was put in charge of a group helping to close down RAF stations after the war. He married his long-time girlfriend and came to Canada, settling in Toronto. Eventually he retired to a small town in eastern Ontario. He was not interested in the POW associations and did not turn up at any of the events.

Harry Levy

Harry Levy and I had been good friends at Lamsdorf. In 2002 I received an email from Harry, who had enquired of some POW contacts in Britain if they knew what had happened to his friend Andy Carswell. We were soon corresponding, after a lapse in our friendship of forty-seven years. While he was being sheltered by the underground in Belgium after being shot down, Harry learned to speak French. He was eventually captured by the Gestapo and ended up as a POW in Lamsdorf. Harry used his wartime experiences wisely and became a college teacher of French. Harry and his wife came to visit us in Ontario in 2004, and we toured Canada, ending off with an Alaska cruise. My wife, Dot, and I reciprocated by visiting Harry and his wife, Joan, at their home in Yorkshire. Harry also wrote a book on his wartime experiences called *The Dark Side of the Sky*. He now keeps himself busy translating French classics into English.

Jim "Jock" Martin

Jock Martin, our flight engineer, came from Edinburgh, Scotland, and was formerly a policeman. After the war he rejoined the Edinburgh police and stayed with them until he retired. I saw him several times after the war on visits and reunions. He died a few years ago.

When Jock died, his son phoned to tell me that his dad had been a flight engineer to the very last, giving instructions to feather engines in the moments before he passed. Perhaps he was replaying that terrifying night in January 1943 when we struggled with our flaming Lancaster.

"Taffy Mac" McLean

Bill McLean – "Taffy Mac" to his friends – was one of my best friends. I drew a book of cartoons (reproduced in this book) for him when he was shipped out on a prisoner exchange after contracting TB. Mac was my partner in my second escape, and we spent many days and nights together in prison. When I went to see him in the hospital in Wales after I had been liberated, he looked pretty bad. I hardly expected him to live very long at all, but he fooled everyone.

He recovered, took an accounting course, married a nurse he had met at the hospital, and got a job with British Airways, eventually becoming its chief internal auditor. I met him many times at POW reunions when he came to Canada and when I visited England. Sadly, he too passed away a few years ago. His second wife, Joan, still lives in Cardiff, Wales, and kindly allowed me to reproduce the book of cartoons I drew for Mac, in this book.

Jack "Paddy" McMahon

Jack "Paddy" McMahon emigrated from Ireland after the war and worked in the grocery business in British Columbia. By a strange coincidence, I met him in Vancouver when I was stationed there in 1952. My wife and I had gone to a local grocery store. Sitting in the car awaiting Dorothy, I noticed that the young man helping her

Left to right: An unidentified friend of Pete Skinner's, Jack "Paddy" McMahon, Andrew Carswell, Bill "Taffy Mac" McLean, Pete Skinner, Jim "Jock" Martin, Lloyd Kidd. RAF POW Association reunion, London, England. July 1995.

with the grocery cart looked familiar. It was Paddy, one of my table mates at Lamsdorf. We had many interesting visits before I left Sea Island. Paddy was a senior executive with a major grocery company by the time he retired. He is still living on Saltspring Island, near Vancouver Island, BC. Jack also wrote, and published, a book on his wartime experiences, called *Almost a Lifetime*.

Eddie Phillips

Eddie was our wireless operator/air gunner. He was English – from London, I believe. His ankle had been broken from his parachute jump, and he had been removed from the Luftwaffe station where we all had been imprisoned to a German military hospital, and probably another prison camp. None of us ever saw him again, and he did not turn up at any military POW reunions that I attended, and of which we had many. Perhaps, like some, he did not want to remember his wartime experience. Perhaps he died on that long march. If you read this, Eddie, please contact me.

VE Day

'Inside the fence there was bedlam'

➤ Pilot From A1

opens Jan. 17, 1943. The night the Lancaster Bomber he was piloting took a fatal hit on the starboard wing.

You're with him at 25,000 feet as the flames — an angry orange glow through the frost-coated windshield — eat closer to the fuel tank. You see the altimeter as it loops counter-clockwise, hear the engines whine as the dive sends the props spinning ever faster. You're there as the teenager from the Beaches, struggling with the reluctant controls, makes the reluctant call to bail.

"Paddy Hipson, our Irish bombardier, pulled the release pin on the forward escape hatch," he writes, "and the pad on which he had been lying minutes before, as well as the hatch, was ripped downward into the roaring darkness.

"The front cockpit of the Lancaster was now full of engine noise from the three remaining Rolls Royce Merlin 1,250-horsepower engines screaming above the roar of the wind, with papers, maps and debris being sucked into the dark void. Paddy hesitated, then stepped into the black hole, and disappeared."

It was a far cry from the James Cagney movie *Captains of the Clouds* Andy had recently seen.

my face, mixing with the dirt."

In mid-March, Andy arrived at Stalag XI-B at Fallingbostel, in northwest Germany. The sound of air raids soon became a nightly affair; it was only a matter of time before the camp would fall. Finally, on April 16, it happened. A convoy of tanks heralded the arrival of the British 2nd Army.

"Inside the fence there was bedlam!" Carswell writes. "Wire cutters appeared, from where I'll never know, and the fence virtually disappeared in minutes. Men were cheering, yelling and laughing and crying and hugging the embarrassed soldiers who jumped off the tanks. All of the tanks going by now were throwing off boxes of rations, chocolate bars, and cigarettes."

Two hours later, a truck arrived with freshly baked bread. Andy still remembers it as the best meal he's ever had in his life. In a few days, the PoWs were taken by truck to an airstrip. There, one after another, DC-3 Dakotas took the former prisoners to England in a seemingly endless stream of aircraft that went like taxis all day long. Andy boarded the day's final flight. He'd somehow in his travels wound up wearing an old army uniform, but he'd sewn wings on the shoulders to show his RCAF heritage. The co-pilot noticed and invited him up to

Andrew Carswell is shown with a painting of a Lancaster Bomber like the one he piloted with the Royal Canadian Air Force during World War II before being shot down over Germany in 1943. He spent much of the remainder of the war as a prisoner in Stalag VIII-B camp.

RICK EGLINTON/TORONTO STAR

Toronto Star newspaper article by Scott Simmie, May 3, 2005.

Robert Burgener

Although not a member of our air crew or a POW, Robert Burgener, a fellow veteran from Toronto, played an important role in the writing of this book. He had arrived in England about the time I returned back to Bournemouth, came up to my room, and listened for most of the night as I related in detail what had happened to me over the previous twenty-seven months. After the war, when he was running a business selling copiers, printers, and computers, he offered to print my book of cartoons, which I had borrowed from Taffy Mac. I accepted his generous offer and had many copies made, which were distributed to ex-POWs at reunions. Years later, thanks to his excellent memory, he again assisted me, helping me to fill in many of the details in this story.

PHOTO CREDITS